Gender, Supernatural Beings, and the Liminality of Death

Gender, Supernatural Beings, and the Liminality of Death

Monstrous Males/Fatal Females

Edited by Rebecca Gibson
and James M. VanderVeen

LEXINGTON BOOKS
Lanham • Boulder • New York • London

Published by Lexington Books
An imprint of The Rowman & Littlefield Publishing Group, Inc.
4501 Forbes Boulevard, Suite 200, Lanham, Maryland 20706
www.rowman.com

6 Tinworth Street, London SE11 5AL, United Kingdom

British Library Cataloguing in Publication Information Available

Library of Congress Cataloging-in-Publication Data

Names: Gibson, Rebecca, 1981- editor. | VanderVeen, James M., 1973- editor.
Title: Gender, supernatural beings, and the liminality of death : monstrous
    males/fatal females / edited by Rebecca Gibson and James M. VanderVeen.
Description: Lanham : Lexington Books, [2021] | Includes bibliographical
    references and index. | Summary: "Gender, Supernatural Beings, and the
    Liminality of Death: Monstrous Males/Fatal Females examines how gender
    changes and manifests in stories and film through several different
    types of beings. With sections on social death, the walking dead, and
    the undead, this is a multifaceted look at myth, legend, and popular
    culture creatures"— Provided by publisher.
Identifiers: LCCN 2020056225 (print) | LCCN 2020056226 (ebook) | ISBN
    9781793641359 (cloth) | ISBN 9781793641366 (epub) | ISBN
    9781793641373 (paperback)
Subjects: LCSH: Sex role in mass media. | Monsters in mass media. | Death in
    mass media. | Liminality in mass media.
Classification: LCC P96.S5 G4573 2021 (print) | LCC P96.S5 (ebook) | DDC
    302.23081—dc23
LC record available at https://lccn.loc.gov/2020056225
LC ebook record available at https://lccn.loc.gov/2020056226

The editors dedicate this book to the ghost of Mary Wollstonecraft Shelley, who inspires us all to write fearlessly and powerfully, to the spirit of Zora Neale Hurston, who tells us that research is poking and prying with a purpose, and to the power of a good cup of tea.

Contents

Acknowledgments   ix

Preface   xi
Rebecca Gibson

Part I: Introduction   1

1 Transformation and Liminal Space within Fiction and Folklore   3
Freya Fenton

Part II: Social Death/Cyborg Transformation   21

2 Vengeful Monsters, Shapeshifting Cyborgs, and Alien Spider
   Queens: The Monstrous-Feminine in Netflix's *Love, Death &*
   Robots   23
Sarah Stang

3 "We're All, in the End, Part of the Same Great Thing": Gender,
   Death, and Memory in Aliette de Bodard's *The Tea Master and*
   the Detective   41
Alex Claman

4 "The House Wants Me to Stay": Mothers, Wives, and Sex
   Objects in the Haunted House Subgenre   53
Victor Hernández-Santaolalla

Part III: Between Life and Death   65

5 To Slay or Not to Slay: Gender, Liminality, and Choice in *Buffy*
   the Vampire Slayer   67
Chelsi Slotten

6 Fear Itself: The Vampire as Moral Panic   85
   Holly Walters

7 Gay Bloodsucker or Post-Soviet Buzzkill?: Vampiric
   Possibilities in Sektor Gaza   101
   Lev Nikulin

8 From Femme Fatale to Fatal Female: Vampiric Power as Coded
   Female in *A Girl Walks Home Alone at Night* and *Only Lovers
   Left Alive*   113
   Rebecca Gibson

Part IV: Reanimation with Sentience   **133**

9 Masculinity, and Not Femininity, as Gendered "Nature" in
   Cinematic Adaptations of Mary Shelley's *Frankenstein*   135
   Devi Snively and Agustín Fuentes

10 The Animated Dead: Reimagining the Beautiful Corpse in Tim
   Burton's *Corpse Bride*   149
   Gillian Wittstock

11 Sexual Encounters Between the Living and the (Un)dead in
   Popular Culture   161
   Matt Coward-Gibbs and Bethan Michael-Fox

Part V: Reanimation without Sentience   **175**

12 Behind the Door: Sukuma *Mitunga* (Zombie) Narratives as
   Social Critique in Northwestern Tanzania   177
   Amy Nichols-Belo

13 Does Death Destroy the Binary?: A Look at Gender Roles
   during Human/Zombie Interaction in the *World War Z* Universe   191
   Rebecca Gibson and James M. VanderVeen

Afterlife and Afterword   203
   James M. VanderVeen

Index   209

About the Editors and Contributors   213

Acknowledgments

Rebecca Gibson: My deepest thanks to my parents, John and Judy Horwitz—the best parents ever—from whom I get my love of life's dark and weird little things, for their continual support; and my coeditor, Jay VanderVeen, whose soft-heartedness balances out my more ruthless nature, for ten years of everything—here's to decades more partnership.

Jay VanderVeen: My *undying* gratitude to the students who participated in my senior-level seminars about the anthropology of zombies for challenging my own understanding of how to study the supernatural; and to Rebecca Gibson for her initiative, guidance, and the occasional nudging elbow.

Joint: We are in debt to our editors at Lexington Press, Judith Lakamper and Shelby Russell, for their guidance and skill; and to the authors of the chapters included herein, as well as the authors, actors, writers, directors, and singers of the works about which we wrote, for without them there would be no book.

Preface

Rebecca Gibson

My journey to the supernatural began far before I was exposed to any theoretical ideas that influenced my research, and before I had honed my writing skills in college, when my mother handed me Anne Rice's *Interview with the Vampire* sometime not very long after I turned twelve. I was a self-contained and extremely creepy child, with a vocabulary far beyond that of others my age, a voracious love of the written word, and an intense appetite for all things dark and spooky. I longed for a world populated by the cold, dead, romantic embrace of vampires, where blood flowed like wine, and relationships, be they love affairs or feuds, lasted centuries. I was comfortable with the concept of death, and wanted to explore ideas about what came after, even though I do not believe in an afterlife. It was the speculation, the "what if," that made things fun for me. A few years later, in my mid-teens, I began playing *Vampire: The Masquerade* and *Vampire: The Dark Ages*, tabletop and live-action role playing games from White Wolf publishers, with a group of friends at various gaming stores in the Elkhart and South Bend, Indiana, areas. We would pop in plastic fangs, and don our best vampiric clothing, and see in the midnight hour with sinister intrigues and fancy-dress balls and fake blood by the gallon. It was quite the fun Friday night for a young goth, and, though the gaming groups broke up, my love for the theatrical aspects of the supernatural never faded.

This book began, as many good partnerships do, with a shrug and a shared glance between friends. "I'm in if you are." I have been wanting to write about the supernatural with Jay VanderVeen since being accidentally too late to take his course on the anthropology of zombies. I had graduated in 2011, the year before it was offered, and my senior capstone in the Department of Sociology and Anthropology at Indiana University South Bend was the much less cool, but still quite useful, economic anthropology. Since leaving my undergrad days behind, Jay and I have formed a solid writing and editing partnership, and at the time of this publication are currently colleagues, teaching in the same university department where my zombie dreams were first thwarted.

Luckily, one lost opportunity does not close the door on all future ones—I was initially approached by our editors here at Lexington Books for an entirely different project, my book on corseting, which was already in production with another publisher, and I decided to see if I could interest them in a book on the supernatural instead: this book you now hold. However, rather than doing another monograph, I wanted to try to highlight the diversity of voices in the field of supernatural studies—I wanted to do an edited volume, and I asked Jay to be my coeditor. A shrug and a shared glance, and here we are.

In this edited volume, you will find many varied elements of the supernatural; not just zombies and vampires, but the spiritual lives of haunted houses, the blending of flesh and technology that makes a cyborg, the resurrection of humanity in various retellings of *Frankenstein*, and a tea making, sentient spaceship. The authors were chosen for their diverse viewpoints, their creativity, their unique take on those beautiful dark elements that make up the supernatural, and their ability to tell stories that tap into our collective desire to know more about death. Specifically, Jay and I wanted to get their takes on the question of what happens to gender when you die? Do you keep it, intact, or is it more ephemeral, like personality, something that is lost when you transition through death's liminal space and move from natural to supernatural? Does this vary in the different types of supernatural beings? When people become zombies, or vampires, or the undead, are they still . . . people?

These questions and more are contained in the chapters of this book. The answers are far from intuitive, and you will be introduced to versions of these creatures from films, books, TV shows, and from life—living mythologies—who will confound your expectations of the "typical" supernatural. But don't take our word for it: allow us to show you what awaits, as we walk through death's door, and meet the beings on the other side.

The author of our introduction, Freya Fenton, discusses what all the creatures, monsters, and beings have in common: transformation. To transform, to change from one thing to another, is integral to liminality—that process by which we ritually move from one state of being through a period of betweenness, to a new state. Each of the supernatural inhabitants of this book are somewhere between human and not, between gendered and ungendered, between life and death, and those gradations of transformation give the book its sections.

The first section begins the journey from alive human to transformed supernatural being, looking at the social death inherent in cyborg creation. Cyborgs—human-machine hybrids—exemplify the question of what it means to be human and where the divide between human and nonhuman occurs. This is one of the oldest philosophical inquiries (recall the perhaps apocryphal exchange between Plato and Diogenes, where the former stated that man was a featherless biped, and the latter held up a plucked chicken proclaiming "behold: a man!"), and involves the literal "supernatural"—that which is beyond nature, and unexplained.

While great strides are being made in cybernetic technology, with brain-body interfaces being tested as I write, our three chapters in this section are more fanciful, more magical, more spiritual than that. In Chapter 2, Sarah Stang looks at female autonomy and power in three of the short films from the Netflix series *Love, Death & Robots*, "Sonnie's Edge," "Good Hunting," and "Beyond the Aquila Rift." All three involve a human or humanoid being that uses technology to interact and influence their surroundings and their lives. They present as human . . . but with modification or augmentation. The crisis of each tale, whether for the main character or the supporting characters, comes when that modification or augmentation is made explicit—when Sonnie's autonomous humanoid body is destroyed, and her neural nature reverts back to the monster where it is stored; when Yan's friend finds a way to reverse her implants, allowing her to shapeshift again; when Greta admits to projecting her reality into Thom's mind and he sees her true shape for the first time. Each one examines her own gender, her own sexuality, in light of her supernatural-cyborg nature.

A sentient ship is the focus of chapter 3, where Alex Claman does a deep analysis of death symbolism and gender roles in Aliette de Bodard's *The Teamaster and the Detective*. The ship is comparable to some of the earliest cyborgs in fiction—the brainships of Anne McCaffrey's Central Worlds universe. Claman's analysis shows how the changeable journey between life and death can involve social, physical, and psychological deaths, and rebirths as an amalgam of human and machine, grief and love, and ship and its partner. These amalgams, like the cyborgs analyzed by Stang, are still very much physically alive, however, unlike the next amalgam, that of house and woman.

In Victor Hernández-Santaolalla's chapter 4, we see disembodied entities, the houses that are being haunted, as in conversation with the female inhabitant characters. These characters themselves fit into the supernatural as well, being that they are the ones who pick up on the nature of the houses—they are in tune with the unnatural, haunted character of their locations. This analysis of several literary and cinematic hauntings asks quite a different question regarding gender and death: what would happen in these stories if we simply . . . believed women about their experiences? The gaslighting (literal and figurative) involved in haunted house stories continues into our next section, on the shadowy world between dusk and dawn, inhabited by vampires.

More than any other of the traditionally supernatural creatures, vampires have one foot on each side of the line between life and death. They have died an unnatural death, yet if they are properly careful, they can blend in with humans, live normal (though nocturnal) lives, take jobs, even, and fall in love. They are the focus of the next four chapters, beginning with Chelsi Slotten's chapter 5 on their nemesis: Buffy the Vampire Slayer. Buffy is indeed a supernatural being, and Slotten's analysis focuses on the liminality involved in being a supernatural teenager, trying to have a normal life, but being so wrapped up in dealing with the undead that Buffy becomes literally torn between worlds, on occasion, straddling that threshold between life and death. Slotten looks at several episodes where that liminality comes to the fore, and places them in a larger narrative context of strong, supernatural female led shows from the 1990s and 2000s.

But what is a vampire, at its very nature, and what does it symbolize? Chapter 6, by Holly Walters, takes us on an historical journey through the mythologies of the vampire, following the themes of death, blood, and sex and how the advent of modern Christianity mingled with various folklores to produce the modern literary vampire. Moral fears of the taint of death's corruption lead to the uncleanliness and sin of the vampiric existence, connecting the first Vampyr, to Dracula, to Edward and Bella in *Twilight*.

One of those moral fears, as discussed in Walters's chapter, is homosexuality, and the queerness of the vampiric state. Our next chapter, chapter 7 by Lev Nikulin, discusses this attraction/repulsion/compulsion between humans and vampires as shown by the music of Sektor Gaza, a post-Soviet punk metal band. Here we see counterculture music combining with non-normative sexualities to create a new and unprecedented outlet for supernatural mythos, and we see the same ideas of contamination and infection reflected in the secular as we have seen in the Christian moralities above, with an added reflection of the HIV/AIDS panic of the late twentieth century, before PrEP and other medication combinations made HIV preventable and treatable. Yet not all vampires are counter-morality or indicative of contagion. As times change, so too do the vampires, and the next chapter looks at such undead evolutions.

My chapter, chapter 8, delves deeper into the idea of gender and its relation to the state of undeath by highlighting two very modern vampires—The Girl from *A Girl Walks Home Alone at Night* and Eve from *Only Lovers Left Alive*. Where Slotten focuses on vampires who are incapable of humanity in their own right, but who can regain it, (and thus the ambiguous role of the Slayer), and Walters discusses how vampires are divorced from being seen as moral or righteous beings, this chapter looks at the most recent iteration of female vampiric existence. These two characters, The Girl and Eve, show distinctly different types of femininity, and find love on their own terms, retaining their humanity despite their undead states and epitomizing the mother and the lover, respectively.

The next section, on reanimation with sentience, deals with mothers/ creators and lovers as well, as we take a look at several very unconventional corpse reanimation stories in two chapters on Frankenstein adaptations, and *The Corpse Bride.* Chapter 9 by Devi Snively and Agustín Fuentes addresses Snively's own Frankenstein story *Bride of Frankie*, wherein the titular Frankie, wife of Dr. Stein, creates her own version of a reanimated corpse. Snively and Fuentes contrast this short film with other cinematic creations, from the original 1931 adaptations, to the comedic works of Mel Brooks (*Young Frankenstein*) and Frank Henenlotter (*Frankenhooker*) to demonstrate the masculine "natural" world of the traditional creator role is contrast against the feminine "civilized" world created in *Bride of Frankie*. In many of their examples, gender is bent almost to the breaking point when a new creation joins the legions of Franken-beings, but in the next chapter we see gender and gender roles being retained, even through reanimation.

Beautiful corpses have a long symbolic history in myth and in representation, with idealized corpse sculptures often represented on top of tombs or coffins. However, whether made pretty or shown in *transi*, the transition between dead and skeletonized, they remained with their catafalques. In chapter 10, Gillian Wittstock discusses a corpse reanimated with the power of love and marriage in the Tim Burton film *The Corpse Bride*. Not idealized, but still beautiful, Emily falls in love with her accidental suitor and must win him away from his former love. Here Wittstock shows how gender remains in the reanimated corpse, and how that representation becomes camp when dramatically overemphasized in Emily's representation.

Emily and the Franken-beings are sentient and stay within their own genre—the sentient reanimated corpse, but our next chapter highlights those genre bending beings that have begun to emerge in recent iterations of the supernatural in film and TV: Chapter 11 by Bethan Michael-Fox and Matt Coward-Gibbs looks at recent entries into various supernatural genres which give them just a little more warmth, life, and humanity, bending the genres and inviting us to contemplate sex with the undead. By examining *In the Flesh*—where zombies can manage their condition and mate with humans; *The Strain*—where stingers replace genitalia in transmitting vampirism as an STD; and *American Horror Story: Coven*—where a young witch discovers the ability to use sex to kill, Michael-Fox and Coward-Gibbs turn the questions of this book around, asking how the living, of any gender, relate to the dead.

In the final section, two chapters examine the final stage of the transition from life to death—reanimation without sentience. Chapter 12 gives us our second mythological/cultural experience of the supernatural, with Amy Nichols-Belo's ethnographic research on Tanzanian zombie narratives. In her work, we see echoes of Walters's chapter on the history of vampires—zombies, too, make explicit the moral fears of a culture, and employ the narrative modes of contamination, sin, and corruption, in the social mores of Tanzania and other African and Afro-Caribbean locations. While the social zombies are ambulatory, and able to follow directions, they lack functional sentience in that they are unable to decide, desire, or act without direction or instruction.

Furthermore, while they do not quite meet the "Western" qualifications for "dead"—they can return to normal life, they still have breath and heartbeats and reduced, but present, metabolism—they are dead in that they live apart from normal society, are mourned as though they are dead, experience lowered metabolic functions including a decreased need for food, and others in society consider them to be dead. They are, for all intents and purposes, dead—reanimated without sentience. They have no wants or desires, apart from doing the bidding of the witches that have enchanted and ensnared them. They are not the only zombies, however, although their prototype, the shambling, agency-less, single-minded undead, are the inspiration for the rest. In the final chapter, Jay and I examine literary zombies who are only after one thing—your body.

Ravenous, relentless, and without thought, the zombies in Max Brooks's *World War Z* are our focus for chapter 13. In this examination of Brooks's universe, we look at survivors and zombies alike to see if the dead are gendered, and how the survivors' gender roles are altered by the war through which they fought. These zombies are very much the literary creation with which we are all familiar; shambling, moaning, mindless killing machines that cease to have needs or desires for anything other than their next meal of human flesh. The survivors, however, retain thoughts and feelings and desires long after the war, and the psychological need to meld their experiences with the horror and unreality of their fight creates new ways of existing in gendered realities.

These zombies are the epitome of undead, and though not malicious (malice implies sentience) they are malevolent in that they almost uniformly produce harm and have no ability to produce or feel pleasure or comfort. The equivalent of an uncontrolled plague, they are also the final stop on the way to final death—where cyborgs retain their human natures, and Franken-beings can exist without killing, and vampires do not need to drain their victims when there are blood banks, there are no true zombies who find redemption or stop killing when sated. They are never sated, and so if not defeated by the remaining humans, they will eat and kill and destroy living humans until there are none left on earth but other zombies.

Thus, we see the threads of liminality and transformation, which began in our introductory chapter by Fenton, conclude in the final chapter. We hope you will enjoy reading these works by these superlative authors. We hope their arguments will be thought provoking, and that their examples will make you want to seek out the books, novellas, TV shows, movies, and songs discussed within. We invite you to step across the threshold, and read more about gender, supernatural beings, and the liminality of death.

Part I

Introduction

Join us on this journey through death's door . . .

Chapter One

Transformation and Liminal Space within Fiction and Folklore

Freya Fenton

INTRODUCTION

Fiction, as a medium, is possessed of many transformative beings. Some are permanently changed from one state to another, either against their will or by choice; some changes are lifelong but transient; all have different causes and results. Whether partial or full-body, human or inhuman, many of these changes generally have one thing in common—they are often regarded as monstrous. But how does one demarcate the concept of transformation? Is it spiritual? Physical? Mental? Or all three? And is it always monstrous? One definition of transformation is listed as "A complete change in the appearance or character of something or someone, especially so that that thing or person is improved" (Cambridge Dictionary 2019). An example of this in modern fiction would be when the Fantastic 4 are exposed to the cosmic radiation that gives them their superpowers; they are fully transformed (and improved, due to their abilities, aside from Ben Grimm/The Thing whose new status is somewhat less positive) (Carey et al. 2005).

NATURAL TRANSFORMATION

In everyday life, banal transformation is everywhere. The diet industry is entirely built around personal physical transformation. Television shows detail how we can transform our looks, our style, our homes; countless books have been written about changing our points of view, our personalities, our jobs and friendships. Societally, we are encouraged every year to commit to change in the form of a New Year's Resolution—most of which do not generally last beyond February, taking on a liminal existence of their own. These are all seen as positive examples of transformation—the choice presented being work hard or fail, as a general rule. We do not, however, possess the same capacity for transformation as fictional and mythological characters—shapeshifters, supernatural beings, creations, repurposes of the human form. A primary example of transformation within fiction, one that almost every person knows a version of thanks to the lasting cultural power of Walt Disney, would be when the prince from *Beauty and the Beast* (originally written as *La Belle et la Bête* in 1740) regains his human form after years as a hideous beast (De Villeneuve and De Beaumont 1740/2013). This immediately takes him from monster to man, with the requisite changes in his societal standing and acceptance—but of course, a negative transformation had to occur first, as he was cursed by a vengeful witch. Romantically, it is the finding of 'true love' that is the rescuing factor—his humanity is restored by his acceptance by another party, one who can see beyond his physical mutation. Whether his temperament will change along with his body is of course a different question.

It is, however, the "non-improved" versions of transformations that generally hold the public's interest—those that are reluctant, or artificial; ones that require great sacrifice or death; ones that have a generally negative impact on the person being transformed and upon those around them. Is this because of our fear of unnatural change? Or even, our fear of natural change? The fear of loss of control is something referenced in stories and legends all over the world. Stories like *The Curious Case of Benjamin Button* (1922) present the natural changes of ageing, reversed (Fitzgerald, West, and Hardcastle 1922/2017); *The Picture of Dorian Gray* (1890) examines the retention of perfect youth, despite the corruptions of life (Wilde 1890/2000); while the *Strange Case of Dr Jekyll and Mr. Hyde* (1886) presents two very different facets of the human condition. Jekyll is presented as a mild-mannered, intelligent, kind man—one who fears the darker side of his personality, and so attempts to remove any negative and unsociable urges via the scientific method, creating a serum that he believes will permanently restrain (and perhaps even remove) them (Stevenson 1886/1997). Of course, this does not work, and leads to the creation of and his transformation into a twisted alter ego, whose morals and behaviors are entirely based around what Jekyll was fighting so hard to deny. While modern depictions of Hyde generally show him as a mutated monster, with unnatural strength and size, the original novella actually describes the unfettered alter ego as a small, diminutive man, the opposite of his original self. Eventually, Jekyll's transformations into Hyde become unwilling, his loss of control over his creation leading to his suicide due to the lives Hyde has taken and the unacceptable behavior that has deeply tarnished his reputation as a doctor and a good man. These stories, and the films based on them, are presented as instructional tales, expressing morality—guidelines for existence that we are told we should be obeying. Just like in *La Belle et la Bête*, there is an expectation that the reader will look at these examples of transformation and be horrified, to a certain extent—and then choose not to follow the paths depicted, for fear of the fate of these characters happening to them (Dorian Gray, for example, winds up dead after seeing the portrait he had been using to save himself from the darkness of a hedonistic lifestyle).

NON-CONSENSUAL CHANGE

On the darker side come those transformations that are unwillingly enforced on both the living and the dead—Frankenstein's Monster, HR Giger's Alien, Star Trek's Borg, the human batteries in *The Matrix*. These are less moral, presented as far more horrific; there is a lack of consent, a lack of knowledge about what is happening, and usually far more pain and strife involved. All include an artificially induced change of state. Dr. Frankenstein's creation is assembled from human remains and reanimated through science; the Xeno-morph uses captured humans as incubators, and was itself a creation of the android David; the Borg seek perfection through assimilation and the total subjugation of self; and the human batteries are used as an energy source for a conquering force of self-aware technology, machines given enough autonomy to realize their disadvantaged position. There is a liminality to all these changes, a point at which all participants cross the threshold from one state to another, from alive to dead (and back to alive), human to monster, consenting to unwilling. For a moment, those taking part in the transformation will occupy both states at the same time—the point when the Borg inject their victims with their nanoprobes, for example (Frakes 1996).

Until these nanoprobes reach the brain and the full assimilation process begins, the victim is trapped between two states; watching and feeling their humanity recede and their Borg identity be fully realized. Full assimilation includes multiple implants and limb replacements, as depicted rather viscer-ally in the film *Star Trek: First Contact*, and the total loss of individual self as their distinctiveness is absorbed by the Borg hive mind (Frakes 1996). Captain Picard is portrayed as permanently emotionally scarred from his assimilation into Locutus, and the Borg's use of his knowledge and experi-ence with Starfleet to nearly cripple them at the battle of Wolf 359 (Bole 1990). The first long-term Borg we are shown that is severed from the collec-tive and recovers his humanity is Hugh, an ex-drone who later works toward the rescue and rehabilitation of an entire Borg Cube (Lederman 1992). He possesses a level of childlike naivety upon his first awakening, as much of his individuality was lost due to the long-term effects of assimilation. An-other character who undergoes a similar transformation is Seven of Nine/

Annika Hansen, who was assimilated in the Delta Quadrant as a child and accidentally kidnapped by the Starfleet ship Voyager while serving as an envoy (Burton 1997). Her slow rediscovery of humanity as she transforms from full Borg to an individual highlights the liminality of the Borg themselves—while rare, the process is still somewhat reversible, meaning the death of the individual can be in itself as fleeting as their pre-Borg existence.

Another example of artificially induced transformation comes from the video game series Dead Space. The process begins with the discovery of a Black Marker, an enigmatic helix-shaped stone sculpture of extraterrestrial origin that travels through space until it locates a biologically suitable planet (Bueno 2008). Once grounded, the Marker sends out an electromagnetic signal, encouraging the evolution and population of sentient beings. Once the planet hits overpopulation and the inhabitants run out of energy supplies (something stated to have happened on Earth within the game's universe) the control the Marker has leads to its discovery, as it is able to provide a free and abundant source of energy. The unlucky species then creates copies of the Black Marker, known as the Red Markers, and disseminates them as energy sources to the entire populace (Bueno 2008).

After enough time has passed and there are a large spread of Red Markers within the various colonies and populations of the initial planet and beyond, all Markers begin sending out a new signal. This particular wavelength triggers hallucinations, early onset dementia, desperate paranoia, terror, and leads the majority of the populace into mass homicidal and suicide sprees, abruptly increasing the number of dead bodies within the population. This act is a deliberate one, required for the next phase of the transformative activity. This begins with the broadcast of a further, more concentrates signal, one that reanimates corpses by mutating them at the cellular level, twisting the dead into nightmarish, hive-minded creatures with only one goal—spreading the contagion further through death, exponentially increasing the amount of biological matter available. Dubbed Necromorphs by humans, there are multiple varieties of monster, with the different forms specialized for particular tasks. These infected creatures then spread the Necromorph contagion further, exposing unwitting subjects to a microbial pathogen that will immediately reanimate them as Necromorphs once they have been killed (which is extremely likely) (Bueno 2008). The final step in this process is the creation of a Brethren Moon during a Convergence Event. Once the Necromorph count is high enough, any able-bodied creatures are summoned to the Markers, where they have also been seen to deposit any dead tissue they come across. The Black Marker levitates into the stratosphere of the planet, linking to and summoning all Red Markers within range. It will then draw all necrotic flesh from the planet to it, creating the aforementioned Moon, which will then become dormant and has been theorized to work as an amplifier for other marker signals (Bueno 2008).

This particular horror tale satisfies multiple tropes. There is Cosmic/inter-galactic horror—nobody knows who created the Black Markers or where they come from, although it has been suggested that they are at least partially sentient, displaying self-preservation tendencies; indeed, the Red Marker aboard the USG Ishimura in the first game will send waves of Necromorphs to attack the player if they get too close or threaten it. There is body horror by the bucketful—from dangerous hallucinations to the monstrous forms of the various animated corpses, which range from adults to children right through to murderous babies, as found in the second game while traversing a school. Death truly is a liminal state for the physical body here, as it is stated plainly that the Markers are only capable of resurrecting dead flesh. The mutations cannot be triggered among the living, hence the Markers reliance on ensuring most exposed to them are deprived of their sanity and converted to killers of themselves and of others (Bueno 2008).

This reanimation and repurposing of the dead is a transformative experi-ence that can be found across many types of story. Hailing from many tales of the Middle Ages and even earlier are Revenants, the European folkloric reanimated corpses (Lindahl, McNamara, and Lindow 2002). These are less often described as being raised by artificial means, and are more often found to be independently returning to life; although they are generally not overly malevolent and more confused as to why they cannot continue their existence from before their deaths (Keyworth 2007). An opposite to this lies in the classic zombie—a once-living creature transformed into a monster, usually depicted as only interesting in feasting on the flesh of humans.

There are now many types of zombie, far outreaching their Haitian folk-loric origins. From *Night of the Living Dead* to *Resident Evil, Shaun of the Dead* to *28 Days Later*, they are at present more overexposed within popular culture than ever before. The idea that the entire populace can be easily and quickly converted into dangerous mass killers, without the concepts of thought or reason, is a terrifying one for many. There are, of course, other non-consensual transformations of people that do not necessarily require their deaths—the myth of the werewolf, for example. Werewolves are a widespread concept within European folklore, and spread globally with the spread of Christianity, although animal transformation concepts are found far earlier in the myths and beliefs of many cultures (Otten 1986).

The film *Ginger Snaps*, for example, uses lycanthropy as a parallel for the onset of womanhood—the main character is bitten because she has begun her first period, which draws the werewolf to her (Fawcett 2000). It can be said that Ginger's transformation into a woman is a non-consensual one—until she embraces the confidence and strength (and the ability to murder) becom-ing a werewolf provides, she is reluctant to face or admit that she is becom-ing an adult. The liminality of teenagerhood is highlighted by the loss of her humanity, as she crosses the boundary of the death of her childhood.

Another version of transformation is that from a sentient, animate being into an inanimate object, or at least being forced into the form of one. The core principle of the Matrix films centers around an artificial reality that humans are trapped in without knowledge, while their living bodies float in pods, providing bioelectricity to their mechanical overlords. Once made aware of this reality, one must make a choice—to forget, and to remain in the Matrix with no memory of this knowledge, or to face a second transformation as they are rescued from this mass hallucination and abruptly disgorged into a barren wasteland of a planet, with their lives then spent avoiding and fighting the machines that now rule what remains of Earth (The Wachowskis 1999). Here, the liminality of the tale lies within the barrier between real and imaginary, and whether it is even possible to tell the difference if the illusion is powerful and realistic enough. The character Cypher's betrayal of his shipmates to the AI beings known as Agents, who exist to keep the false reality from being revealed to the millions of minds within it, would indicate that for some this illusion is preferable—there is, after all, no steak in the real world.

REPAIR, RE-USE, RECYCLE

Of course, occasionally the steak, while real, is not actually made of animal. The psychiatrist and budding chef Hannibal Lecter's penchant for transforming people into food brings us both the body horror of the change, and the idea that one's food may not be what it purports to be (Harris 1999). Is there within this tale not a hidden transformation of the people at Hannibal's table as the food is eaten, from everyday human to unwitting cannibal? And also, for some, a change from human to foodstuff? While the good doctor's philosophy of "eat the rude" is admirable to many, he forces his visitors to occupy a liminal space where they have become unaware of who they have become. This is revised in the prequel book into being an experience that mirrors Hannibal's own—when his sister is murdered and eaten by a criminal militia group during a cruel winter, he is later informed that he, too, became an unwitting cannibal at that point, crossing the same liminal space that his later visitors will (Harris 2006).

Of course, cannibalism both willing and unwilling has a mythological past. The Titan Cronos from Greek myth devoured five of his own children, to prevent them from deposing him after he did the same to his father, Uranus (Grant and Hazel 1973/1993). In another myth, the Argonian princess Harpalyce killed, cooked, and served her child (or younger brother, depending on the source) to her incestuous father as vengeance for his treatment of her (Grant and Hazel 1973/1993). A similar concept to the cannibalism of the dead and the re-use of human remains is practiced within the world of Bioshock, a series of games that began as an Ayn Rand-inspired tale about an attempt at building a utopia somewhere in the Atlantic Ocean.

Conceptualized by the business magnate Andrew Ryan, the city of Rapture was built to be free of the constraints of human morality and accepted behavior, with the idea being that any denizen could rise to the top if they just put in enough work (Shirley and Levine 2011). Without scientific ethics as a restraint, the gene-altering substance ADAM is discovered within a particular type of sea slug. For human consumption, ADAM is refined into a serum known as a Plasmid, an extremely addictive substance that promotes the stem cell alterations required for the different abilities to manifest. Plasmids can give their users supernatural abilities such as telekinesis, pyrokinesis, and the control of swarms of bees, for example. As there is no such thing as a true human utopia outside of Star Trek, class divisions soon appear within the underwater city, resulting in the creation of cheap ADAM producers by Ryan's opponent, Frank Fontaine—little girls, usually kidnapped, were implanted with the slugs, creating up to thirty times the usual dosage due to a symbiotic relationship (Shirley and Levine 2011).

As the city's ADAM addiction grew, even these child hosts were not enough, and the transformed Little Sisters (as they came to be called) were eventually psychologically conditioned to travel throughout Rapture with their protective guardians, collecting ADAM from the many dead bodies of the city in an attempt to satisfy the rapidly crumbling society. The mental conditioning ensures that the Little Sisters do not see the ruined city of Rapture as it truly is—they exist within a dreamlike state that makes the leaking, dangerous, corpse-ridden city appear to be a beautiful haven, with the corpses they are extracting ADAM from disguised as angels (Thomas 2009). It is, however, the innocence of the Sisters that separates them from the usual cannibal—they have no concept of life outside of their conditioned existence, and do not understand the potential ghoulishness of their actions.

CREATIONS AND CRAFTED CREATURES

The Little Sisters, like so many other characters within fiction, were not born monstrous, however—they were created. A question often asked of created creatures, from Frankenstein's monster to the android Data, is whether they are truly alive—or do they exist in a liminal space between life and death, having never been born but still being able to be destroyed? One of the first robots ever shown in film is the Maschinenmensch from Fritz Lang's Metropolis, an archetypal example of Isaac Asimov's Frankenstein Complex—where artificial beings turn against their creators (Lang 1927). The robots in *The Matrix*, the Cylons from *Battlestar Galactica*, Ava from *Ex Machina*, the two AI beings in William Gibson's *Neuromancer* and Data's brother Lore are all examples of this. However, unlike more basic robots such as Robbie or R2-D2, these creations all have something in common—independently formed sentience, in many cases formed by the creations themselves. But does this sentience bring them across that liminal void between being alive, or not?

In season 2 of *Star Trek: The Next Generation*, the status of artificial beings as lifeforms is brought to the forefront, as Commander Bruce Maddox seeks to dismantle Data and discover whether he can be replicated (Scheerer 1989). Data is naturally concerned that the outcome will not be positive—that Maddox would be incapable of reassembling him as he was—and refuses, resigning his Starfleet commission in the process. Maddox fights this, stating that Data is property and not a person, and so a battle is fought in the courtroom for Data's rights as a sentient lifeform. With the aid of Captain Picard as his defense counsel, and the wise words of the El-Aurian bartender Guinan, he is able to successfully defend his right to life. This concept is revisited multiple times within TNG's canon, a primary example of which is when Data builds his own child, Lal (Frakes 1990). Lal is far more advanced than Data, able to use contractions and feel emotions, but ceases to function due to a cascade failure within her positronic net. Due to the Enterprise crew's acceptance of both Data and Lal as sentient lifeforms, her loss is treated as a death among the crew, despite Data's lack of emotion toward her loss.

The novel *Metamorphosis* explores Data's personhood in a different way; when an alien race grants Data his deepest wish—to become human—he must learn to live with the idea of his frailty and death, accepting a lifespan far shorter than his would have in a positronic body (Lorrah 1990). This transformation is very similar to the tale of Pinocchio, which was of course referenced by Commander Riker during his very first meeting with Data, and again when the human Data is trying to prove he is who he claims to be. Data is eventually restored to his artificial form by being sent back in time by the alien beings, after the loss of his android abilities results in the deaths of a number of the crew and a serious war breaking out in the local star system. He carries no memory of his transformation, as in this new timeline it never happened. Data is eventually permanently killed in action during the events of the film *Star Trek: Nemesis*, when he sacrifices himself to save Captain Picard from doing the same for his crew (Baird 2002). This is, however, retconned to a certain extent during the events of the series *Picard*, where it is revealed that while his physical body was destroyed, the contents of his neural net had been safely uploaded to a computer, enabling the Captain to say a final goodbye to his friend before deactivating the memory storage as per Data's request (Goldsman 2020). Data, as a sentient being, chose the path of his existence and its ending—indicating that he was something more than simply an artificial intelligence within an android body. Certainly his friends and coworkers treat him as though he were alive in the fully human sense of the word, especially after he wins against Maddox in court (aside from Dr. Pulaski, whose very human prejudices mean she never treats him as better or more of a person than any other computer (Scheerer 1989)).

The character of Deadpool is another created one, and despite being an antihero there are times when the things he does seem truly monstrous (such as his murder of all primary Marvel heroes and then his jump into fiction and the resulting deaths of many other literary characters during his Deadpool Killustrated arc) (Cullen Bunn et al. 2014). Deadpool's human alter ego is the mercenary-for-hire Wade Wilson, who while dying of cancer agreed to a highly dangerous and experimental treatment. The result of this was his incredible healing factor—while it has not cured his cancer, it keeps it permanently from killing him—as well as preventing most other forms of death (including healing from decapitation, dismemberment, incineration and multiple gunshot wounds, among others). He is functionally immortal as he cannot age due to his cells' regenerative properties, although he has been killed and resurrected in the past more than once (Nicieza, Liefeld, et al. 2008). It is also responsible for his primary side effect from the treatment, psychosis (he often hallucinates a second version of himself which he holds entire conversations with). His dry sense of humour and fourth wall-breaking have made him a solid fan favorite, although it would be a struggle to describe him as a "good" person. At some point during his character arc he falls in love with Marvel's personification of death, after meeting her multiple times during a number of near-death experiences (Nicieza, Liefeld, et al. 2008). Deadpool literally straddles the barrier between life and death, passing between the two on several occasions.

Far less human creations are the preserve of the fictional company Umbrella, from the *Resident Evil* games. Presenting to the public as a pharmaceutical and health science research group, they are also producers of a number of viruses and other bioweapons, including many types of genetically engineered monster (Perry 1998). As expected, the virus escapes into the local environment and then into the nearest city, and the decision is made to use Raccoon City as a test environment for several BOW, or Bio-Organic Weapons (Perry 1999). These range from animals mutated due to viral exposure, such as giant spiders and vicious attack dogs, through to fully artificially created monstrosities such as Mr. X and the Tyrant (from the second and third video games respectively). This also ties back into the liminality of death enforced by pulling human bodies back across the brink—the primary and most-encountered antagonist in the Resident Evil games is once again the classic zombie. It also, in later games, once again asks—what makes one human?

The character of Albert Wesker deliberately infects himself with the T-Virus, although due to his prior genetic manipulation (as a child) it does not mutate him in the same way as it did his compatriots—instead, he melds with it, gaining supernatural strength and speed as well as a powerful healing factor (Seto and Kotake 2007). Of course, Wesker is the primary antagonist in multiple games, first working for Umbrella and then going freelance and being hired by other bioweapon researchers, such as Tricell. It could be stated, however, that it is not his being freed from the standard shackles of humanity that made him evil; he was already a master manipulator and rogue agent long prior to his transformation into the enhanced version of himself. His death in Resident Evil 5 during the climactic volcano battle comes after several further transformations, including his mutation into a giant and rather tentacled creature (Anpo and Ueda 2009). In a way, Wesker is a perfect metaphor for the Umbrella Corporation itself—self-serving from the outset with multiple hidden agendas, and with no regard for the suffering caused to others as long as there was enough scientific test data for study.

Frankenstein's creature is somewhat more of a sympathetic creation, having undergone immediate rejection by his creator and triggering abject horror in all those who can see him, due to his physical appearance (Shelley and Groom 1818/2019). It speaks volumes that his only friend throughout the novel is a blind old man, one who cannot see his face and thus cannot reject him simply at (literally) face value. It could but argued that he is less of a villain and more of a tragic character—forced into existence, dragged back across the liminal space between life and death, he never asked to be created—and, when he asks for a companion of his own, is denied even that simple choice for himself (Shelley and Groom 1818/2019). It seems little wonder that he chooses a life of exile deep within the arctic wilderness; he has no reason to attempt to join society, as nobody will accept him for who he is. Yes, he is a murderer, but it does not necessarily follow that it was something he initially wished for (his vengeful killing of Frankenstein's bride aside, but by that point in the tale the creature has entirely given up on his humanity).

The character of Blodeuwedd from Welsh mythology could also be seen as another creation driven to murder by events outside of her control. In her tale, the seer and witch Arianrhod has cursed her son Lleu Llaw Gyffes with never taking a human wife (Davies 2008). To counter this, the magicians Gwydion and Math create a beautiful woman from the flowers of three plants (oak, broom and meadowsweet respectively) and name her Blodeuwedd, and she is married off to Lleu in a human woman's place. Sometime later, Lleu is away on business and she meets and falls for the lord of Penllyn, Gronw Pebr. They conspire to murder Lleu, and Blodeuwedd persuades Lleu to tell her the secret of how he can be killed, as he is functionally immortal due to being Arianrhod's son. Once the secret is divulged, the lovers make an attempt at it, only to fail due to Lleu's eventual rescue by Gwydion and Math (although they do rule both Penllyn and the lands belonging to Lleu for a short time). Lleu is healed, regains his lands, and Blodeuwedd is punished by being transformed into an owl—cursed to be nocturnal due to all other birds having a hatred for her owl form. Gronw is killed by Lleu using the spear he attempted to use as a murder weapon, and the tale ends with Lleu's acceptance of the throne of all Gwynedd (Davies 2008). It is possible to see this tale through a more sympathetic lens—Blodeuwedd did not ask to be created, much like Frankenstein's creature, and she was never truly given the option to realize her own destiny, due to her enforced marriage to Lleu. She also undergoes multiple transformations throughout her tale—from flowers, to human, to wife, to traitor, and finally to an owl. She is not asked at any point what her wishes are, or whether she desires to marry Lleu—instead, as she is a creation, it is assumed that she will simply obey the commands given to her.

All creation tales have far earlier examples. Judaism has some early stories of artificial lifeforms; Golems, which are usually created from inanimate substances such as clay or mud. The earliest known written account of how to create a golem can be found in Sodei Razayya by Eleazar ben Judah of Worms, of the late twelfth/early thirteenth century CE. It is said that removing the name of the golem would cause it to disintegrate, but that it could later be revived if needed.

Even earlier than this is the ancient Greek myth of the Talos—a colossal automaton made of bronze, and in some sources crafted by the god Hephaestus himself (Grant and Hazel 1973/1993). The Talos's purpose was to protect Europa, the mother of King Minos in Crete, and so he circled the island three times daily and attacked approaching ships. He was ordered to be created by Zeus, who was enamored of Europa, and had made her the first queen of the island. Neither golems nor the Talos are sentient or independently intelligent, however, despite their ability to follow orders; which separates them from other automated creations such as Data. The most famous depiction of the Talos can be seen in the 1963 film Jason and the Argonauts, where in a departure from the myth he is guarding the "Isle of Bronze," and is awakened when Hercules attempts to steal from the island, despite a warning from the goddess Hera to only take provisions (Chaffey 1963).

As can be seen from the multiple examples described here, the idea of the darker side of transformation through creation has seized the imaginations of many over the centuries. Again, this would seem to tie directly back into a societal fear of a loss of control—but instead of control over the self, it is a loss of control within everyday life and the upending of the normal that is highlighted here. Much like the old idea of adults fearing teenagers, it is the exposure to the unknown that is the fearful part, the transformation of all that is known from the familiar to the strange.

LIMINAL SPACES AND PLACES

A person can, of course, also be transformed by a place, especially one of liminality. The spaces of life and death and the gap between them have been explored in much popular fiction and many folktales. There are multiple examples, from Hades to fairy rings; the Twilight or sumrak from Lukyanenko's Night Watch series of novels; Death as a plane within Garth Nix's Abhorsen books; or the concept of the Warp from Warhammer, an alternate dimension from which the visitor is unlikely to return from fully human, if at all. The Silent Hill series has layers of planes of existence built on top of each other, each a transformation of the previous. A place affected by the thoughts and dreams of its visitors and inhabitants, it follows an eerie cycle, almost mimicking REM sleep as it changes. On the outside, it is normal, everyday Silent Hill, a tourist town with a dark past—an ancient place of worship which was colonized, with the spiritual power of the area eventually being affected by the powerfully psychic character of Alessa and becoming malevolent (Heath 2003).

As the player character travels further into Silent Hill, they become engulfed in Alessa's nightmares and the alternate dimensions and realities she has created within the town (and eventually beyond, as her influence spreads to nearby towns). The first layer of Alessa's influence is the Fog World, which truly lives up to its name; swathed in vision-distorting mist and constant snow, there are few inhabitants here that are not trapped visitors or twisted manifestations of a person's psyche. Next, deeper, lies the Otherworld, which mirrors the Fog World with a corrupted reflection—it is a place of decay and despair, barbed wire and blood. The monsters are more prevalent and dangerous here, and it is permanently night, the walls made of pulsating flesh and rusting metal. The last area, the deepest layer of Alessa's nightmares, is named Unknown or Nowhere depending on the game.

Nowhere is a maze-like amalgamation of different areas of Alessa Gillespie's nightmares, including areas previously visited in the Otherworld and Fog World. Nowhere is generally where the primary boss battles of the game series are fought and depending on the player's actions throughout the game can result in the character's escape from Silent Hill or their death or entrapment within the Fog World (Heath 2003). Characters who have failed their test may find themselves stuck within a loop, repeating the same actions within the Fog World—such as the mailman from Silent Hill: Downpour; or dead and trapped within the various planes forever, like Angela Orosco in the second game. The liminality of this location is most obvious in the first three games, with characters passing between life and death on many occasions. In the original game, one of the achievable endings indicates that Harry Mason died as a result of crashing his car (while avoiding Alessa) at the beginning of the game, and his experiences within Silent Hill have been akin to a spiritual purgatory—death's "waiting room," as it were, experienced while dying or immediately after death, depending on his injuries (Heath 2003). While this is not the canonical ending in terms of story, it adds an extra layer of liminality to his experiences—was he alive or dead, while wandering through the nightmarish town?

Silent Hill 2 gives the protagonist, James Sunderland, a far more torturous procession in and out of Alessa's world. As a man burdened with the guilt of suffocating his terminally ill wife, which he has psychologically blocked out to protect his mental health, the town and/or Alessa conjures a nightmarish hellscape deliberately designed to ensure he suffers, because he subconsciously believes it to be necessary but does not remember why. When his dead wife suddenly steps back across the veil in the form of Maria, a transformed conjuration that is her opposite and everything he dreamed of while she was slowly dying of cancer, he is forced to see her die again and again and suffer the mental trauma of the constant loss, however short-lived. In this particular chapter of the town, the male monsters are punishment incarnate, murderous beasts and twisted unreal creatures representing how James sees himself—and the female monsters, such as the nurses and mannequins, are highly sexualized; femme fatales that have no qualms about attacking and murdering James while teasing him with what he cannot have (Heath 2003). *Silent Hill 3*, the direct sequel to the first game, takes the thinness of the veil between worlds even further. If the player character Heather Mason is killed, then a creature or god named Valtiel can often be seen dragging her body away before the load/quit screen appears—within the Silent Hill universe, Valtiel represents cycles and rebirth, and it is suggested that it is he who pulls Heather's spirit back across the boundary to try again (Heath 2003). Valtiel can be seen in the background in multiple locations, turning valves and wheels which sometimes change the plane of existence for Heather—from the Fog World to the Otherworld and back again, a constant cycle that occurs as Alessa draws Heather, the good part of her soul, further into her world.

Of course, there are many other manifestations of a liminal plane within storytelling, some with more fatal consequences than others. The Abhorsen series by Garth Nix centers around magical spell-casters, some of whom tie their power into a series of bells, the ringing of which can bind souls and send them into Death—or, draw them out, reanimating corpses both as sentient beings and as transformed Hands, mute servants with no free will (Nix 1995). In these novels, Death is a river with a series of waterfalls (known as Gates) that go ever deeper into this liminal space; it is a dangerous space to navigate and will murder (and thus entrap) unwary visitors. In the first book, the protagonist Sabriel is forced down as far as the Fifth Gate seeking her father's spirit; she frees him and he returns to life for "a hundred hundred heartbeats" to help her destroy a great evil, after he became trapped beyond the gate himself during a magical battle (Nix 1995).

Similar to this realm is the Twilight or Gloom (translated from the Russian word sumrak), found in Sergei Lukyanenko's Watch series. These books tell stories about the magic-using "Others," a group who can step into a shadow realm outside of the usual planes of existence. Each Other must, eventually, choose a side—Light or Dark, essentially Good or Evil, although something that is made clear in the books is that both sides are as hypocritical and self-serving as each other (Lukyanenko 1998/2007). There is a clear delineation between each faction, and each faction possesses a bureaucracy—the Night Watch, who serve the light, and the Day Watch, who serve the dark. Both factions are bound by a treaty of balance, and cannot unduly influence humanity one way or the other; this pact was signed due to centuries of devastating wars, with millions of casualties on both side. The Light includes conjurers, magicians, and shapeshifters; the Dark has the stereotypically "evil" vampires, werewolves, dark magicians, and similar. The Twilight is supposedly neutral ground, and similarly to other depictions of liminal spaces, has levels within it. The deeper the level, the more magically powerful and experienced the visitor must be to safely arrive and leave. By stepping into the Twilight, one can see destinies, revive the dead, travel great distances, and so forth (Lukyanenko 1998/2007). And once again, like many of these planes of existence, one can become trapped there and thus die in the "normal"/human world. Discovering that one can access the Twilight is one of the earliest steps on the path to transforming into an Other, and is usually done accidentally—after that point, their choice of path apparently depends on their actions and temperament (as well as whichever faction finds and educates them first). However, one's destiny is usually predetermined, and they do not truly have the free will to decide their side.

Warhammer's Immaterium, also known as the Warp, is described as a separate dimension inhabited by the essences of twisted monsters and corrupted gods, an ocean of psychic energy that thirsts to break through into our universe and devour it (Merrett and Robert 2013). There are four primary Gods of Chaos, corresponding somewhat roughly to the tradition of the four Horsemen of the Apocalypse—Tzeentch (change and sorcery), Slaanesh (pleasure and excess), Nurgle (pestilence) and Khorne (blood; skulls; generally a messy death). Some humans serve these gods willingly, in return for promises of personal grandeur and success; some are enslaved; and some are corrupted by objects such as books, swords or other cursed items. Humanity is regularly exposed to this dimension due to the mechanism of their faster-than-light travel—using a beacon on Earth known as the Astronomican, specialized psychic Navigators can use the Warp as a shortcut, travel within the Warp taking far less time than in real space. Of course, this travel into and through the Warp is what draws the attention of the beings within it, and so many ships have been lost to the vast psychic sea over the millennia (Merrett and Robert 2013). Rifts within the Warp have also been responsible for the unleashing of unspeakable demonic horror on unsuspecting planets within realspace, often leading to the planet's populace being corrupted and devoured by the dark psychic energies, all to better serve whichever Chaos god was the most interested or powerful at that point in time. A full transformation of both body and soul can be expected from exposure to the Warp and the gods within it—with passage from man to monster being a painful and sometimes deadly one, if the human involved is not physically strong enough to withstand the mutations (Merrett and Robert 2013).

One final example of a transformative liminal space within pop culture comes from the video game *Death Stranding*, a complex narrative detailing the adventures of one Sam Porter Bridges, a deliveryman in post-apocalyptic North America (Kojima 2019). Sam is a repatriate—someone with the ability to return to life after death. In this game's universe, the globe was struck by a series of simultaneous explosions, later titled the Death Stranding or an Extinction Event. This event resulted in the worlds of the dead and living becoming connected via a place known as the Beach, a place existing in the liminal space between the two states of being. Each person has their own timeless Beach, a limbo that one can travel to and from given certain abilities. Between the land of the living and the Beach lies the Seam—an underwater area where Sam's essence or soul is sent after death. For most, this is a one-way passage—but for repatriates like Sam, they can follow a strand back to their bodies in the real world, meaning that he literally cannot die unless he deliberately chooses to pass through the beach and into the afterlife (Kojima 2019). Beginning immediately following the global (and thought to be sixth) Death Stranding, whenever a person dies in the living world but their soul does not succeed in crossing their Beach to the afterlife, their corpse becomes a Beached Thing or BT unless destroyed before it begins to necrotize.

Bodies are usually incinerated, although there is only a small window of time that this remains an effective method of destruction. These souls, if given enough time, become 'stranded' in the living world due to the overlap between life and death and an inability to pass beyond their Beach (hence, Beached Thing; beached whales are used often as a metaphor within the game). These entities, if allowed to consume any other living person, will cause another gigantic explosion just like those of the initial global wave. These explosions have been named "voidouts" due to the native matter of the Beach reacting like antimatter with the victim's body. The most common type of BT seen during the game is a Gazer—a ghostly human form, floating in midair, attached to their Beach via an umbilical cord (Kojima 2019).

There are other types of BT, including several gigantic and monstrous ones. BTs can be perceived by sufferers of the condition DOOMS, which is essentially an enhanced connection to the Beach and the other side, giving them certain abilities which vary by level. Sam, as the primary protagonist, has a DOOMS level of 2, meaning that he can sense BTs but is unable to see them without connection to a Bridge Baby (an unborn fetus removed from a brain-dead mother, which strengthens links to the other side when used). Yes, it's a complicated one. But at its core, the game is about transformation, the liminality of death and the ability (or inability) to reach it—indeed, there is even a character named Heartman who is killed and then resurrected via automated external defibrillator (AED) every twenty-one minutes, as he searches for his lost family and researches the Beach phenomenon in three-minute bursts of death. When the player character of Sam encounters Heartman, he states that he has died and visited his Beach over 800,000 times in this quest, which has of course had a serious physical effect on him, seriously weakening his heart (Kojima 2019).

The character of Fragile, another porter, was once forced to run through Timefall with no protective gear by the antagonist of the game, and as a result her body is scarred and withered, looking far older than Fragile's actual physical age. It is revealed during the game that even Sam has undergone a radical transformation, from being the first Bridge Baby to being granted the power of repatriation to who he is during the story. The United States (and indeed possibly the entire globe) has been transformed by the Death Stranding phenomenon, a dangerous rain called Timefall prematurely aging and killing anything exposed to it, including plant and animal life. The world of Death Stranding is bleak and empty, with scattered groups of humans desperately trying to connect with each other through the porters, such as Sam and his fellow DOOMS-sufferer Fragile (Kojima 2019). At the same time, it carries a level of quiet beauty—looking much like unpopulated areas of Iceland for large segments of the game, from grassy lowlands to snowy mountaintops, with the Knot cities scattered across it like star grouping of Orion's Belt. As can be seen from the examples listed, there are many liminal spaces within fiction, for good or for ill. Some are definitely hostile, such as the Warp; some have dangerous effects on the world around themselves; and some are simply a steppingstone to another plane of being. They are all, however, places of transformation and transition.

CONCLUSION

So to answer the question posed at the beginning of this chapter—what is transformation? As can be seen from the examples described and dissected within this piece, it is a process that can be both internal and external, physical and mental, obvious and subtle. It can be monstrous—either through the creation of monsters or the suffering of the transformed. It can happen through direct intervention or accidentally, as punishment or as a blessing. It can be a route to godhood or madness. It can involve liminality, or not—as the creator prefers. From life to death and back again, from animal to person to monster, the concept plays a vital part within our folklore, religion, and fiction, and stories featuring it as a core mechanic are likely to be written and rewritten for millennia to come—provided the Death Stranding, the last extinction event, does not reach us first.

BIBLIOGRAPHY

Anpo, Yasuhiro, and Kenichi Ueda, dirs. 2009. *Resident Evil 5*. PlayStation 3. Capcom.
Baird, Stuart, dir. 2002. *Star Trek: Nemesis*. DVD. Paramount Pictures.
Bole, Cliff. 1990. "The Best of Both Worlds [Star Trek: The Next Generation]." TV Series Episode. Paramount Studios.
Bueno, Fernando. 2008. *Dead Space: The Official Game Guide*. Roseville, CA: Prima Games. https://archive.org/details/Dead_Space_Official_Game_Guide/mode/2up.
Burton, LeVar. 1997. "The Raven [Star Trek: Voyager]." TV Series Episode. UPN.
Cambridge Dictionary. 2019. "TRANSFORMATION | Meaning in the Cambridge English Dictionary." *Cambridge.Org*. https://dictionary.cambridge.org/dictionary/english/transformation.
Carey, Mike, Mark Frost, Michael France, and Dan Jurgens. 2005. *Fantastic 4*. New York: Marvel Comics.
Chaffey, Don, dir. 1963. *Jason and the Argonauts*. DVD. Columbia Pictures.
Cullen Bunn, Matteo Lolli, Sean Parsons, Veronica Gandini, and Joe Sabino. 2014. *Deadpool. Killustrated*. New York: Marvel Worldwide, Inc.
Fawcett, John, dir. 2000. *Ginger Snaps*. Canada: Motion International.
Fitzgerald, F Scott, Clare West, and Nick Hardcastle. (1922) 2017. *The Curious Case of Benjamin Button & Other Stories*. Oxford: Oxford University Press.
Frakes, Jonathan. 1990. "The Offspring [Star Trek: The Next Generation]." TV Series Episode. Paramount Studios.
———. dir. 1996. *Star Trek: First Contact*. DVD. United States: Paramount Pictures.
Gabrielle-Suzanne De Villeneuve, and Jeanne-Marie Leprince De Beaumont. (1740) 2013. *La Belle et La Bête*. Paris: Chêne.
Goldsman, Akiva. 2020. "Et in Arcadia Ego [Star Trek: Picard]." TV Series Episode. Amazon Prime.
Grant, Michael, and John Hazel. (1973) 1993. *Who's Who in Classical Mythology*. London: J M Dent.
Harris, Thomas. 1999. *Hannibal*. New York, N.Y.: Delacorte Press.
———. 2006. *Hannibal Rising*. New York: Delacorte Press.
Heath, Nora, trans. 2003. *Hiru 3 Koshiki Kanzen Koryaku Gaido Ushinawareta Kioku Sairento Hiru Kuronikuru.*: Konami, Tokyo. https://web.archive.org/web/20171003193903/http://www.translatedmemories.com/book.html.
Keyworth, David. 2007. *Troublesome Corpses: Vampires & Revenants, from Antiquity to the Present*. Southend-On-Sea, United Kingdom: Desert Island Books.
Kojima, Hideo, dir. 2019. *Death Stranding*. PS4. Sony Interactive.
Lang, Fritz, dir. 1927. *Metropolis*. DVD. Parufamet.
Lederman, Robert. 1992. "I, Borg [Star Trek: The Next Generation]." TV Series Episode. Paramount Studios.
Lindahl, Carl, John Mcnamara, and John Lindow. 2002. *Medieval Folklore: A Guide to Myths, Legends, Tales, Beliefs, and Customs*. Oxford; New York: Oxford University Press.
Lorrah, Jean. 1990. *Metamorphosis: The First Giant Novel*. London: Titan Books.
Mary Wollstonecraft Shelley, and Nick Groom. (1818) 2019. *Frankenstein, or, The Modern Prometheus: The 1818 Text*. Oxford: Oxford University Press.
Merrett, Alan, and Neil Robert. 2013. *Visions of Heresy: War, Darkness, Treachery and Death*. Nottingham: Black Library.
Nicieza, Fabian, Rob Liefeld, et al. 2008. *Deadpool Classic Vol.1*. New York, NY: Marvel Publishing; [London.

Nix, Garth. 1995. *Sabriel*. London: HarperCollins.

Otten, Charlotte F. 1986. *A Lycanthropy Reader: Werewolves in Western Culture; Medical Cases, Diagnoses, Descriptions; Trial Records, Historical Accounts, Sightings; Philosophical and Theological Approaches to Metamorphosis; Critical Essays on Lycanthropy; Myths and Legends; Allegory*. Syracuse, NY: Syracuse University Press.

Perry, S D. 1998. *The Umbrella Conspiracy*. New York; London: Pocket.

———. 1999. *City of the Dead*. New York; London: Pocket.

———. 2000. *Nemesis*. New York; London: Pocket.

Scheerer, Robert. 1989. "Measure of a Man [Star Trek: The Next Generation]." TV Series Episode. Paramount Studios.

Sergei Lukyanenko. (1998) 2007. *The Night Watch*. Translated by Andrew Bromfeld. London: Arrow Books.

Seto, Yasuhiro, and Hiroaki Kotake, dirs. 2007. *Resident Evil: The Umbrella Chronicles*. Wii. Capcom.

Shirley, John, and Ken Levine. 2011. *Rapture*. London: Titan.

Sioned Davies. 2008. *The Mabinogion*. Oxford; New York: Oxford University Press.

Stevenson, Robert Louis. (1886) 1997. *The Strange Case of Dr Jekyll and Mr. Hyde*. London: Dorling Kindersley.

Thomas, Jordan. 2009. *Deco Devolution: The Art of Bioshock 2*. Marin: Take-Two Interactive.

Wachowski, Lana, and Lily Wachowski, dirs. 1999. *The Matrix*. DVD. Warner Bros.

Wilde, Oscar. (1890) 2000. *The Picture of Dorian Gray*. Oxford: Oxford University Press.

Part II

Social Death/Cyborg Transformation

Where human and machine meet, where cyborg transformation occurs, there
exists a social death. Not un-alive, but not . . . human. Not anymore.

Chapter Two

Vengeful Monsters, Shapeshifting Cyborgs, and Alien Spider Queens

The Monstrous-Feminine in Netflix's
Love, Death & Robots

Sarah Stang

Scholars have long noted that the monster polices the symbolic borders of what is permissible, and to step outside of social norms risks being labelled monstrous and categorized as "other." This dehumanization is particularly common for transgressive women in mythology and popular culture, as "the woman who oversteps the boundaries of her gender role risks becoming a Scylla, Weird Sister, Lilith, . . . or Gorgon" (Cohen 1996, 9). The cyborg could easily be added to this list because, while technology can be empowering for women, the portrayal of the female cyborg body in popular culture—a body often designed by men—instead tends to dehumanize and so further marginalize women (Balsamo 1996; Doane 1992). Whether monstrous, cyborgian, or both, this literal dehumanization of women is ubiquitous: As feminist film scholar Barbara Creed (1986) has argued, "all human societies have a conception of the monstrous-feminine, of what it is about woman that is shocking, terrifying, horrific, abject" (44). Creed's foundational work demonstrates that the monstrous-feminine is more than just a female version of a male monster; rather, she is terrifying within patriarchal society because of her female physicality, as the female body is perceived as simultaneously attractive and dangerous, and the threat she poses to her male victims as a seductive, sexually predatory, and castrating figure. Rosi Braidotti (1994) has echoed Creed's observations, noting that there exists a "traditional patri-archal association of women with monstrosity" (80), and so female monsters are found in mythologies, legends, folklore, and artwork across cultures.

Female monsters often either take the form of the vengeful *femme castratrice* (see Creed 1993) or the beautiful but deadly *femme fatale* (see Doane 1991).

This chapter builds on Creed's concept of the monstrous-feminine, together with considerations of abjection, hybridity, and the cyborg body, to analyze the portrayal of nonhuman, hybrid, and/or monstrous women in Netflix's 2019 science fiction anthology series, *Love, Death & Robots.* Following Creed's approach to analyzing female monstrosity in visual media, I conduct a close reading of three characters from the series: Sonnie, a scarred cyborg and sexual assault survivor whose consciousness resides inside a monstrous bioengineered beast; Yan, a shapeshifting mythological nine-tailed fox with a cyborg body; and Greta, a spider-like alien creature who appears as a beautiful woman in the mind of her male captive. All three of these women have monstrous forms and are presented through a clearly gendered lens. Greta is portrayed as a horrific monstrosity who keeps her true form hidden from her lover/prisoner so he will accept her. Both Sonnie and Yan are victims of masculine violence with broken, unnatural bodies who become violent, vengeful cyborg-monsters. As this chapter demonstrates, *Love, Death & Robots*, like much science fiction, repeats problematic tropes of female representation by framing hybrid female bodies as broken and horrific, and presenting women as victimized yet also deceptive, predatory, violent, and most importantly, *not quite human* or even *entirely monstrous*. That these monstrous women prey on male characters demonstrates Creed's (1986) point that "the feminine is not per se a monstrous sign; rather, it is constructed as such within a patriarchal discourse which reveals a great deal about male desires and fears" (70). Given that all three episodes I discuss here were written and directed by men, their focus on sexual assault, rape revenge, seduction, sexualized female bodies, and female monstrosity reveals the same kinds of preoccupations men have had regarding women's bodies and behavior since antiquity.

SONNIE'S STORY: VICTIMIZATION, VIOLENCE, AND QUEER MONSTROSITY

Episode 1, "Sonnie's Edge" (Wilson 2019), is set in a futuristic, dystopian version of London in which massive bioengineered beasts are forced to engage in vicious underground battles as entertainment. These beasts are remotely linked to the minds of their owners, who control their actions from outside the arena. Sonnie, a scarred, dour woman who controls a beast named Khanivore, is a champion of these battles. At the beginning of the episode, a boisterous and arrogant man named Dicko approaches Sonnie, together with a beautiful blonde woman on his arm, to request that she throw the match. The conversation is tense and full of meaning: admiring Khanivore, Dicko exclaims "He's magnificent!" to which Sonnie responds "Yes. *She* is" (Wilson 2019). However, Sonnie was staring at Dicko's companion when she responded, thereby establishing her lesbian desire—an element that becomes important later in the episode. Sonnie refuses to throw the match, regardless of how much bribe money Dicko offers her. Sonnie's teammate informs Dicko that Sonnie does not fight for glory or money, rather each victory is symbolic vengeance against the men who raped and mutilated her, leaving her covered in scars—that is what gives her an "edge" in battle. This initial set up is important because it communicates to viewers that this story might be unique in the context of mainstream science fiction, in that it seems to be centralizing queer female empowerment—and since this is the first episode in the series, it potentially establishes the tone for the rest of the anthology. Although the writers likely believed this is what they were doing, as the episode progresses, it becomes clear that this story instead relies on over-used, regressive, and misogynistic tropes.

At the start of the fight, Sonnie's opponent—who controls a beast called Turboraptor—threatens her sexually, exclaiming that she's "a sweet little girl" who is going "down, down, down" while gesturing at his crotch as though forcing someone to give him oral sex (Wilson 2019). Once she starts winning the fight, he changes his tone and calls her a "fucking little cunt" (Wilson 2019)—an extremely misogynistic term that might be especially triggering for a rape survivor. Khanivore uses spiked, whip-like tentacles in battle, stabbing Turboraptor several times and thereby wielding penetrative phallic power—imagery that returns throughout the episode. This imagery evokes the eponymous (and female) monster in the film *Alien*, which Creed (1993) has discussed in relation to the way it reproduces by violently penetrating its victims and laying eggs inside them (130). A female monster enacting penetrative violence is therefore claiming phallic power for herself and occupying a dominant position. At this point in the episode, this act of penetration could be interpreted as Sonnie—who is directly controlling Khanivore—enacting vengeance for her own rape by violently penetrating her opponent, which is controlled by the man who made sexually aggressive gestures and verbally abused her.

Creed (1993) has argued that although the monstrous-feminine is designed by men to represent male fears of female power, it also presents women as an active, phallic, terrifying embodiment of "avenging female fury" (86). This is certainly apparent in this monstrous battle, as Khanivore stabs Turboraptor several times, but then he retaliates by slicing off several of her tentacles (thereby symbolically castrating her). He reclaims that phallic power and stalks her as she crawls back from him on the ground, slams her against the arena wall, and stabs her in the lower abdomen as she cries/roars in pain. The viewers are then shown a close-up shot of Turboraptor thrusting his blade even deeper into Khanivore's body, imagery which, as Kelly Williams (2019) points out, is reminiscent of sexualized violence, since "the position of the monsters—male pinning the female against the wall and penetrating her, graphically—is obviously reminiscent of a sexual position" (para. 13). While pinned against the wall, Khanivore manages to stab Turboraptor in the chest, killing him, and then decapitates him (thereby symbolically castrating him in turn).

By emerging victorious from this vicious battle of castration and penetration, Khanivore is the very image of the monstrous *femme castatrice* of rape revenge films as discussed by Creed (1993): she who embodies the "castrating female psychotic . . . and the woman who seeks revenge on men who have raped or abused her" (123). This battle is only a taste of what is to come, however, because after the match Dicko's companion, a woman named Jennifer who was previously shown clinging to Dicko's arm, comes to Sonnie's private chamber and seduces her. The seduction is intimate and tender, albeit with unnecessary shots of Jennifer's naked breasts pressed up against Sonnie's chest, evocative of lesbian porn intended for a heterosexual male gaze. Sonnie opens up to Jennifer, revealing that she is not driven by revenge or hate but by primal fear—she is not "the angry little girl, out for revenge" that everyone thinks she is (Wilson 2019). While Jennifer pretends to be innocent and "even a little bit frightened" of Sonnie (Wilson 2019), she is actually a deceptive *femme fatale* and stabs Sonnie through the skull while they kiss with sharp mechanical claws that extend from her fingers.

Jennifer is not only a *femme fatale* but a cyborg *femme fatale*—a seductive, treacherous, beautiful woman whose technologically enhanced body becomes a weapon in the most intimate of moments. She is also acting on Dicko's orders, telling Sonnie that she made him "so very, very angry" (Wilson 2019). In this moment, Dicko appears and begins to gloat, asking "are you scared now?" then calling Sonnie a "silly fucking girl" (Wilson 2019). Bleeding on the ground, Sonnie coughs out the words "neat . . . trick," which enrages Jennifer, who starts stomping on her head, smashing it in with her stiletto heel (Wilson 2019). This gruesome death leaves Sonnie's head crushed and broken, with blood and brains splattered around it and her eyeball popped out of its socket. Sonnie's body begins to convulse as she laughs, choking out the words "not good enough," before her disembodied voice reveals that the men who raped and maimed her had actually cracked her skull and left her for dead (Wilson 2019). Her friends were able to partially save her, but her human body is actually "just a couple of bioware processors spliced to a spine" while her consciousness resides in the body of her monstrous beast, Khanivore (Wilson 2019). As the creature slowly appears behind Dicko and Jennifer, Sonnie's voice plays out of a nearby speaker explaining that every time she steps into the ring, she is fighting for her life—"that fear of death" is her edge (Wilson 2019). Seeing Khanivore, Jennifer gasps and turns to run away, only to be stabbed through the back of the head by one of the creature's sharp tentacles—the writers seem to delight in the phallic imagery of Sonnie/Khanivore being stabbed and stabbing in turn. Khanivore then wraps a tentacle around Dicko's body, squeezing him and bringing him close to her massive, fanged jaws. The episode ends with Sonnie's voice asking Dicko "Are you scared now?"—repeating what he had said to her earlier—before fading to black (Wilson 2019).

While this story might be interpreted as satisfying or empowering since Sonnie wins the battle and kills her seducer and would-be murderer as well as the man who ordered her death, its portrayal of Sonnie as a victimized, violent, damaged, queer woman who literally becomes a monster after being raped and nearly killed by a group of men is decidedly problematic. In addition, the amount of gratuitous, graphic violence directed at Sonnie echoes the misogyny underpinning rape revenge films such as *I Spit on Your Grave*, with lingering and almost fetishistic shots of sickening violence against women even as the filmmakers claim to be telling a story of female empowerment (Creed 1993). This connection to rape revenge films might not be coincidental, as the series was coproduced by David Fincher, the director of notorious rape revenge film *The Girl with The Dragon Tattoo* (2011) which also uncomfortably lingers on the protagonist's brutal sexual assault and naked body. Fincher has made several films that involve sexualized violence against women, presented, as Richard Lawson (2011) notes, "from an unabashedly male perspective" (para. 1), and *The Girl with The Dragon Tattoo* specifically embraces "garish nastiness, rape as titillation" (para. 5). As Creed (1993) notes, in rape revenge films "woman, pleasure and death are intimately related" (129), and even though the woman's violence might be justified or even satisfying for the audience, she is still presented as monstrous—literally, in Sonnie's case.

Sonnie was completely stripped of her humanity when she was sexually assaulted, mutilated, and left for dead, and although she is indeed a "survivor," she is entirely defined by her trauma. That she became a monster after being raped echoes the ancient Greek myth of Medusa as recounted by Ovid in *Metamorphoses*: Medusa, once a beautiful human woman, was raped in Athena's temple by the god Poseidon. Angered by this desecration of her temple, Athena took her wrath out on Medusa, transforming her into a monster as punishment for her own rape. Medusa has since been claimed as a symbol of feminist rage—an embodiment of the misogyny that has shaped Western society for millennia as well as the injustice women face within patriarchal society, blamed and punished for their own victimization at the hands of men (Valentis and Dovane 1994). Creed (1993), drawing on and critiquing Freudian psychoanalysis, sees Medusa as a castrating figure, threatening to the male psyche and therefore used to oppress and control women's behavior. Indeed, Elizabeth Johnston (2016) considers Medusa the "original nasty woman"—a figure that haunts Western patriarchy, "materializing whenever male authority feels threatened by female agency" (para. 5).

As she notes, "in Western culture, strong women have historically been imagined as threats requiring male conquest and control, and Medusa herself has long been the go-to figure for those seeking to demonize female authority" (Johnston 2016, para. 1). Portraying woman-as-monster is, then, a means to punish and dehumanize women, and while female monstrosity might be empowering in some contexts, the creators of "Sonnie's Edge" have uncritically remediated the harmful misogynistic assumptions and beliefs that equate "rape survivor" with "monster."

That Sonnie is queer only adds salt to the wound, as queer women are especially marginalized and victimized within patriarchal society. For Sonnie, her queerness is framed as tragic rather than celebrated in any way, as she is violently betrayed by her would-be lover, and Jennifer being a *femme fatale* sends the message that bisexual women cannot be trusted—an unfortunately common trope in popular culture (Hart 1994). The *femme fatale* trope is one in which "woman's nature is represented as deceptive and unknowable" (Creed 1993, 136), and the fact that this treacherous, seductive, violent, queer woman is also a cyborg underscores the association between femininity, queerness, and monstrosity/nonhumanness—an association that seems to be the entire thematic focus of this episode. Feminist theorists have interpreted many kinds of female monsters as queer, and Creed (1996) has argued that "within homophobic cultural practices, the lesbian body is constructed as monstrous in relation to male fantasies" (87). The association between female homosexuality and female monstrosity has existed since antiquity and gives the example of the popular image of "the lesbian as a deadly siren who waits for her male prey while savoring an erotic embrace with her amoral sisters" (Creed 1996, 86–87). In this case, Sonnie is the monster preying on men while Jennifer is the deadly siren, and in both cases, they are punished for their transgressions. Sonnie's body is the recipient of horrific, gratuitous violence which completely destroys it and although it did not kill the "real" her, it did force her to reveal her "true" monstrous form and remove any possibility for her to "pretend" to be human again. And Jennifer, like most deadly sirens or *femme fatales*, is punished for her transgressions with a violent, penetrative death.

As Kelly (2019) has argued, Sonnie's story "is emblematic of the failure to find ways to represent female power (or empowerment) as anything other than monstrous" (para. 25). The men behind this story might have intended for Sonnie to be a "strong female protagonist," a trope that has long been critiqued by feminist critics skeptical of female empowerment that seems to always come as a result of the character's violent, horrific backstory (one that usually involves past sexual assault, sometimes with an added dash of rape revenge) and still results in women being portrayed in mostly one-dimensional ways (Chocano 2011; Dunn 2013; Gin 2017). Regardless of authorial intent, turning a queer woman into a violent monster, especially as a result of her sexual assault, is *not* in fact a very progressive choice. While she is technically the victor in the story, her existence is that of a victim—doomed to a life of violence, rage, dehumanization, and heartbreak.

YAN'S STORY: OBJECTIFICATION, SEXUAL SLAVERY, AND TRANSFORMATION

As if one story that dooms victimized women to a life of tragedy, sexual assault, bodily mutilation, and vengeful violence was not enough, the eighth episode of *Love, Death & Robots,* "Good Hunting" (Thomas 2019) features another nonhuman/monstrous woman who suffers countless violations at the hands of men. Yan is a *huli jing*, a mythological nine-tailed fox with the ability to shapeshift between animal and human forms. Her mother was murdered in front of her by a spirit hunter—"one of the brave *men* who protects humanity from spirits" (Thomas 2019; emphasis added)—hired to kill her because she had supposedly "bewitched" a man and was "draining" him through sexual intercourse like a succubus. Together with his son Liang, the story's protagonist and narrator, the hunter springs a trap on Yan's mother whom he claims "cannot resist the cries of the man she's bewitched" (Thomas 2019), tossing urine on her as she tries to shapeshift back into a fox in order to trap her in a hybrid form so she cannot flee as effectively from him.

Meanwhile, Liang finds the woman's daughter Yan, a frightened fox cub who transforms into a naked human girl to talk to him. Yan explains that her mother never bewitched the man, rather he was the one who fell in love with her and would not stop bothering her. Liang angrily insists that Yan's mother "lured men in and feeds on them for her evil magic" and Yan retorts that "a man can fall in love with a huli jing just like he can with a human woman" (Thomas 2019). Again, this upsets Liang, who declares that "it's not the same!" Yan replies "not the same? I saw how you looked at me," suggesting that Liang has been admiring her naked body while they talked (Thomas 2019). Suddenly, Yan's mother appears in the doorway right before the hunter's blade slices through her neck from behind, decapitating her. Yan flees, Liang covers for her as she escapes, and the hunter gathers the *huli jing*'s head, taking it as proof so he can collect his bounty.

Five years later, Liang and Yan are friends and he has been bringing her food because her ability to hunt has been declining. She is struggling to return to her fox form because increasing industrialization initiated by English colonizers is draining magic from the world. Liang moves to a steampunk-inspired Hong Kong, working with machinery and building automata while enduring racist treatment from the white English men who rule there. While walking, he sees a group of white men accosting Yan, who apparently also moved to Hong Kong at some point, and he saves her from them (they are inexplicably frightened of

Liang even though they outnumber him). She explains that she is now permanently trapped in her human form and has turned to sex work in order to
survive—"All I have is my beauty. Now I live by the very thing you accused my
mother of: I bewitch men for money" (Thomas 2019). She dreams of returning
to her animal form, hunting and "growl[ing] in the faces of all the men who
believe they can own me" (Thomas 2019).

After an undisclosed amount of time passes, Yan comes to Liang once
again in need of his help. She reveals that her body is now completely robotic
from the neck down. The governor, one of her regular clients, drugged her
and she woke up strapped to an operating table. The audience is shown a
flashback of white men in lab coats and medical masks peering down at her
before they start sawing into her leg, blood spurting everywhere as Yan
thrashes helplessly and screams in agony. The governor "could only get hard
for machines, and he wanted the ultimate machine to serve that twisted
desire" so he turned her into a cyborg against her will (Thomas 2019). Her
body is entirely mechanical, with the skin of her face and her long, dark hair
the only organic parts left, perhaps because, as she lamented previously, all
she has (that is, all she is valued for) is her beauty. The audience is shown a
scene of her naked body on display for white men to admire, and although
this was likely intended to be a critique of racist and sexist objectification,
the episode itself continuously puts Yan's body on display for the viewer,
clearly catering to the heterosexual male gaze. In a flashback, she explains
how she finally said no to the governor, refusing to continue being his sex
toy/sexbot. She murders him, declaring that "a terrible thing had been done
to me, but I could also be terrible" while the camera lingers on her naked
body (Thomas, 2019). While this was likely intended to be a potentially
empowering scene, as she violently murders the man who mutilated her and
turned her into a living sexbot, the gratuitous nudity positions Yan's body as
a site of voyeuristic-fetishistic spectacle. This titillating combination of violence and sexualization is an unfortunately common way in which the female
cyborg body is presented in mainstream science fiction (Cornea 2007; Gillis
2005; Lan 2012; Melzer 2006; Springer 1996).

Knowing that Liang is skilled with machines, she asks him to help her
regain the ability to hunt, to exact vengeance against "the men who perpe-
trate evil, but call it progress" (Thomas 2019). Liang agrees to help her, and
the montage that follows presents Liang as an active and creative inventor/
genius, while Yan is shown laying passive, waiting for him to alter her body.
She groans in pain from the procedures, and several of the positions she takes
while he works on her are decidedly sexual—the audience is even shown a
close-up of her buttocks as Liang removes the metal plate covering them and
her metal breasts with Liang's hands on them as he places a new breastplate
on her. Once Liang's work is complete, Yan undergoes a painful transformation, screaming as her mechanical body extends and shifts into nine-tailed

fox form. Liang wishes her "good hunting" as she leaps from his balcony into the night (Thomas 2019). In the final scene, an Asian woman is being harassed and assaulted by a group of white men, and Yan leaps down from above to attack them as the episode ends.

The unnecessary additions of Yan moaning in agony during this process, plus the horrific medical procedure the audience was shown earlier, suggest a sadistic desire to put her torment on display for the viewer. This reinforces Abby Robinson's (2019) point that the series relishes in a "display of female suffering and degradation for the sole purpose of entertainment" (para. 12). Like "Sonnie's Edge," this episode focuses on a sexually victimized woman with a tragic backstory whose body is mutilated and technologically altered by men. Perhaps worse, in "Good Hunting" Yan is dependent upon a man to help her survive and adapt—her life, agency, and possibility for vengeance are given to her by Liang. In this sense, as seen from Yan's perspective, the story is technophobic—technology led to the loss of her powers and then the loss of her bodily integrity, and although she becomes a robotic fox in the end, it is a poor, artificial substitute for her original magical form. From Liang's perspective, though, the story is technophilic—he finds his calling as a genius mechanic, engineer, and roboticist, and technological development is the one thing that keeps Yan in his life, dependent upon him.

Donna Haraway (1991) has argued that the cyborg could be an empowering figure for women because it collapses boundary distinctions and so potentially challenges patriarchal ideologies embedded in technology. However, this episode seems to disagree, instead hinting that technology is good for men and bad for women—men get to master it, while women are at its mercy. This point has been articulated by several feminist scholars concerned with the intersection of gender and technology. Anne Balsamo (1996), for example, has argued that regardless of the potentials of technological development, it is still heavily influenced by patriarchal gender norms and boundaries. Similarly, as Mary Anne Doane (1990) has demonstrated, the representation of "techno-femininity" in science fiction cinema is used to reinforce rather than destabilize gendered stereotypes. In science fiction, there is a clear distinction between strong, resilient, and resourceful female heroes who use violence to save the day, such as Sarah Connor in *The Terminator* and Ripley in *Alien*, and "the vicious female cyborg that represents the patriarchal fear of female sexuality" such as Maria in *Metropolis* or the Borg Queen in *Star Trek: First Contact*, who are both sexually attractive and dangerous (Lan 2012, 195; see also Melzer 2006; Springer 1996). The latter can be understood as a version of the monstrous-feminine, in that her hybrid technologically enhanced body is what gives her the (phallic) power to threaten men, yet, as Brown (2011) argues, the female cyborg is fetishized, combining sexual attractiveness and violent capability. These critiques certainly apply to the portrayal of Yan.

The writers of "Good Hunting" could have attempted to develop a more nuanced, less misogynistic story of survival and adaptation but chose not to. Certainly, Yan gets her revenge, but like Sonnie her empowerment comes at a high cost. While there is something appealing about her final embrace of a robot animal form—not her "true" form but as close as she can get now—and the freedom and power it affords her, the trauma, abuse, dehumanization, and literal objectification she undergoes sours the story. She is victimized, sexualized, and mutilated—the same misogyny, violence, and discrimination that lead to her mother's murder ruined Yan's life. Like Sonnie trapped in Khanivore's body, as a fox all Yan has left is violence. There are no happy endings for hybrid, monstrous, magical women in *Love, Death & Robots*—only suffering, pain, and death.

GRETA'S STORY: DECEPTION, HORROR, AND UNREQUITED LOVE

Episode 7, "Beyond the Aquila Rift" (Bérelle et al. 2019) presents a different kind of female monstrosity. Instead of centralizing female despair, victimhood, physical mutilation, and vengeance, this episode engages more with the trope of the deceptive, seductive, sexually predatory woman. Thom, the protagonist, is a likeable, middle-aged spaceship captain returning home with his crew after a successful mission. Due to a routing error, their ship ends up lightyears off course, and Thom wakes up from his cryogenic slumber to alarms blaring. The doors open and he is greeted by a familiar face—his former lover, Greta. Thom thinks that he is just stuck at a repair facility for a few weeks, and Greta is excited to rekindle their romance. Greta meets Thom in her private quarters wearing a tight, short golden dress, and the camera focuses on her buttocks as she walks, the sound of her high heels clicking on the floor. As she walks in front of Thom, she asks if he likes the view, and while she could be referring to the view of space out of her large windows, the playful smile on her face suggests that she is referring to her own cleavage, prominently on display thanks to the low-cut dress. Their conversation is friendly and flirty, with Thom referring to their previous tryst as a "fling" and Greta insisting that it was more than just a fling, recalling when they broke a bed in a hotel room and that she "never knew anyone could fuck that hard in zero-G" (Bérelle et al. 2019).

The episode shifts into an unsurprising montage of Thom and Greta having passionate sex, after which Greta reveals that she was not completely honest with him—he is actually much farther from Earth than she let on, and he will never get back home. Thom wakes up his crew member Suzy to tell her the bad news, but she is uncontrollably agitated and hostile, insisting that Greta is not who she says she is, begging Thom to "look at her!" (Bérelle et al. 2019). Suzy attacks Greta, cutting her neck in the process, but later in bed Thom notices that the cut is gone. This confirms his suspicions that the woman is not really Greta, and he confronts her about it. Greta reveals that she is feeding him a fake reality and he grows increasingly angry and violent toward her, pushing her back against the same window they had sex against earlier. Greta tearfully insists that Thom is not ready to know the truth, as she has "been through this" with countless other "lost souls" who ended up there and that she does not want to hurt him (Bérelle et al. 2019). He demands to see her true form, and she reluctantly agrees though she asks him to understand that she really does care for him.

The scene cuts to a much older, emaciated Thom, who wakes up and looks around, shocked and horrified by what he sees. The ship is caught in and covered by thick webbing, giving it an unpleasant organic appearance while the music rises in an unsettling crescendo. This image is particularly disturbing because the messy, visceral, possibly sticky organic substance covers every clean, crisp, metallic surface of the ship, rendering the space dark and creepy. The image is horrifying for Thom not only because the substance likely came out of some creature's body, but also because it has fully dominated the human technology it covers—the ship (and Thom) is completely engulfed by it with no hope of escape.

Thom hears Greta's distorted, uncanny, echoing voice, greeting him with a sultry "hello, Thom" (Bérelle et al. 2019). As it echoes around the ghastly chamber, a figure emerges from a shadowy cave. At first, it appears to be a shapely human woman but as she continues to step into the light, the music intensifies and her full body is revealed to be a giant, horrifying spider-alien creature with dozens of eyes and legs, and a pink, puckered, circular mouth. The creature's pale pink skin, stretched taut over bones and muscles, appears to glisten as if covered in slime, and it makes a creepy chittering noise. Horrified at what he is seeing, Thom screams while the scene flickers between a close-up of his terrified face and wide eyes and the spider-alien's grotesque body and blinking, beady eyes. The flickering shot-reverse-shot effect intensifies until the scene cuts to younger, healthy Thom once again waking up in his pod, with human Greta there to greet him with a friendly "hello Thom" (Bérelle et al. 2019). He asks if it is really her, and she dodges the question, instead saying "It's good to see you, Thom" and the scene proceeds with him once again shocked that his ship has gone so far off course and Greta acknowledging how upsetting it is but reminding him that "at least there's a friendly face here" (Bérelle et al. 2019). The scene flickers between a regular version of Thom's ship in the repair station and the true version of it surrounded by dense webbing before the credits roll.

In the original short story on which this episode is based, the author Alastair Reynolds makes it clear that the creature is benevolent, and truly means no harm to Thom. She sees herself as a caretaker—although she knows that Thom will eventually die, like the rest of the "lost souls" who have ended up in her web, she still wants him to live out the remainder of his life in a comforting, happy illusion. On Twitter, the screenplay writer Phillip Gelatt has confirmed that the creature is "benevolent & horrible at the same time" (Gelatt 2019a) but that the "horrible" part is referring specifically to her appearance (Gelatt 2019b). However, he does acknowledge that "the way it is going about being benevolent is questionable, if not outright horrible. But it's [*sic*] intentions are pure. It does love, I think" (Gelatt 2019b). He goes on to say that "it wants him to be happy. And it wants him to come to some kind of acceptance of his circumstance" (Gelatt 2019c). And yet, the episode's portrayal of Greta does not really reflect this interpretation: The use of unsettling music and sounds, flickering shot-reverse-shot, the "bait-and-switch" reveal of her initially appearing as a voluptuous naked woman as she emerges from the shadows, and the close-ups of the creature's body and Thom's terrified reaction make it clear that this was intended to be a horrific surprise reveal. As Thom looks around his nearly unrecognizable ship in horror, he sees the corpses of his crew members, and he himself appears on the verge of death. In addition, the ship seems to be trapped in the creature's webbing, suggesting that she catches ships like prey. Although this is not suggested in the original story, the show's portrayal makes it difficult to sympathize with the creature and instead frames her as predatory. In addition, the fact that she traps people in illusions and, at least in Thom's dream, disguises herself as a seductive, beautiful woman and takes advantage of him—after all, she tricked him into thinking she was Greta, flirted with him aggressively, and had sex with him—reinforces that same *femme fatale* message that women are untrustworthy, deceptive, and sexually manipulative. The audience is expected to react with horror and revulsion toward the creature, aligned as they are with Thom's perspective. In this sense, regardless of the creature's motivations, she is designed to appear repulsive, predatory, and entirely monstrous.

Although Gelatt uses the pronoun "it" to refer to the creature, in the original short story, the creature is unambiguously female, the queen of a kind of colony, residing in "a matriarchal chamber" (Reynolds 2016, 69). In the show, Greta's true form is framed as female in both overt and symbolic ways. This is important because her femaleness, together with her spider-like design, is directly connected to her monstrosity and abjection. Most male spiders do not build webs, or at least build them less often than female spiders because they are not as territorial and need to travel to find mates (Foster 2020). Even when males do build webs, they are usually not as large, thick, or extensive as those made by female spiders because the latter live, eat, and breed in those webs for their entire lives—both their food and their mates come to them (Foster 2020). Greta's web network is incomprehensibly vast—so thick and large it can engulf an entire spaceship—and, given how the webs seem to stretch out into the distance and Greta claims that she's been through this "a million times" (Reynolds 2016, 68), it is likely that her web has caught many ships and that the creature is ancient. If she is anything like Earth arachnids—and even if she is not, her design was at least clearly inspired by Earth arachnids—her massive web-lair suggests that she is indeed a female creature.

According to Julia Kristeva (1982), the abject is that which elicits reactions of disgust, horror, and fear. Spiders are abject creatures, the cause of a relatively common phobia, and so the choice to give Greta multiple legs and eyes was clearly done to elicit those intertwining reactions of fear and disgust. In addition, the upper part of Greta's body almost appears humanoid, with arms reaching out to either side. The placement of the eyes and mouth, then, is roughly where a human's genitals would be. This is not incidental: the creature's mouth—puckered, with pink lips surrounding a dark hole—resembles either a vagina or an anus. It could arguably be a kind of *vagina dentata* or "toothed vagina," a common trope of female monstrosity as well as a misogynistic legend found in cultures from around the world that symbolizes "the threatening aspect" of female genitals (Creed 1993, 105). According to Creed (1993), "woman . . . terrifies because man endows her with imaginary powers of castration" (87). The locus of these powers is the vagina—an organ that, according to Creed (1993), heterosexual men both desire and fear because although it is pleasurable for most men to penetrate the vagina, it also means that the penis must be "devoured" by the woman's body, disappearing inside of her. The vagina is often symbolically associated with the mouth precisely because of that act of devouring the penis, and not only does the myth of the *vagina dentata* symbolize "male fears and phantasies about the female genitals as a trap, a black hole which threatens to swallow them up," it also "points to the duplicitous nature of woman, who promises paradise in order to ensnare her victims" (Creed 1993, 106). Greta's sexually charged illusions could be interpreted as exactly that deadly promise of paradise.

As Braidotti (1994) has demonstrated, women's bodies have been "forever associated with unholy, disorderly, subhuman and unsightly phenomena" (80). Like all unsightly bodies, a spider creature like Greta is fascinating even as it is abhorrent, and since she was initially presented as a sexualized, conventionally attractive woman, and has the ability to become that woman again at any time, she is simultaneously both desirable and repulsive. Greta is also described in the short story as having waited there "for eternities" wanting "nothing more than to care for the souls of the lost" (Reynolds 2016, 60). These details paint a picture of some kind of ancient alien spider queen or goddess—an important element in the discussion of female monstrosity given how patriarchal rewritings of myths "recast [the] goddess as devil, monster, and whore" (Caputi 2004, 13). As powerful women signify a threat to patriarchal society, they must be made monstrous and therefore dehumanized and categorized as evil (Caputi 2004). As with Sonnie and Yan, an extremely effective way of dehumanizing someone is to make them literally a nonhuman monster/cyborg/alien—a framing that also categorizes them as an abject subject. According to Kristeva (1982), one of the reasons the abject is so disturbing is that it challenges the divide between self and other, human and nonhuman—the abject subject is one who embodies the "in-between, the ambiguous, the composite" (4) and is "heterogenous, animal, metamorphosed, altered" (207). Because it draws one "toward the place where meaning collapses," the abject must be "radically excluded" or repressed (Kristeva 1982, 2). One way of repressing the abject is by framing it as monstrous and horrific, and, in Thom's case, rejecting it altogether in favor of a more pleasant, normative illusion.

THE FEMALE MONSTER AS A SITE OF MALE SEXUAL ANXIETY

Although these three episodes are not the only ones with problematic portrayals of women—"The Witness" is similarly pornographic, male gaze-y, and violent—these are the ones that seem particularly preoccupied with framing women as monstrous nonhumans. Cristina Santos (2016) has argued that phallocentric discourse exercises dominance over the female body by depicting women "who fail to accept their predefined roles within their culture and society as monstrous" (xv). From a vengeful and monstrous rape survivor, to a bewitching mythological cyborg/sexbot, to a horrific and deceptive alien spider queen, the female characters in these episodes all embody and reinforce misogynistic ideas about women. The show's creators claim that they wanted to write a "love letter to nerds" (Long 2019), and in doing so they have uncritically remediated some of the worst tropes related to female representation in speculative fiction.

As Robinson has argued, this series is full of "gratuitous female nudity" (para. 6) and audiences "see women's bodies in disturbing, threatening scenarios, where very real trauma is used as a prop" (para. 18). Her criticisms are cogent and worth quoting at length:

> Women in varying states of undress are littered throughout the series, serving no purpose other than to be ogled at—and when you consider that this is a series which has been overseen by two men, with all of the writing and directing credits (that we can see) also male bar one, there is no way to frame this as anything other than problematic (para. 13).

Similar criticisms have been levied at the series by others, such as Ben Travers' (2019) point that the whole series has "a gross male gaze problem" (para. 4). Peter Rubin (2019) sees the series as "an endless parade of stoic supermen and the women who deceive or escape them," suggesting that this love letter is aimed at a "particularly retrograde subset of genre fans" (para. 6).

I would agree with these critiques, as the show's representation of women falls into long established tropes that serve to oppress, constrain, and police the borders of permissible female behavior. Women's positioning is particularly fraught and contradictory because they are forced into the role of both victim and monster, as seen with Sonnie and Yan. Echoing Creed's earlier work on female monstrosity, Braidotti (2011) has observed that "woman, as a sign of difference, is monstrous . . . the female body shares with the monster the privilege of bringing out a unique blend of fascination and horror" (226). Indeed, this idea—that within patriarchal society rife with misogynistic discourse, woman is not just framed as sexual other but is so feared and reviled that she is categorized as *nonhuman* and *monstrous*—has been repeated by feminist theorists concerned with highlighting the oppressive function of monstrosity as a label used to other, categorize, and marginalize non-male (and non-white, non-heterosexual, non-normative) bodies. The presence of female monsters in popular culture is therefore not surprising (Caputi 2004; Creed 1993), especially in science fiction, which often features nonhuman, cyborg, and/or monstrous others.

But, as I have discussed, Sonnie, Yan, and Greta are all ambiguous women—powerful and capable, even while they are simultaneously victimized, abused, tortured, sexualized, and rejected as horrific and monstrous. Sonnie and Yan are survivors, doing what they can to exist in a world that has broken them and changed their bodies forever. But Sonnie is a champion and Yan will, presumably, go on to save more women from predatory men. Greta might be a horrific monstrosity, but that is only because Thom is too weak to accept her as she is. Regardless of her appearance—she is not human so why should she be held to human beauty standards?—she is clearly an ancient, powerful creature, able to weave both extensive web networks and convincing telepathic illusions. She does not need Thom's approval, as much as she would like him to accept his fate. For feminist scholar Deborah Covino (2004), the abject woman is subversive and liberating: she "immerse[s] herself in the significances of the flesh, becoming willfully monstrous as she defies the symbolic order" (29). Patricia Yaeger (1992) has similarly proposed that women should seek a grotesque and sublime feminist aesthetic by embracing their own unruly bodies. Regardless of the problematic way they are victimized, abused, and/or presented as eldritch horrors, these characters all draw on that image of a powerful, willfully monstrous woman. In this sense, within the ambiguity of these characters lies the potential for feminist reclamation and empowerment. However, Sonnie, Yan, and Greta were written and designed by men, and given the overwhelming dominance of male directors and authors in science fiction, the feminist potential of these characters is undercut by authorial intention and bias. This is not to diminish the power of oppositional or subversive reading, nor am I arguing that there should be no female monsters, aliens, and cyborgs in science fiction. However, space must be made for powerful, active, willfully monstrous women who do not need to be victimized, abused, tortured, raped, or framed as deceptive, seductive *femme fatales* in order to exist. Given the negative critical reception of the show, it is clear that popular science fiction needs to move past these harmful tropes and instead allow viewers, who are hopefully stronger than Thom, to see, accept, and celebrate those women in all their hybrid, monstrous, abject glory.

BIBLIOGRAPHY

Balsamo, Anne M. 1996. *Technologies of the Gendered Body: Reading Cyborg Women*. Durham: Duke University Press.

Bérelle, Léon, Dominique Boidin, Rémi Kozyra, and Maxime Luère, dir. 2019, March 15. "Beyond the Aquila Rift." *Love, Death & Robots*. Netflix.

Braidotti, Rosi. 1994. *Nomadic Subjects: Embodiment and Sexual Difference in Contemporary Feminist Theory*. New York: Columbia University Press.

Braidotti, Rosi. 2011. *Nomadic Subjects: Embodiment and Sexual Difference in Contemporary Feminist Theory*. Second Edition. New York: Columbia University Press.

Caputi, Jane. 2004. *Goddesses and Monsters: Women, Myth, Power, and Popular Culture*. Madison: University of Wisconsin Press.

CD Projekt Red. 2007–2015. *The Witcher* series. CD Projekt. Microsoft Windows.

Chocano, Carina. 2011. "'Tough, Cold, Terse, Taciturn and Prone to Not Saying Goodbye When They Hang Up the Phone.'" *The New York Times*. July 3. https://www.nytimes.com/2011/07/03/magazine/a-plague-of-strong-female-characters.html.

Cohen, Jeffrey Jerome. 1996. "Monster Culture (Seven Theses)." In *Monster Theory: Reading Culture*, edited by Jeffrey Jerome Cohen, 3–25. Minneapolis: University of Minnesota Press.

Cornea, Christine. 2007. *Science Fiction Cinema: Between Fantasy and Reality*. Edinburgh: Edinburgh University Press.

Covino, Deborah C. 2004. *Amending the Abject Body: Aesthetic Makeovers in Medicine and Culture*. Albany: SUNY Press.

Creed, Barbara. 1986. "Horror and the Monstrous-Feminine: An Imaginary Abjection." *Screen* 27, no. 1: 44–71. https://doi.org/10.1093/screen/27.1.44.

Creed, Barbara. 1993. *The Monstrous-Feminine: Film, Feminism, Psychoanalysis*. New York/London: Routledge.

Creed, Barbara. 1996. "Lesbian Bodies: Tribades, Tomboys and Tarts." In *Sexy Bodies: The Strange Carnalities of Feminism*, edited by Elizabeth Grosz, and Elspeth Probyn, 86–103. New York: Routledge.

Doane, Mary A. 1990. "Technophilia: Technology, Representation and the Feminine." In *Body/Politics: Women and the Discourses of Science*, edited by Mary Jacobus, Evelyn Fox Keller, and Sally Shuttleworth, 163–76. London and New York: Routledge,

Doane, Mary A. 1991. *Femmes fatales: Feminism, film theory, psychoanalysis*. New York: Routledge.

Dunn, Sarah. 2013. "Enough With the 'Strong Female Characters,' Already." *Mic*. October 9. https://www.mic.com/articles/66469/enough-with-the-strong-female-characters-already.

Fincher, David, dir. 2011. *The Girl with the Dragon Tattoo*. Sony Pictures Entertainment.

Foster, Steve. 2020. "Do Male Spiders Spin Webs? Not What You Expected." *School of Bugs*. https://schoolofbugs.com/do-male-spiders-spin-webs/.

Gelatt, Philip (@pmjeepers). 2019a. "Yes, benevolent & horrible at the same time." Twitter post, April 16, 2019. https://twitter.com/pmjeepers/status/1118148989117796352?s=20.

Gelatt, Philip (@pmjeepers). 2019b. "It's appearance, certainly." Twitter post, April 18, 2019. https://twitter.com/pmjeepers/status/1118948350672297984?s=20.

Gelatt, Philip (@pmjeepers). 2019c. Yes. "It wants him to be happy." Twitter post, April 18, 2019. https://twitter.com/pmjeepers/status/1118953583867621376?s=20.

Gillis, Stacy. 2005. "Cyber Noir: Cyberspace, (Post)Feminism and the Femme Fatale." In *The Matrix Trilogy: Cyberpunk Reloaded*, edited by Stacy Gillis, 74–85. London: Wallflower

Ginn, Sherry. 2017. *Marvel's Black Widow from Spy to Superhero: Essays on an Avenger with a Very Specific Skill Set*. Jefferson: McFarland.

Haraway, Donna. 1991. "A Cyborg-Manifesto: Science, Technology, and Socialist-Feminism in the late Twentieth Century." In *Simians, Cyborgs and Women: The Reinvention of Nature*, 149–81. New York: Routledge.

Haraway, Donna. 1992. "Promises of Monsters: A Regenerative Politics for Inappropriate/d Others." In *Cultural Studies*, edited by Lawrence Grossberg, Cary Nelson, and Paula A. Treichler, 295–337. New York: Routledge.

Hart, Linda. 1994. *Fatal Women: Lesbian Sexuality and the Mark of Aggression*. London: Routledge.

Johnston, Elizabeth. 2016. "The Original 'Nasty Woman.'" *The Atlantic.* November 6. https://www.theatlantic.com/entertainment/archive/2016/11/the-original-nasty-woman-of-classical-myth/506591/.

Kristeva, Julia. 1982. *Powers of Horror: An Essay on Abjection*. Translated by Leon S. Roudiez.New York: Columbia University Press.

Lan, Kuo Wei. 2012. "Technofetishism of Posthuman Bodies: Representations of Cyborgs, Ghosts, and Monsters in Contemporary Japanese Science Fiction Film and Animation." PhD diss., University of Sussex. http://sro.sussex.ac.uk/id/eprint/40524/.

Lawson, Richard. 2011. "'The Girl with the Dragon Tattoo': We Only Hurt the Ones We Love." *The Atlantic.* December 21. https://www.theatlantic.com/culture/archive/2011/12/girl-dragon-tattoo-we-only-hurt-ones-we-love/333985/.

Long, Christian. 2019. "SXSW: Love, Death & Robots is Tim Miller's 'Love Letter to Nerds.'" *SyFyWire.* March 11. https://www.syfy.com/syfywire/sxsw-love-death-robots-tim-miller-love-letter-to-nerds.

Melzer, Patricia. 2006. *Alien Constructions: Science Fiction and Feminist Thought*. Austin: Texas University Press.

Reynolds, Alastair. 2016. *Beyond the Aquila Rift: The Best of Alastair Reynolds*, edited by Jonathan Strahan and William Schafer. London: Gollancz.

Robinson, Abby. 2019. "Netflix's Love Death + Robots has one very big problem and it's not okay." *Digital Spy.* March 18. https://www.digitalspy.com/tv/ustv/a26856709/love-death-and-robots-netflix-sexist-misogynistic/.

Rubin, Peter. 2019. "Love, Death & Robots and the Rise of NSFW Netflix." *Wired.* March 15. https://www.wired.com/story/love-death-and-robots-review/.

Santos, Cristina. 2017. *Unbecoming Female Monsters: Witches, Vampires, and Virgins*. Lanham:Lexington Books.

Springer, Claudia. 1996. *Electronic Eros: Bodies and Desire in the Postindustrial Age*. Austin: Texas University Press.

Thomas, Oliver, dir. 2019, March 15. "Good Hunting." *Love, Death & Robots.* Netflix.

Travers, Ben. 2019. "'Love, Death & Robots' Review: David Fincher and Tim Miller's Netflix Shorts Are One-Dimensional Beauty." *IndieWire.* March 10. https://www.indiewire.com/2019/03/love-death-robots-review-netflix-series-david-fincher-1202050029/.

Valentis, Mary and Anne Devane. 1994. *Female Rage: Unlocking Its Secrets, Claiming Its Power*. New York: Clarkson Potter.

Williams, Kelly. 2019. "What Exactly is 'Sonnie's Edge?': Thinking About Women's Bodies in Love Death + Robots." *The Vault of Culture.* April 14. https://www.vaultofculture.com/vault/feature/williams/sonniesedge.

Wilson, Dave, dir. 2019, March 15. "Sonnie's Edge." *Love, Death & Robots.* Netflix.

Yaeger, Patricia. 1992. "The 'Language of Blood': Toward a Maternal Sublime." *Genre* 25, no. 1: 5–24.

Chapter Three

"We're All, in the End, Part of the Same Great Thing"

Gender, Death, and Memory in Aliette de Bodard's The Tea Master and the Detective

Alex Claman

INTRODUCTION

Memory is a notoriously fickle thing; it shifts and changes over time, lending new cadences and rhythms to past times. Both mind and body remember positives and negatives, joys and traumas. As humans' reliance on external storage continues to grow, the meaning of *embodied* memory is shifting and adapting—the "cyborgification" of humanity is not a question of whether it has happened, it is a question of extent. In light of this, it is increasingly important to consider questions of memory and the persistence of that memory after death. Use, reuse, and misuse of memory can take place at every scale from the personal to the sociocultural (Stoler 2016).

Throughout the (ongoing) course of her Xuya universe, Aliette de Bodard has pondered questions about death, gender, and memory. In this chapter, I will examine her novella, *The Tea Master and the Detective*, through queer and (post)colonial theoretical lenses to tease out how she posits these questions and suggests answers to them. The Xuya universe presents a far-future alternate history in which the Americas were primarily colonized by southeast and central Asian empires, namely China and Vietnam.[1] Proceeding forward from that divergence point, the stories examine life within a galaxy under the dominion of a Confucian-inspired Chinese and Vietnamese space-faring empire. Within this world, *The Tea Master and the Detective* unfolds a beautifully complex story that addresses embodied trauma, memory, varied experiences of physical and emotional intimacy, and legacies of and resistance to imperial expansion. In this respect it builds on the anti-establishment nature of the *roman scientifique* (Stableford 2017). The Shadow's Child is, in some sense(s), monstrous: she is not traditionally human, her form and appearance are reconfigurable, and she can survive unaided in space and deep space (with its perception and temporal warping).

The novella's core genre DNA is that of the space opera, infused with elements of murder mystery.[2] Westfahl (2003) identifies the two key characteristics of space opera as spaceships and adventures that frequently involve conflict.[3] As the subgenre has continued to grow, it has inevitably spawned multiple subgroups and tropes, frequently positioning aliens as explicitly *nonhuman* species with no historically shared worlds or ancestry, who can be friendly, aloof, or antagonistic, but usually Other. It is worth noting that aliens have historically been used as vehicles to express and/or explore anxieties about race, class, gender, and sex, with varying degrees of self-awareness and concern for dehumanization on the part of the author and the narrative (Pearson 2017). *Tea Master* does not have aliens, but it does present humans living in "alien" environments, on other worlds and in space itself. Although humanity's journey to the stars is not elaborated upon within the novella, de Bodard provides a detailed alternate history on her website. By the events of the novella, North America has long since been colonized by a Confucian Chinese/Vietnamese empire. The influx of land and resources allowed the empire to thrive and maintain power, as opposed to the insularity and British machinations that doomed its real-world counterpart. This fictional empire is also more egalitarian, allowing all people (not just men) to enter the imperial service (de Bodard n.d.). All of the characters in *The Tea Master and the Detective* thus operate within or are (at least) heavily influenced by the structures of this spacefaring, human, Confucian, and Vietnamese-Chinese empire.[4]

The novella opens with The Shadow's Child and Long Chau meeting for the first time. Long Chau requests a custom tea blend to enable her to function well in deep space. The ship eventually agrees, with the caveat that she wishes to accompany her client to ensure that the blend works as intended; based on her response, Long Chau deduces that The Shadow's Child is afraid of deep space, and states that she is looking for a corpse. After crafting the blend and worrying about being able to make rent for her berth at the station, the ship serves the scholar and they make their way into deep space. Long Chau expertly deduces the reasons and circumstances behind The Shadow's Child leaving the military and her reluctance to enter deep space, apologizing when she realizes that she's hurt the ship. The two make their way to the derelict of another mindship, recovering a corpse from the wreckage, a corpse that Long Chau determines was not a part of the wreck. The Shadow's Child visits a fellow mindship and learns more about Long Chau, including that she was tortured by the militia. Reconvening, the women identify the body—a woman who worked at the nearby orbital—and visit the sisterhood to which she belonged. The ship and the detective manage to figure out that the woman died as part of the sisterhood's initiation ritual. With Long Chau's support, The Shadow's Child braves deep space again to save both Long Chau and the youngest member of the sisterhood.

The final significant element of the story's world is "deep space." It is a space between space, an inherently liminal expanse that allows for faster-than-light travel between the disparate planets and orbitals of the empire.[5] This is useful for transportation of all kinds, but particularly military deployments—this is, after all, an *empire*. In this respect, it is roughly analogous to the seas and oceans of Earth during the so-called Age of Sail. However, just like the sea, deep space is dangerous and ultimately unknowable in its entirety. De Bodard's descriptions are haunting and vaguely menacing; deep space has shoals, ebbs, and *movements*.[6] It alters perceptions of space, time, and bodily senses, necessitating the brewing of teas to calm humans' minds and help them "to bear the unknowable space" (4).[7] The Shadow's Child is a brewer of these specialized medicinal teas (the titular Tea Master).

I argue that deep space, this space outside of space, is a metaphor for "the void of not-knowing" (Wilchins 2004, 42).[8] While inside it, both characters exist outside their normal sociocultural contexts, and are thus separated from imperial structures. By traveling through and interfacing with this liminal space, ship and human are able to challenge and reconstruct notions of gender and resistance to empire while confronting embodied realities of death and memory.

Untethered from the need to abide by real-world social, historical, even planetary restrictions, de Bodard is free to construct a new future for the human race. It is therefore noteworthy that she has chosen empire as the hegemonic social unit. While significantly more egalitarian than actual imperial powers (particularly Western European colonial and American neocolonial entities)—multi-partner relationships are recognized, indigenous languages and cultures are preserved, queer identities are widely accepted and welcomed—*The Tea Master and the Detective* is still inherently a story about empire. However, as Stoler argues, colonialism is inherently multitemporal and multivalent such that what is past is not necessarily over, colonial relations have been "disparately and partially absorbed into social relations and ecological disparities," and histories (especially as articulations of past and present) may recede and experiences periods of latency before resurfacing (2016, 25–26). Observing and analyzing the real world, she argues that colonial systems still exist today; in most instances they have been transformed, hidden, occluded, or adapted, but they persist. I follow her preference for the moniker "(post)colonial" as opposed to "postcolonial," since the parentheses add some level of acknowledgement of the inherently problematic nature of imposing temporal and spatial boundaries on something as complex as colonialism (Stoler 2016, ix). *The Tea Master and the Detective* has often (correctly in my opinion) been identified as a (post)colonial narrative, due to its focus on characters who question or challenge imperial structures and the heritage of Aliette de Bodard herself, since she is of Vietnamese-French descent and lives in Paris.[9]

GENDER

The Xuya universe is noteworthy for its varied representation of queer identities and characters. Multiple-partner marriages, same-sex relationships, and nonbinary gender identities (to name a few) are all accepted. Within the novella, most of the speaking characters identify as women and use she/her pronouns; the only character identified as nonbinary is one of The Shadow's Child's fellow ships, Sharpening Steel into Needles. Although definitively not an issue with *The Tea Master and the Detective*, this has been problematic in other narratives, since within science fiction as a whole, nonbinary characters have historically been represented as not human, whether that means an alien species or synthetic beings like robots or, as here, spaceships. Despite the fact that these implications are not generally intended, such portrayals can contribute to real-world stigma against nonbinary people, since they may be narratively connected with the inhuman, uncanny, or disturbing.[10] This is *not* the case with *The Tea Master and the Detective*, since de Bodard is careful to acknowledge the emotional states and care for each other that both Sharpening Steel into Needles and The Shadow's Child have.

The Shadow's Child is a character innately connected to empire: she is a spacefaring vessel who was a warship. She served as a member of the imperial military, a piece of the vast machine that continually (re)inscribed and expanded imperial hegemony and dominion. Repressive social systems like colonizing empires exert control by codifying boundaries and enforcing classification. The creation of limits, "wild" and "unknown" lands, and less-than Other(s) permits conquest to take on a veneer of acceptability.[11] This is further bolstered by technological development, which is one of the key driving forces behind imperialist projects (Csicsery-Ronay 2017). As a character, The Shadow's Child *physically* embodies this formulation, but actively resists it. She was directly involved in colonial efforts, transporting and deploying troops as an element of the imperial military complex; she mentions a former lieutenant (4) and her last captain (19). Viewed as merely a ship, an unthinking mass of metal, she can be construed as a tool that allowed her empire to extend, maintain, and consolidate its control via its technological superiority. Yet while this is true on one level, it is untrue at others, because the Shadow's Child is *she*. *She* is a living, thinking, feeling being.[12] This is why she is so traumatized by the accident in deep space: she is trapped, injured, and has to watch her entire crew die slowly (5, 15–18). As a result, she suffers from PTSD, and is therefore no longer useful in the view of the imperial service. The military is able to repair the physical damage, but is either unable to recognize or unable (unwilling) to acknowledge her psychological damage. This reflects the reality of war- and combat-related trauma, but is perhaps noteworthy for the fact that her gender never plays a role.

Gender, and by close (social) relation sexuality, has historically been, and unfortunately continues to be, one of the primary vectors of social classification, control, and subjugation. This is no less true of science fiction than any other literary genre (i.e., Russ 2017).[13] Despite the broad reach of Haraway's cyborg (i.e., Balsamo 1996; Haraway 2017; Hayles 2017), examinations of gender are frequently based on an explicitly binary and essentialist view which often fails to take into account nonbinary, gender nonconforming, and nonhuman people and bodies.[14] The same can also be said of many media presentations of (alternate) futures in print and on screen, including the still-ongoing *Ghost in the Shell* franchise. Despite its narrative generally being centered on someone with an entirely artificial body, the show (in its various iterations) is either unwilling or uninterested in actually questioning what gender means in a world of cyborgs and wholly artificial bodies.[15] *The Tea Master* addresses these questions by, essentially, not engaging with them; I read *The Shadow's Child* as a ship, not a cyborg in the more literal sense of splicing human and artificial (although she is certainly one of Haraway's cyborgs). It has been repeated enough to become partially meaningless, but the point is still true: gender is a construct. As Wilchins puts it, gender is "a repeated doing that is always in danger of failing" (2004, 136). The Shadow's Child challenges over-simplified views of gender as social and sex as biological, as well as the unquestioned reproduction of that imposition vis-a-vis artificial bodies.

Morgan (2020) addresses this in the context of human-robot romantic relationships (although limiting discussion to artificial *humanoid* beings), while Dalton (2020) traces a gradual replacement of male-male nonsexual human "bromances" with unequal human-AI relationships. Extending and building on both arguments, I would argue that The Shadow's Child (and indeed all sentient spaceships) is inherently queer, because her identity, form, and presentation(s) are effectively self-determined and mutable.[16] As a character she also lends herself to an asexual reading, although this is not made explicit in the text. As O'Connacht (2020) has noted, many narratives with asexual and/or aromantic characters reinforce their differences from more "normal" characters by exiling them from their society. Within the novella, The Shadow's Child's PTSD resulted in her leaving the military (her previous community), but she is still a part of her birth society and exists as a valued member of her new community (which further expands when Long Chau arrives), even if she herself does not fully understand that fact. I read this as a direct result of her proximity to deep space, in terms of both its connectivity and its uncanniness. The Shadow's Child is a woman not because of her physical form or gender performance in any kind of human sense; she is a woman because that is *who she is*.[17] Her return(s) to deep space, despite her fear and traumatic memories, open a path toward reclamation of her selfhood and reconnection with her body.

DEATH AND MEMORY

Since the narrative focuses closely on The Shadow's Child's perspective, readers experience deep space through the ship's eyes. For her, death is a constant presence in deep space, felt as the persistent *weight* of her trauma. At the beginning of the novella (even in normal space), she is haunted by memories of her crew, especially their deaths. The Shadow's Child is also meta-narratively haunted by Dr. John Watson, with whom she shares a degree of literary DNA even as she is a response to him.

Both Watson and Sherlock Holmes have transcended their original publication materials and copyright restrictions to become established literary archetypes, but they are still heavily rooted in the context in which Conan Doyle wrote and set his stories. The basic premise—brilliant detective and (usually) his everyman foil—has been adapted numerous times since the stories' initial publication, but few of those adaptations have engaged meaningfully, if at all, with the colonialism inherent in a story set in late nineteenth-century London where one of the two leads is an army veteran.[18] Partially following the success of the BBC's recent modern-day version—titled simply *Sherlock*—fan communities have increasingly begun to read Holmes and Watson's relationship as romantic (i.e., Greer 2015; Hofmann 2018; Valentine 2016).[19] Such readings, unfortunately, continue to downplay or ignore the British imperialism inherent in the originals, and even unquestioningly reflect the fundamental belief in the police as good (if generally inept). In *The Tea Master and the Detective*, Aliette de Bodard actually grapples with these issues meaningfully.

The Shadow's Child is a traumatized veteran with medical expertise and a strong sense of duty, as is Watson. Besides the gender swap, the most significant differences between the two are that The Shadow's Child is aware and *critical* of the colonial system of which she is a part and, further unlike her literary counterpart, she lives and works in a "provincial backwater" (1). Partially due to the location and partially due to her own efforts to keep herself apart, the ship evidently does not form any strong friendships or tell anyone about her experiences since she left military service—probably about five years. She does not address her trauma in any meaningful way, shying away from memories of her former crew and her time stuck, drifting alone, in deep space. In Malabou's formulation, minds (and thus memories and personalities) are plastic and malleable and thus respond to trauma by changing their shape, in some cases causing the identity of a person to metamorphose entirely (2012). The Shadow's Child does not experience such a drastic change, but she consciously and unconsciously reshapes her mind around the trauma so that she thinks about it as little as possible, even as the source of her pain is only a short jump away. She thus differs from Breq/Justice of Toren, the protagonist of Ann Leckie's *Imperial Radch* series, whose trauma and memories were deliberately occluded by a third party. Eventually Breq begins to trust people enough to talk through her experiences; The Shadow's Child does not have such a gentle experience. Long Chau, in true Holmesian fashion, blithely ignores all social mores and baldly states the ship's trauma—hardly a caring or supportive action, although it does seem to shock The Shadow's Child out of her paralysis, and Long Chau is demonstrably more supportive in the novella's denouement, albeit in a suitably irritable and prickly fashion.

All of which is not to say that the ship is only able to remember death, pain, and loss; The Shadow's Child was born to a human mother, and remains a recognized part of her family, preserved in their ancestral memory and carrying within herself extensive records of family history.[20] This is illustrated poignantly through her meal with Sharpening Steel into Needles. Since they are both ships, they cannot eat actual food; instead they share and replay memories and recordings of past meals:

> On the low table was an overlay of various dishes from caramel pork to noodle soup, and green tea the colour of verdigris. None of it was real, and neither of them ate, per se, but food for them was memories—of feasts and places and people, accumulated and refined through the centuries of their lives (32).

In the Xuya universe, ships live for multiple generations of their family, acting as living bridges, archives, and links to ancestral memories. Such long lives mean that ships must inevitably experience the deaths of their human-bodied relatives and any crew with whom they travel. The Shadow's Child is still part of her family despite the distances that separate them, remaining tied into long-distance kinship networks which are producer and product of the imperial structures within which they exist. It is this same imperial structure that ultimately separated the ship emotionally from her family. The accident that caused the loss of her military crew violently removed her immediate community and trapped her alone with her grief and without hope of rescue. Ships are as social as humans, and loss of community and support is mentally and emotionally damaging. Once she was rescued, The Shadow's Child responded by closing herself off from other people so that she wouldn't have to experience that pain again—her brain's plasticity being affected by the accident.

Nor is it an accident that she only begins to open back up to people when forced to interact with someone who is not interested in accepting excuses. As mentioned previously, Long Chau easily figures out the reason behind the ship's reticence to enter deep space, but once the detective *understands* that reason she exhibits a more caring side, talking The Shadow's Child through the worst of her anxiety (68–70). In this respect, Long Chau is unlike most of the other characters in the novella, who seem to either ignore or downplay the ship's trauma. This is a frequent occurrence in imperial and/or (post)colonial systems, wherein trauma is frequently weaponized at an institutional level as a means of social control, and which is frequently accompanied by the creation of unwritten social stigma around open and honest discussion; the same is true of hetero-patriarchal societies, in which those same methods are used to construct and perpetuate rigid gender roles. The Shadow's Child's fellow ships do not understand her reluctance, since they cannot understand her trauma. Through her willingness to work to understand the ship's trauma, and her care for those frequently overlooked or ignored by society, Long Chau also works to resist the imperio-colonial hegemony. She bears physical and mental scars from militia interrogation (31) and aided her student in escaping their family, leading to her travels and consultation (68–69). Her partnership with The Shadow's Child is thus both a rejection of the state's classification of the ship as damaged and not useful, and an acceptance of her as she is. This is also a powerful statement from a queer found-family perspective: accepting someone on their own terms, not questioning them, and supporting them is (unfortunately) still a radical act.

CONCLUSION

This is all possible because of deep space, the liminal space outside of real space replete with possibility, a version of Wilchins' "void of not-knowing" (2004). Its effects on unprotected human minds and bodies, and on injured ship Minds, are admittedly terrifying, but it is that same awesome power that allows it to remain wholly (or even partially) uncontrolled. While it is true that the ruling empire of *The Tea Master and the Detective* uses deep space for transportation, it cannot truly possess it. Both colonialism and imperialism are predicated on "seizing lands . . . and changing the function, prior purpose and meanings of the now-colonized terrain" (McLeod 2007, 2). Deep space has no land to seize, and so it remains unknowable in its entirety; it will forever exist outside of imperio-colonial dominion. And while it is both the cause and source of the ship's trauma, it simultaneously provides her with the freedom to live outside of the hegemonic sociocultural structures and strictures that impeded her healing. With Long Chau's somewhat cantankerous help, The Shadow's Child is able to reclaim her sense of self and begins to help others lost in the fringes.

NOTES

1. European colonization still happened, and the United States does exist, albeit much diminished and confined to the eastern seaboard.

2. The current system of genre classification has both merits and disadvantages (as do all such systems).

3. He identifies what he calls a third trait, but which reads more as a critic's exhaustion: that space opera "often succumbs to formulaic plots and mediocrity" (Westfahl 2003, 198). Indeed, the same could be said of any genre.

4. Sohn (2017) has a well-researched history of the dismal history of Asian representation in the genre, although this is thankfully (albeit slowly) improving.

5. For the basic concept, see also Star Wars' hyperspace, Star Trek's warp drive, Farscape's jump drive, "The Flow" in John Scalzi's *Interdependency*, etc., although most of these examples are more in line with a high-speed tunnel as opposed to the tidal deep space.

6. In many ways, deep space is an intriguing instantiation of the abject (Kristeva 1982), as it exists both literally and figuratively at the edge(s) of space and consciousness. See Farstadvoll (2019) for a material view on the abject.

7. Parenthetical page numbers like this refer to pages of a PDF version of the novella, counting page 1 as the first page of story text.

8. The void, or lack, of clear labels and categorizations is an essential component of queerness.

9. It is worth noting that post-colonial theory has a troubled history within French academia and still meets with resistance; see Bennington (2016) for more.

10. For example, this is what makes the Godmade in Elizabeth Bear's *The Red-Stained Wings* (2019), or all of the Mind avatars (and the Minds themselves) throughout Iain M. Banks' *Culture* series, potentially problematic; they are all explicitly described as genderless and referred to as "it." However, Becky Chambers's *A Close and Common Orbit* (2016) and Martha Wells's *All Systems Red* (2017), among others, treat embodied gender among artificial *humanoid* beings with care and empathy.

11. In terms of American science fiction, see Mogen (1993) for more on the influence of the frontier western, although the more recent success and popularity of "space western" media franchises like *Cowboy Bebop* (1998), *Firefly* (2002–2003), and *The Mandalorian* (2019–present) may indicate that his conclusions are no longer as true. See Rivera (2012) for more on the U.S. Southwestern borderland.

12. Within the Xuya universe, ship Minds are essentially human—birthed by a human mother using certain methods to ensure their development, and then placed into their ship body (8). Speace (2020) has argued that these Minds can be read as direct responses to the brainships in Anne McCaffrey's 1969 novel *The Ship Who Sang*.

13. The field is, thankfully, changing and adapting to increased social awareness of these issues; part of this process is also the reclamation and (in some cases) rediscovery of neglected sections of the genre's history (i.e., Newell and Lamont 2005).

14. This is one of the primary issues with Lester del Rey's short story *Helen O'Loy* (originally published in *Astounding Science Fiction* in 1938). See Geczy (2017) for more on human/humanoid artificial bodies and Pearson (2017) for more on queerness in science fiction.

15. Most scholarship that engages with the franchise also seems to unquestioningly accept a gender binary (i.e., Brown 2008; Correa 2013; Endo 2012; Johnson 2007; Yuen 2000), although both Schaub (2001) and Silvio (1999) resist this to varying degrees.

16. See Yoon Ha Lee's *Beyond the Dragon's Gate* (Tor 2020), which addresses dysphoria in AI ship-minds who have been unwillingly moved into new ship bodies. To the best of my knowledge it is one of only a few speculative stories to even name the topic in the context of ships.

17. To date, there has been very little academic scholarship in this vein; Kennedy partially examined the topic, albeit solely within the context of C.J. Cherryh's Alliance-Union universe (1990, 104–24).

18. Scholarship, on the other hand, has engaged with the Holmes stories through multiple theoretical lenses, including feminist, queer, and (post)colonial (i.e., Fathallah 2017; Frank 1996; Miller 2008).

19. In the context of the Holmes canon, Watson (on whom The Shadow's Child is partially based) is a stereotypically straight, heterosexual everyman, while Holmes lends himself strongly to an asexual reading—he never shows much if any romantic or physical interest in anyone else. His fascination with Irene Adler, in particular, is predicated on her mental acuity and ability to outsmart him.

20. The topic of emotional bonds between family members, of whom some are human and some are ships, is treated poignantly in one of my other favorite Xuya stories, *Three Cups of Grief, by Starlight* (Clarkesworld 2015, Issue 100).

BIBLIOGRAPHY

Balsamo, Anne. 1996. *Technologies of the Gendered Body: Reading Cyborg Women*. Durham; London: Duke University Press.

Barbini, Francesca T., ed. 2020. *Ties that Bind: Love in Fantasy and Science Fiction*. Academica Lunare CfP Series, Vol. 4. Edinburgh: Luna Press Publishing.

Bennington, Alice. 2016. "(Re)Writing Empire? The Reception of Post-Colonial Studies in France." *The Historic Journal* 59 (4): 1157–89.

de Bodard, Aliette. n.d. "The Universe of Xuya." https://aliettedebodard.com/bibliography/novels/the-universe-of-xuya/.

Brown, Steven T. 2008. "Machinic Desires: Hans Bellmer's Dolls and the Technological Uncanny in *Ghost in the Shell 2: Innocence*." *Mechademia* 3: 222–53.

Correa, Marie Deanne Therese O. 2013. "Ghost in the Shell: A Cyborg-Feminist Review of Mamoru Oshii's Animated Film." *Plaridel* 10 (2): 115–19.

Csicsery-Ronay, Istvan, Jr. 2017. "Science Fiction and Empire." In *Science Fiction Criticism: An Anthology of Essential Writings*, edited by Rob Latham, 443–57. New York: Bloomsbury.

Dalton, AJ. 2020. "The Decline of the Bromance and the Rise of Human-A.I. Relationships in Science Fiction Tv and Films." In *Ties that Bind: Love in Fantasy and Science Fiction*, edited by Francesca T. Barbini, 48–61.

Endo, Yoshie. 2012. "Ambivalent Portrayals of Female Cyborgs in Oshii Mamoru's *Ghost in the Shell* and *Innocence*." *Journal of Literature and Art Studies* 2 (5): 507–19.

Farstadvoll, Stein. 2019. "A Speculative Archaeology of Excess: Exploring the Afterlife of A Derelict Landscape Garden." PhD thesis, The Arctic University of Norway.

Fathallah, Judith May. 2017. "The White Man at the Centre of the World: Masculinity in *Sherlock*." In *Fanfiction and the Author*, 47–100. Amsterdam University Press. http://www.jstor.org/stable/j.ctt1v2xsp4.7.

Frank, Lawrence. 1996. "Dreaming the Medusa: Imperialism, Primitivism, and Sexuality in Arthur Conan Doyle's "the Sign of Four."" *Signs* 22 (1): 52–85. http://www.jstor.org/stable/3175041.

Geczy, Adam. 2017. *The Artificial Body in Fashion and Art: Marionettes, Models and Mannequins*. New York: Bloomsbury Academic.

Greer, Stephen. 2015. "Queer (Mis)recognition in the BBC's Sherlock." *Adaptation* viii (1): 50–67. http://search.proquest.com/docview/1746469290/.

Haraway, Donna. 2017. "A Cyborg Manifesto: Science, Technology, and Socialist-Feminism in the Late Twentieth Century." In *Science Fiction Criticism: An Anthology of Essential Writings*, edited by Rob Latham, 306–29. New York: Bloomsbury.

Hayles, N. Katherine. 2017. "Virtual Bodies and Flickering Signifiers." In *Science Fiction Criticism: An Anthology of Essential Writings*, edited by Rob Latham, 330–51. New York: Bloomsbury.

Hofmann, Melissa A. 2018. "Johnlock Meta and Authorial Intent in Sherlock Fandom: Affirmational or Transformational?" *Transformative Works and Cultures* 28.

Johnson, Rebecca. 2007. "*kawaii* and *kirei*: Navigating the Identities of Women in *Laputa: Castle in the Sky* by Hayao Miyazaki and *Ghost in the Shell* by Mamoru Oshii." *Rhizomes* 14.

Kennedy, Samuel H. 1990. "Aspects of Linguistics and Communication in Selected Works of C.J. Cherryh." Master's Thesis, Texas Tech University.

Kristeva, Julia. 1982. *Powers of Horror: An Essay on Abjection.* Translated by Leon S. Roudiez. New York: Columbia University Press.

Malabou, Catherine. 2012. *Ontology of the Accident: An Essay on Destructive Plasticity.* Translated by Carolyn Shread. Cambridge: Polity Press.

McLeod, John, ed. 2007. *The Routledge Companion to Postcolonial Studies.* London: Routledge.

Miller, Elizabeth Carolyn. 2008. "PRIVATE and Public Eyes: Sherlock Holmes and the Invisible Woman." In *Framed: The New Woman Criminal in British Culture at the Fin de Siècle,* 25–69. University of Michigan Press. http://www.jstor.org/stable/j.ctv65swhm.6.

Mogen, David. 1993. "Science Fiction 'Westerns' and American Literature." In *Wilderness Visions: The Western Theme in Science Fiction Literature,* 2nd ed., 11–21. San Bernardino, CA: Borgo Press.

Morgan, Cheryl. 2020. "Robot Love Is Queer." In *Ties that Bind: Love in Fantasy and Science Fiction,* edited by Francesca T. Barbini, 34–47.

Newell, Diane, and Victoria Lamont. 2005. "House Opera: Frontier Mythology and Subversion of Domestic Discourse in Mid-Twentieth-Century Women's Space Opera." *Foundation: The International Review of Science Fiction* 34 (95): 71–88.

O'Connacht, Lynn. 2020. "Aromanticism, Asexuality, and the Illusion of New Narratives." In *Ties that Bind: Love in Fantasy and Science Fiction,* edited by Francesca T. Barbini, 99–120.

Pearson, Wendy. 2017. "Alien Cryptographies: The View from Queer." In *Science Fiction Criticism: An Anthology of Essential Writings,* edited by Rob Latham, 246–67. New York: Bloomsbury.

Rivera, Lysa. 2012. "Future Histories and Cyborg Labor: Reading Borderlands Science Fiction After NAFTA." *Science Fiction Studies* 39 (3): 415–36.

Russ, Joanna. 2017. "The Image of Women in Science Fiction." In *Science Fiction Criticism: An Anthology of Essential Writings,* edited by Rob Latham, 200–210. New York: Bloomsbury.

Schaub, Joseph Christopher. 2001. "Kusanagi's Body: Gender and Technology in Mecha-anime." *Asian Journal of Communication* 11 (2): 79–100.

Silvio, Carl. 1999. "Refiguring the Radical Cyborg in Mamoru Oshii's "Ghost in the Shell."" *Science Fiction Studies* 26 (1): 54–72. http://www.jstor.org/stable/4240752.

Sohn, Stephen Hong. 2017. "Alien/Asian: Imagining the Racialized Future." In *Science Fiction Criticism: An Anthology of Essential Writings,* edited by Rob Latham, 503–16. New York: Bloomsbury.

Speace, Gillian. 2020. "Readers' Advisory: Past Is Prologue: Science Fiction and Ways of Working." *Reference and User Services Quarterly* 59 (2): 96–102. https://doi.org/http://dx.doi.org/10.5860/rusq.59.2.7273.

Stableford, Brian. 2017. *The Plurality of Imaginary Worlds: The Evolution of French Roman Scientifique.* 2nd edition. Encino, CA: Black Coat Press.

Stoler, Ann Laura. 2016. *Duress: Imperial Durabilities in Our Times.* Durham; London: Duke University Press.

Valentine, Amandelin A. 2016. "Toward a Broader Recognition of the Queer in the BBC's *Sherlock.*" *Transformative Works and Cultures* 22.

Westfahl, Gary. 2003. "Space Opera." In *The Cambridge Companion to Science Fiction,* edited by Edward James and Farah Mendlesohn, 197–208. Cambridge University Press.

Wilchins, Riki. 2004. *Queer Theory, Gender Theory.* Los Angeles, CA: Alyson Publications.

Yuen, Wong Kin. 2000. "On the Edge of Spaces: "Blade Runner," "Ghost in the Shell," and Hong Kong's Cityscape." *Science Fiction Studies* 27 (1): 1–21.

Chapter Four

"The House Wants Me to Stay"

*Mothers, Wives, and Sex Objects
in the Haunted House Subgenre*

Victor Hernández-Santaolalla

The stories about haunted houses found their origins in eighteenth-century English Gothic literature, influenced by French and other European literature. In particular, they can be traced back to the publication of *The Castle of Otranto* written by Horace Walpole in 1764, which is also recognized as the first Gothic horror novel (Grider 2007). However, stories about haunted houses found a different development in the American popular culture (Bailey 1999). Since Edgar Allan Poe's description of the House of Usher in 1839, and through Hawthorne's *The House of the Seven Gables*, "the haunted house becomes a strikingly versatile metaphor; [. . .] it drags into light the nightmarish tensions of gender, class, and culture hidden at the heart of American life" (Bailey 1999, 24). This appreciation, which could be extrapolated to the most horror stories, takes here a special tenor since in these stories the characters must deal with a series of supernatural forces that threaten to destroy their home life, besieging them in what is expected to be their ultimate safe place. In that regard, Stephen King identifies the haunted house with a Bad Place, an archetype in which he also includes haunted hotels or haunted cars.

However, although he points out that all these spaces "are nasty," he recognizes that there is a particularly serious problem when what is haunted is the home: "Our homes are the places where we allow ourselves the ultimate vulnerability: they are the places where we take off our clothes and go to sleep with no guard on watch" (King 2010, 281). Anne Rivers Siddons, author of *The House Next Door*, expresses herself in similar terms, while incorporating her vision as a woman:

> The haunted house has always spoken specially and directly to me as the emblem of particular horror. Maybe it's because, to a woman, her house is so much more than that: it is kingdom, responsibility, comfort, total world to her . . . to most of us, anyway, whether or not we are aware of it. It is an extension of ourselves; it tolls in answer to one of the most basic chords mankind will ever hear. My shelter. My earth. My second skin. Mine. So basic is it that the desecration of it, the corruption, as it were, by something alien takes on a peculiar and bone deep horror and disgust [in King 2010, 287].

In this sense, since the home has traditionally been perceived as a "woman's sphere," it is understandable—as Carpenter and Colmar point out—that stories of haunted houses have attracted the interest of women writers (in Bailey 1999, 28). Their restriction to the domestic sphere makes these ghost stories stress the duties that women are expected to fulfill within the home. Along these lines, it is no accident that in 1892 Charlotte Perkins Gilman used the resource of haunted houses to denounce the vices of a patriarchal society in "The Yellow Wallpaper" (Bailey 1999; Davison 2004). Likewise, decades later, in 1959, Shirley Jackson, another female author, will publish *The Haunting of Hill House* in which she will again highlight the oppressive patriarchal ideology symbolized, in this instance, by Hill House, simultaneously place and character, which will lead Eleanor Vance to madness and, finally, to death.

Shirley Jackson's novel reveals, in the words of Bailey, "the alienation of an ambitious woman torn between her loyalties to family and her personal dreams and imperatives in the circumscribed upper middle class world of the 1940s and 1950s" (1999, 26). For the author, the figure of Eleanor Vance, as would Jennie, the sister-in-law of the protagonist of Gilman's story, internalizes the oppression imposed by her culture, establishing a connection with the Cult of True Womanhood, by which a true woman must cultivate the four cardinal virtues: piety, purity, submissiveness and domesticity. "Put them all together and they spelled mother, daughter, sister, wife-woman. Without them, no matter whether there was fame, achievement or wealth, all was ashes" (Welter 1966, 152). The cult of domesticity that prevailed in American white upper-middle class households during the nineteenth century identified women as purer than men, too pure to work outside the home. The home became a fundamental value, the center of family life: "a man's home was a testament to his status in society and his wife was the barometer of family virtue [. . .]. Therefore, a man was valued by his ability to provide a secure home, one that did not require his wife to leave" (Keister and Southgate 2012, 229). Therefore, a woman's value was completely circumscribed to that of her home, and it was the home that in turn gave value to the family and its patriarchal leadership.

In line with this, given the particular influence that Shirley Jackson's novel has had on subsequent haunted house stories, it is expected that some of these ideas about the value of domesticity, although updated, will continue to be present in recent works. In fact, beyond this seminal importance, *The Haunting of Hill House* becomes especially relevant currently because, after being brought to the big screen in 1964 by Robert Wise and then in 1999 by Jan de Bon, on October 12, 2018, the television adaptation—the most distant from its literary background to date—was released on Netflix.

In this chapter, the role of women in films and television series about haunted houses will be reviewed. To this end, a broad definition of the supernatural phenomenon will be adopted, which in some cases will go beyond the very "essence" of the term. Thus, for example, it will overcome the classical difference established in *Poltergeist* (Hooper 1982), but also the formulation that Bailey includes in *American Nightmares* (1999, 56). Therefore, titles will be considered in which the haunted is not restricted to the limits of the traditional house, others in which the phenomena are limited to the actions of a particular ghost (or even a demon) rather than a set of paranormal events, and even others in which the supernatural is only a product of a character's mind. After all, as in Henry James's *The Turn of the Screw* and its subsequent adaptations, what is really important is not the veracity of the supernatural incident but how it is perceived and the implications of this.

"WOMAN, NO ONE WILL BELIEVE YOU"

The haunted house subgenre is not too far removed from other horror subgenres in that it has women as its preferred victims. This leads to a greater exposure of female suffering and to the over-sexualization of the female body over the male one, as is shown below. However, this prominence of women as objects of suffering caused by supposed paranormal phenomena also means that women are the first to notice that something strange is happening—or even that something is about to happen. Women are thus given a (extra)sensory capacity only similar to that of children, which sometimes—just like in the case of children—leads them to be silenced under the argument that what they see is only a figment of their imagination.

Therefore, although this sort of special clairvoyance could be seen as a virtue, it turns into condemnation, because men—but also some other women—do not usually give credit to what the protagonists suggest. Films such as *House on Haunted Hill* (Castle 1959), *The Amityville Horror* (Rosenberg 1979), *Darkness* (Balagueró 2002), *Malevolent* (De Fleur 2018), or

Malasaña 32 (Pintó 2020) give a good account of how women (usually young women) are the ones who warn of the danger looming over the family in the face of doubt or rejection by their male companions, whether they are their partners, parents or brothers. It is true that sometimes these fears are unfounded, as in *House on Haunted Hill*, but the key point is that it is usually women who see and experience the events, and it is men who do not believe them, adopting in turn a purely paternalistic position.

In short, either because these women are more sensitive or because they are more fearful, at first most of them are accused of exaggerating and being hysterical, crazy or, if anything, of wanting to draw attention to themselves. This element was already present in Gilman's works. Thus, the protagonist of "The Yellow Wallpaper" indicates "that there is something queer about" the colonial mansion where they will spend the summer. These suspicions, however, will only provoke her husband's jokes, something she accepts as "one expects that in marriage" (Gilman 2006, 1). It is also present in Jackson's novel, because although it is Dr. Montague who leads the three young people there to analyze the supernatural nature of the house, it is Eleanor and Theo—especially Eleanor—who first realize that something strange is happening there. This fact, which is also included in the novel's first film adaptation, is especially relevant in the film directed by Jan de Bon, where the young tenants go to Hill House to participate in a supposed sleep experiment, which, at first, covers up the supernatural nature of the house.

It is true that this mistrust of what women see or experience in the house can be associated with various real mental conditions, sometimes related to a specific suicidal act, like in *Malevolent, The Conjuring* (Wan 2013), or *The Haunting of Hill House* itself. In fact, this notion of suicide is central to Shirley Jackson's novel and subsequent adaptations, and it is also crucial in *I Am a Ghost* (Mendoza 2012) or in *The Orphanage* (Bayona 2007). In any case, regardless of any association with certain illnesses, it is interesting how the partners resort to episodes from the past to discredit the woman's version. A notable example of this can be found in *What Lies Beneath* (Zemeckis 2000). In this one, Norman Spencer, far from believing Claire, his wife, who states that the ghost of a woman is haunting her, sends her to the psychiatrist and even accuses her of trying to sabotage the important conference he has to prepare. The truth is that the woman who appears before Claire is a former lover and student of her husband, who was murdered by him when he saw her as a threat to his career. Claire was supposedly aware of this infidelity, but a car accident that took place a year before erased it from her memory. The accident happened under strange circumstances and it is even suggested that she could have caused the accident herself, so it is used as a way of exposing the woman's mental instability. In the words of Frances A. Kamm, the film "establishes a dialectic relationship between the supernatural and Female Gothic traditions, blurring the boundaries between external threats and a subjective paranoia; the validation of the heroine's experiences and a denial of her perception" (2019, 134). In fact, the husband eventually confesses that he thought she knew the truth and was making up the ghost story to set him up, but even so he tried a sort of gaslight, making her understand that what she was seeing was all just in her head.

This element of doubting the woman's version and resorting to past events to undermine her is also present in *The House on Pine Street* (Keeling and Keeling 2015). In this film, pregnant Jennifer is the first (and practically the only one, except for her friend's child) to notice something strange happening in her new home. Her husband—as well as her own mother—on the other hand, thinks that she is either going crazy or simply stressed out, claiming that her current state reminds him very much of what happened in Chicago some time ago. This argument later turns to accusing her of being incapable of focusing on anything other than herself, while Walter, the character who functions as a sort of "oracle," according to Bailey's approach (1999, 60), tells her that the house "hates" her because she hates the house, her mother, her husband, and her son for hindering her perfect life. Even her mother references this selfishness at the end of the film when, after her husband has died under strange circumstances, Jennifer decides to return to Chicago, and her mother claims to be happy for her because she got what she wanted.

Both films feature two leading women who are stuck at home while their husbands are able to grow professionally and socially elsewhere. In fact, both Claire, who left her job as a cellist to take care of her family after alleged pressure from her husband, and Jennifer, who started a life she does not want in a place she does not like to follow her spouse, interact with their few friendships exclusively within the house. It is also interesting how, at least in the first film, the husband's rationale is endorsed by his profession as a renowned scientist, while Claire is anchored in the art scene. This duality can also be seen in *Hereditary* (Aster 2018), in which Annie Graham, a miniature artist, opposes the reasoning of her husband, psychiatrist Steve Graham. She tries to make her husband believe her, because she is the only one who really knows what is happening, and she even understands that, accidentally, because of her vulnerability and the use of deception, she is to blame for the existing problems. He, however, doubts the truth of what she says, and even tells her, from his professional perspective, that she is sick.

The women in these films thus fulfil the dual role of Cassandra and Eve; that is, they anticipate what is about to happen, yet they are condemned to be believed by no one, while at the same time being portrayed as the ultimate culprits of what is happening. This accusation of women, either by others or by themselves, relates to the role traditionally attributed to them as protectors of the home. In this respect, while the father became the protective figure of the outside, the provider and the one who enforces discipline according to social norms, the mother is the protector of the inside, the caretaker and safeguarder of the family's secrets. Therefore, considering the space in which these stories develop, it is not surprising to see how many of these aspects are repeatedly played out, especially when there are children involved. Thus, the scene where a mother must watch over the safety of her children while the father is away becomes repetitive, while there is no shortage of films in which the origin of the haunting lies precisely in a frustrated motherhood of the past, as in *Secreto Matusita* (Fernández-Moris 2014), in which the woman's house is cursed because her son died in it and was not buried.

This absence of the father—whether temporary or permanent—is also evident in *The Orphanage*, where in the face of her partner's rejection, the mother decides to stay to get her child back, wherever he may be. Thus, after finding the child's body behind a hidden door that leads to some sort of house basement—a space that like the attic, at the other end of the building, which is especially significant in stories of haunted houses (Grider 2007, 152–53)—and aware of her guilt, she decides to commit suicide so that she can be with her child again. In this sense, it is clear that to save children, even if it is only their spirit, the final sacrifice must be made by a woman, a mother; an element also featured in the 1999 film version of *The Haunting*. Women are the ones who must become the heroines of the story because they are, once again, in charge of safeguarding everything behind the walls of the house, even though, normally, it is men who cause the tragedy directly or indirectly. Sometimes this is because they are the ones who absorb the evil of the house, to the point of wanting to murder their family, as in *The Amityville Horror* or *Darkness*, or the hotel in *The Shining*, and other times because they are the ones who urge and convince their female companions to stay in the building.

Of course, there are also examples when the woman is more enthusiastic about the idea of living in the house, while the more rational man thinks that the price of the deal must come with a catch, like in *Burnt Offerings* (Curtis 1976), in which it is the mother, represented as the true and only caretaker of the home, who absorbs the essence of the building—to the point that the woman is totally identified with the house, which anticipates the fateful end.

"THERE IS A GHOST IN MY BED"

As preferred victims of supernatural attacks, women suffer a certain physical and mental violence, but also sexual violence, in their own homes. Actually, female protagonists become objects of desire and suffer some sexual aggression by some male supernatural force, as in *The Legend of Hell House* (Hough 1973) or *The Entity* (Furie 1982), in which the camera does not hesitate to adopt the voyeuristic or predatory gaze of other horror film subgenres (Clover 2015; Mulvey 1999; Rockoff 2002). However, in contrast to the Italian *giallo* or the slasher, where there is usually a murderer lurking, someone who is the epitome of masculinity (Rockoff 2002, 6), in the tales of haunted houses and ghosts, there is generally no corporeal entity that can have a prior sexual interest in the victim, and yet it is women who become the object of desire of the spirits living in the house. In fact, it is women, especially young women, who usually receive visitors at night while they are asleep. Here, we find a new parallel with children—although with clear differences—as they are the ones who traditionally warn parents in the middle of the night that a monster/ghost is lurking. Films such as *13 Ghosts* (Castle 1960), *Poltergeist*, *The Conjuring*, or *Paranormal Activity* (Peli 2007) show, with varying degrees of violence and eroticism, that a woman cannot be at ease in her bed at night.

It is notable how, in *Paranormal Activity*, both the man and the woman are visited on different nights by the spirit that lives in the house. However, it is the woman who receives the greatest shock, with the camera recording how the sheets on her side move, and how it is she who is taken out of the bed and finally urged to go into the garden where, despite the cold, she states that she is comfortable. In this sense, it is no longer just that the ghost has a preference for women, but that the woman seems to accept it, even if only while she is being possessed. This is what happens in *The Legend of Hell House*, with this sexualization targeting the two female protagonists: Ann Barrett and Florence Tanner. The first, who is the wife of the doctor who leads the group—yet again, the voice of reason—observes, while in bed with her husband (whom she certainly cannot wake up, as the show is only for her), sexual scenes that originate in the shadows. Aware that it is only an illusion, she leaves the bedroom. Then, apparently possessed, she tries to seduce Ben Fischer, even stripping off her clothes before him—when men are possessed, they become violent; when women are possessed, they become sexually aroused. This is an advance that she repeats and that he stops by slapping her. For her part, Florence Tanner stars in these erotic moments in her bed. Deceived by the trapped spirit, she agrees to have sexual relations with him as a way of giving him the strength to leave the house, which will allow the ghost to enter her as a way to take control of the situation.

On the topic of sexual violence against women, one cannot fail to mention *Repulsion* (Polanski 1965), a film in which, although there is no ghost, the protagonist suffers from constant visions where she is being sexually attacked. In the film, the protagonist's obsession with becoming a victim of men leads her (and the viewer) to imagine that she is living through paranormal events. In this respect, sometimes the haunted house is used as an alternative explanation—and, arguably, an explanation that is less cruel than the real one—of the reason behind the female characters' fears. This is also the case in *La casa muda* (Hernández 2010) and its American remake, *Silent*

House (Kentis and Lau 2011). Although with some differences, in both versions the young protagonist imagines that there are malevolent intruders in the house she had not visited in years because she seeks to repress a past of sexual abuse, in which her own father was involved.

The film *I Am a Ghost* is also interesting in this respect. In this movie, the protagonist is a female ghost who tries, with the help of a medium, to be released from the house. In contrast to a first vision in which she claims she was murdered, it is finally discovered that she actually committed suicide by stabbing herself; fateful end to a terrible childhood in which her mother used to tell her that she had a demon inside and that she needed an exorcism, although she was actually diagnosed with dissociative identity disorder. However, her vision of her death is that of a naked man; a male monster residing inside her, who stands over her and repeatedly sticks the knife into her. Here, if we associate the knife with the inevitable phallic symbol it represents and pay attention to the position of both, there seems to be a clear analogy of rape.

Likewise, in the television series *Being Human* (BBC Three 2008–2013), Annie Sawyer is a ghost who has been trapped in the house where she lived with her fiancé, and who, after her death, will rent it to John and George, a vampire and a werewolf, respectively; something the fiancé does not know. While it is interesting that, out of the three protagonists, it is the woman in particular who is the ghost that is locked up in the house, the only one that no one but other supernatural beings can see and hear, and whose appearance, and even existence, is closely related to her state of mind, it is especially relevant to note that she was murdered by her own fiancé, who threw her down the stairs after a fit of jealousy—which is also the trigger for Kayako's murder in the *Ju-On* franchise. The murder in *Being Human*, just like the abuse suffered by the young woman in *La casa muda/Silent House*, has been forgotten/silenced by the victim—and just as the former still loves her father, Annie is still in love with her fiancé, and even continues to "look after" him when he is at the house. The discovery of the crime leads her to think that the way she can get out of the limbo in which she finds herself is by taking revenge on him and alerting his current partner.

BACK TO HILL HOUSE

Told in two time-frames, the television adaptation of *The Haunting of Hill House* narrates the story of the Crane family, made up of Hugh and Olivia and their children Steven, Shirley, Theo, and the fraternal twins Nell and Luke. The plot begins when the couple decide to move to Hill House—still free, at least in the public mind, of the dark legend it would later have—to restore it and be able to sell it afterwards. The series again takes up one of the common tropes of haunted house stories: the occupation of the house is temporary, which keeps it from being seen as a real home. Likewise, throughout the episodes the veracity of the supernatural is continually questioned, posing the question of whether everything that has happened (and what is about to happen) is the result of forces from beyond or is merely a product of the human mind, even if it is a collective suggestion. Along these lines, we should mention the story of the girl that Theo must deal with in the third episode, who complains about the existence of a monster that she calls Mr. Smiley. Theo—who, like her namesake in Shirley Jackson's novel, is the most sexual and has a special sensory capacity that is almost divinatory—imagines, while she is in bed at night, a man with a deformed face and a wide smile taking off her duvet. However, it is all a mere suggestion, since it is not a supernatural monster that is harassing the girl, but her foster father.

Returning to the main plot, two suicides by hanging serve as a border between the two time frames in which the series takes place: the first one is that of Olivia Crane, the matriarch of the family; the second one is that of Nell, the youngest daughter, who twenty-six years later decides to return to the house. Both hang themselves on the recurring spiral staircase of the story that Shirley Jackson devised in order to wake them up from a bad dream. The former had stayed in the house after her family fled, and Poppy, one of the spirits in the house, leads her to think that her husband will kill all her children. The viewer knows that Hugh Crane does not kill his children, as they see him leave them in a motel and return to the house, from which he returns hours later with blood on him, which arouses suspicions of his possible guilt. In fact, the audience learns about the real reason for Olivia's death and her previous descent into "madness" sometime later, as at first it is only known that Hugh pushed his wife against the wall and then abandoned her. Olivia's death and the strange behavior of the father mark, from then on, the whole history of the family, to the point that, at present, he has hardly any relationship with his children, thus deepening the idea that the fundamental pillar for the conservation of the family nucleus is the mother. In fact, the father's idea of protection is to hide the truth from his children, the truth being that, before committing suicide, the mother tried to poison the twins and murdered the Dudleys' daughter.

Moments before her fateful end, Olivia Crane was going through episodes of headaches, hallucinations, and nightmares that led her husband, urged by Mr. Dudley, to take her away from the house for a while, as this was the only thing that improved his wife's mental health. Hill House seems to cause particular harm to women, and it is up to men to save them from being completely plunged into the pit of madness; something that has no effect on Olivia, who, by deceiving her family, returns home in the middle of the night. Nell also does the same, returning to the cursed place where, after a brief moment of happiness, she is urged by her mother to wake up in the same way she did, and ends up becoming the woman with the crooked neck, the one who has been chasing her since she was a child, thus fulfilling her destiny of becoming an eternal guest of Hill House. The idea of suicide as a final solution has haunted Nell from the first moment that she set foot in Hill House. In fact, she sees the specter when her husband—who is, coincidentally, the first therapist who actually listened to her—dies in the bedroom after suffering an aneurysm while trying to help her in one of her recurrent sleep paralyses, so she blames the attack on the house, in the face of the logical disbelief of the others. Thus, even if the adaptation differs greatly from the original, Nell remains the shy, insecure girl—literally paralyzed, in this case—whom no one believes. If in the novel and the two film adaptations her story revolves around the care of her mother for years until she dies and is "invited" to Hill House, where she will continue to fulfil in some way that role of caregiver and resigned victim of the patriarchal society, in the television series she seems to be the only one who really keeps in touch with the different members of the family, managing, at the end of it, to officially reconcile the family.

In the face of Nell's warnings, older brother Steven is the most skeptical. However, he is the one who benefits most from the family's misfortune, by writing a book about the events in the house. When presenting one of his books on the supernatural phenomena of the Alcatraz prison, Nell accuses her brother of profiting from stories he himself does not believe in and which he simply deems insane. He, however, defends himself by saying that she has no right to boycott his work and destroy his life, questioning whether she has stopped taking her medication.

Between Steven, the skeptical voice of reason, and Nell, the authentic believer, announcer of what was happening and eternally misunderstood— "Nobody could see me" will complain as a child on the day of the big storm—stand the other siblings, who, with some doubts, are aware of the strange phenomena that revolve around them and the house. One of them is Luke, who is haunted by his personal spirit—The Tall Man—as a child and as an adult, and who has seen his life destroyed by drugs. After Nell's death and aware that the house is the culprit, he decides to go and burn it down; an idea that his namesake had put forward both in the novel and in both film adaptations, and which involves one of masculinity's preferred solutions: if something is wrong, destroy it.

The series *The Haunting of Hill House* thus incorporates some of the main tropes of haunted house stories, and somehow develops the gender conflict that was already present in Jackson's novel. The discrediting of the woman's opinion, her circumscription to the home environment—and even to specific rooms (Bailey 1999, 33)—being relegated to the task of caring for the family—Olivia Crane must bring together the different plans they have of the house, but she is not even capable of accomplishing that—and an idea of sacrifice that can even lead them to commit suicide are some of the issues the series touches upon. In the face of this, men present themselves as the solution: Hugh Crane—just like the protagonist of *Paranormal Activity*—insists that he can solve it, and Luke later tries to solve it his way also. But the truth is that no man can keep the house in order, because, following the assumptions of the patriarchal ideology that seems to permeate these stories, that is not entirely his place.

BIBLIOGRAPHY

Bailey, Dale. 1999. *American Nightmares: The Haunted House Formula in American Popular Fiction*. Madison: The University of Wisconsin Press.

Clover, Carol J. 2015. *Men, Women and Chainsaws. Gender in the Modern Horror Film*. Princeton: Princeton University Press.

Davison, Carol Margaret. 2004. "Haunted House/Haunted Heroine: Female Gothic Closets in 'The Yellow Wallpaper.'" *Women's Studies. An Inter-Disciplinary Journal* 33(1): 47–75.

Gilman, Charlotte Perkins. 2006. *The Yellow Wallpaper and Other Writings*. New York: Bantam Dell.

Grider, Sylvia Ann. 2007. "Haunted Houses." In *Haunting Experiences. Ghosts in Contemporary Folklore*, edited by Diane E. Goldstein, Sylvia Ann Grider and Jeannie Banks Thomas, 143–70. Logan: Utah State University Press.

Kamm, Frances A. 2019. "'There's a Ghost in My House': The Female Gothic and the Supernatural in *What Lies Beneath* (2000)." In *Gender and Contemporary in Horror Film*, edited by Samantha Holland, Robert Shail, and Steven Gerrard, 133–49. Bingley: Emerald.

Keister, Lisa A. and Darby E. Southgate. 2012. *Inequality. A Contemporary Approach to Race, Class, and Gender*. New York: Cambridge University Press.

King, Stephen. 2010. *Danse Macabre*. New York: Gallery Books.

Mulvey, Laura. 1999. "Visual Pleasure and Narrative Cinema." In *Film Theory and Criticism: Introductory Readings*, edited by Leo Braudy and Marshall Cohen, 833–44. New York: Oxford University Press.

Rockoff, Adam. 2002. *Going to Pieces: The Rise and Fall of the Slasher Film, 1978–1986*. Jefferson: McFarland & Company.

Welter, Barbara. 1966. "The Cult of True Womanhood: 1820–1860." *American Quarterly* 18(2): 151–74.

Part III

Between Life and Death

More than any other supernatural, vampires stand on the threshold between life and death. Able to blend in to the mortal world, if they are careful, and sustaining themselves on the blood of humans, they cede the daylight to the living, and rule the darkness of the night.

Chapter Five

To Slay or Not to Slay

Gender, Liminality, and Choice in Buffy the Vampire Slayer

Chelsi Slotten

Buffy the Vampire Slayer (*BtVS*) was a hugely influential TV series that ran from 1997–2004 and changed the TV landscape forever. The show introduced us to the now-common concept of the "Big Bad" who main characters fight at the end of a series, created the monster of the week trope, and upended several gender stereotypes. The petite blonde girl was no longer the victim, but the hero. Buffy was also the precursor to many of today's shows, and the heroine genre society has embraced it to a certain degree. As such, her impact on pop culture and gendered expectations should not be underestimated. Over the course of seven seasons, viewers watched Buffy come into her own as a person and a Slayer. Throughout the series Buffy struggles with her place in the world. The Slayer stands between the human world and the demons, vampires, and monsters who would seek to destroy it. As such, Buffy is constantly being pulled between two worlds, the living and the dead, and struggles to fit into either fully. She wants to belong with her friends at Sunnydale High but cannot fully integrate because of her duties as the Slayer. Conversely, she fails to live up to the expectations and desires of the Watchers Council in her duties as the Slayer because of her desire to fit in at school. It is this desire to exist in both worlds that drives the narrative of this show, particularly in the earlier seasons.

In its time on air, *BtVS* gained a massive and dedicated following. The contemporary, predominantly positive reviews of the show reveal that the characters resonated strongly with female viewers (Magoulick 2016). A plethora of different forms of media dedicated to celebrating the show exist, including its own academic journal—*Slayage*. Debate continues among both fans and scholars about whether *BtVS* lived up to its feminist potential or whether it has rather more conservative underpinnings (Hirmer 2013; Jones 2013; Magoulick 2016; Price 2010). Other studies recognize its importance in creating a new genre, recognizing that the show may have been a neces- sary bridge that led to some of the more radical feminist shows on air today, such as *The Chilling Adventures of Sabrina* (Henesy 2020). This back and forth, intentional or not, is one more way in which liminality has continued to influence how the show is perceived more than 15 years after its final epi- sode aired. The show has, of course, continued in graphic novel form but the analysis provided here pertains only to the TV series.

Over the course of seven seasons, there are four episodes that are particu- larly useful in highlighting the liminal nature of Buffy's life. These episodes can also shed considerable light onto the feminist or not debate mentioned above. It is therefore surprising that no scholar has, thus far, conducted an analysis of how these four episodes shape gender norms and understanding in the show. The episode addresses what happens when Buffy, through choice, betrayal, or supernatural means, ceases to be the Slayer. These glimpses of normality showcase normative gendered expectations, progress in women's rights over the past century, and even call into question the very premise of the show. For this reason, I think a more in-depth analysis of these episodes can shed some additional light on the feminist, or not, portrayals in *BtVS*.

THEORY

Before embarking on a discussion of gender and liminality within *BtVS*, it is important to understand how those terms are utilized in this chapter. Gender is understood to be an emergent property. In other words, it is a culturally constructed concept that acquires meaning through the performance of differ- ent actions (Butler 1993, 1995; Geller 2005; Gilchrist 1999; Joyce 2017; Price 2010). Gender cannot therefore be considered a static concept; it is always changing and adapting to the cultural norms. As gender norms are created through social action and perception, they are constantly in flux, able to change and open to manipulation as a person or society sees fit. Individu- als within a community can either accept and reproduce the gender norms, reject the norm, or seek to redefine gender norms (Conkey and Gero 1997; Pecheux 1981). One site of interaction between cultural gender norms and self-determination is the body.

As members of a community we choose to move and adorn our bodies in certain ways. These choices regarding the clothing we wear, the actions we take, the words we use, and the things we prioritize all contribute to how our gender is perceived by our broader society (Díaz-Andreu 2005; Wesp 2014). While it may be difficult to identify what exactly defines the core aspects of a contemporary gender presentation as they are constantly in creation, "as a society we have little trouble in recognizing it" (Halberstam 1998, 1). One of the difficulties in concretely defining a masculine or feminine gender presentation is intersectionality. Intersectionality "emphasizes that different dimensions of social life cannot be separated out into discrete and pure strands" (Joyce 2017, 4) and that any of these dimensions of social life may be prioritized depending on the situation (Boutin 2016). While it is impossible to separate the Slayer from the high school girl in *BtVS*, different aspects of Buffy's identity are displayed differently depending on who she is talking to and what she hopes to gain. As Butler points out, maintaining one's own identity requires negotiation between cultural norms and personal desires (2004). Buffy's choices can then shed light on what cultural gender norms are being portrayed as important by the show and which ones are up for renegotiation.

One aspect of Buffy's self that makes her such a good vehicle through which gender norms can be reevaluated is her liminality. The idea of liminality was first suggested by van Gennep in his 1909 research of rites of passage. He identified three important phases of any rite of passage—the rite of separation, the rite of margin, and the rite of aggregation. Victor Turner was particularly interested in the middle phase, the rite of margin which is a state of liminality. Turner describes the state of liminality as a state of transition being "neither here nor there . . . betwixt and between" two other known statuses (1987, 7). Turner emphasizes the vital role liminal figures play in society as they allow society to deal with the chaos of important events, such as a coming of age ritual, in a controlled manner that reifies the norm. The liminal state is one that lacks concrete boundaries and one in which both change, and disruption, can occur. As Gilmore states "the power of liminality is to be found in its release from normal constraints, making possible the deconstruction of the normal constructs of common sense, ordinary objects are transformed into novel creations, some of them bizarre to the point of monstrosity" (2003, 20). When the liminal figure chooses to continue into the rite of aggregation, they show how the order can overcome chaos. Before that occurs, the unfettered potential of the liminal figure offers a multitude of possibilities for chaos that could result in destruction and destabilization. The chaos and potential they embody allows them to challenge societal norms and forge new identities. Liminal figures are therefore incredibly powerful forces in society through which norms can be reshaped.

Buffy's liminality manifests itself in a multitude of ways. First, and mostly obviously, Buffy is the person who, as the show introduction states, "alone will stand against the vampires, the demons, and the forces of darkness. She is the Slayer" (Smith 1997). As a result of her fate, Buffy must face the forces of darkness and protect the rest of the human world. In order to do this, she cannot be completely part of the human world as her responsibilities force her to miss out on 'normal' life. However, Buffy also refuses to forgo her normal life. She makes concessions as a result of her slayer duties, but she still has friends, goes to school, attends dances, goes shopping at the mall, and has responsibilities to her family. Buffy's refusal to give up her entire life for slaying, unlike another slayer who is imbued with the powers and strength of the slayer when Buffy briefly dies, highlights the in-between nature of her existence. She does not fit the normal description of a slayer because she lives a normal-ish life, but she is also not a normal teenager because of her slayer duties.

The liminal nature of the slayer is not limited to standing between the forces of darkness and the humans of the world. The power that imbues the slayer is in fact the result of being paired with a demon snake (Petrie 2003). The slayer is therefore both the force that protects humans from the monsters on earth, and partially a monster herself. The slayer was created by men who were too afraid to fight evil themselves, but also wanted to control the actions of the slayer, an action that Buffy sees as cowardly and weak. When we consider Foucault's thoughts on monsters, Buffy's ambivalent state is further highlighted. Foucault believed that monsters are created to oppose socially accepted norms (Foucault 1978). Those that fight monsters are then fighting to maintain those norms. What then does it mean when the individual who is fighting monsters is part monster? She must uphold societal norms to oppose monsters, but as a partial demon herself, also opposes those norms.

In addition to the slayer being a combination of human and demon, Buffy has done another monstrous and liminal thing; she has come back from the dead. Unlike a vampire, she was resuscitated through CPR and still retains her soul. However, the parallel of Buffy both fighting vampires, and herself dying and coming back to the living is poignant. One could argue that, as the next slayer was called up upon her death, Buffy must be dead as two slayers cannot exist at the same time, and yet she is clearly alive. Buffy is neither one thing or another and not fully in either world she inhabits. She is the embodiment of a liminal figure and carries all the unlimited potential for change within herself.

SELF-REFLEXIVITY

As others have mentioned, locating one's own nexus within their work is important for readers to be able to adequately reflect on the authors conclusion and understand where they may be coming from (Watt 2007; Berger 2013). For that reason, I would like you to know that I was a huge *BtVS* fan when I was younger. I remember the show as being inspiring and forward thinking. I loved how Buffy could be strong and capable, yet still live a life close enough to mine that I could relate. I both envied her abilities and confidence and felt sorry for the difficulties she faced because of her slayer duties. She did not fit in at her school but for all the best reasons. She was funny, strong, smart, beautiful, and kind. The supporting characters also grew into themselves over the course of the series and showed other ways of being strong, coping with the difficulties of high school, and navigating interpersonal relationships. The show featured women who could be and do anything and the belief in that ability for women was a powerful draw for me. I loved that show, although I had not watched it in years. I was therefore very excited to undertake this project and have an excuse to re-watch a truly mind-boggling amount of *BtVS*. As I re-watched the show, I found myself relating more to some of the adults in the series than the titular character and her friends, aka the Scooby Gang. I also noticed that some of the gendered tropes in the show were not as radical as I recalled. I have tried my very best to hold onto my younger self's belief in *BtVS* as feminist show, because the belief it inspired is powerful and important, while also recognizing the more socially conservative elements of the show that were not apparent to me when I was younger. I do not wish this analysis to reflect a tumble from the heights of beloved fandom, as I still quite enjoyed the show. Rather I hope to present a balanced approach that can recognize both the successes and failures of *BtVS* as a feminist show. It is up to you to decide how well I manage.

BUFFY'S PLACE IN THE NARRATIVE TRADITION

BtVS was part of a cohort of supernatural themed shows with female leads that were broadcast in the 1990s and 2000s. These shows include *Charmed*, *Sabrina the Teenage Witch*, and *Xena: Warrior Princess*. The success of these shows led to more supernatural themed shows being pitched and picked up by networks, including Buffy's own spinoff called *Angel* (Henesy 2020). The Netflix show *Chilling Adventures of Sabrina* pays homage to the influence of Buffy on the horror genre through the presence of Easter eggs in the show. When the show turned twenty in 2017, a glut of show producers paid tribute to the influence *BtVS* had on their careers and the shows they worked on. *Supernatural*, the long running show on the WB, has had over 30 actors from the Buffyverse on various episodes and is full of callbacks to *BtVS* for the eagle-eyed viewer. The impact of *BtVS* on television shows over the last two decades cannot be overstated.

　BtVS not only helped inspire a generation of TV producers but continues in two earlier narrative traditions—that of the girls' school story and the Gothic drama. The girls' school story was first seen in Sarah Fielding's *The Governess, or The Little Female Academy* (1749) before becoming increasingly popular in the eighteenth and nineteenth centuries. Historically the girls' school story was set in a realistic setting, although may depict an experience that most students at the time would not have lived (Mitchell 1995). These stories highlight girls' accomplishments and tend to focus on a "new girl" who must "progressively learn the rules of the school and earn her place among a friendship group and the esteem of the school community" (Smith and Moruzi 2018, 7). Fitting in in this genre often means adhering to the conservative, heteronormative ideals of femininity. In so doing, the accomplishments of the protagonist can be celebrated, and the failings of the protagonist can be framed in an educational manner. The value in the presentation of positive and negative social perceptions of contemporary femininity allows concepts of femininity and girlhood to be questioned and reshaped. Analysis of these portrayals allows the audience to view contemporary gender expectations and understand the concerns regarding the politics of gender to be uncovered.

BtVS adheres to this storyline, particularly in the earlier seasons of the show. The show begins with a sixteen-year-old Buffy about to start her first day at a new school. Much of the first two episodes revolve around her meeting various different people and cliques at the school and protecting her new friends from harm, while making them aware that vampires are real in Sunnydale. Over the course of the next three seasons Buffy struggles to fit in. She tries out for the cheerleading team, and briefly makes it as an alternate, unsuccessfully runs for Homecoming Queen, and struggles to live a normal life despite her role as the Slayer. Her struggles are magnified because in her old school, before she became the Slayer, Buffy had been popular, on the cheerleading team, and May Queen. Despite her best efforts, Buffy is not popular and does not fit in beyond her small group of friends, dubbed "the Scooby Gang" (Solomon 1997). It therefore comes as surprise to Buffy when, during her prom, the following speech is given:

> Jonathan: We have one more award to give out. Is Buffy Summers here tonight? Did she . . . um. . . . This is actually a new category. First time ever. I guess there were a lot of write in ballots and, well, the prom committee asked me to read this. "We're not good friends. Most of us never found the time to get to know you. But that doesn't mean we haven't noticed you. We don't talk about it much, but it's no secret that Sunnydale High isn't really like other high schools. A lot of weird stuff happens here."
> Student: Zombies!
> Student: Hyena people!
> Student: Snyder!
> Jonathan: "But whenever there was a problem or something creepy happened, you seemed to show up and stop it. Most of the people here have been saved by you. Or helped by you at one time or another. We're proud to say that the class of '99 has the lowest mortality rate of any graduating class in Sunnydale history. And we know at least part of that is because of you. So the senior class

offers its thanks and gives you, uh . . . this. It's from all of us. And it has written[sic] here, Buffy Summers—Class Protector" [Solomon 1999].

The above speech highlights that, despite Buffy never fitting in, her class-mates appreciate her presence in their lives and are aware of all the good she's done for the school community. This is a small but crucial deviation from the girls' school story line because it reveals that difference can be celebrated too.

BtVS also has elements of the Gothic genre. Gothic fiction combines themes of horror, death and sometimes romance. As Buffy navigates her life-Slayer balance, we routinely see her and the Scooby Gang confront horrify-ing monsters and death, while trying to negotiate romantic and sexual rela-tionships. These threats that Buffy and her friends face provide opportunities for the characters to learn new skills and develop their sense of self. The audience therefore is presented the opportunity to see capable and strong women in action. The plotlines and characters within gothic fiction often seem larger than life, but in fact reflect elements of cultural and political events at the time of their creation (Horner 2010). Notably, gothic fictions "has traditionally given voice to those 'unclean' liminal entities that elude binary distinctions by falling somewhere between two opposing ideas" (Madden 2017, 10). As discussed above, Buffy is herself a liminal being, although she is hardly the only liminal character on the show. Buffy also embodies the "ambiguity, mystery, liminality, violence, and monstrosity" that Margarita Georgieva ascribes to gothic children (2013, 12). Her role is ill-defined as she refuses to give up either her slaying or her normal life and her role as the slayer necessitates a level of secrecy while ensuring her life is filled with monsters and the violence necessary to combat them.

There are some important ways in which *BtVS* does not conform to the gothic narrative. Tania Modleski characterizes traditional Gothic heroines as confused, afraid, and helpless individuals. She sees their need for guidance and external control as a "metaphor for the restrictions of the feminine role and as a warning against stepping outside this role" (Modleski 1982, 72). Buffy is very clear in what she wants and is far from helpless, even if she is occasionally afraid. Rather, Buffy's ability to deal with what is in front of her and succeed despite her fears turns this metaphor on its head. It shows what women are capable of if they step outside the bounds society places on them and even encourages them to do so. Even when traditional Gothic heroines move beyond their prescribed roles, they often return to their designated constricted roles, thus "announc[ing] the importance of, and at the end re-stores, sanctioned values and behavior" (Botting 2008, 201–2). As we will see below, Buffy fails, in some ways, to meet this criterion of a Gothic heroine as she refuses to be bound by historical constraints regarding the slayer's behavior and is better for it. In another sense, Buffy does meet this criterion because she always returns to her duties as a Slayer, even as she changes the terms under which she is willing to undertake that role.

TO BE OR NOT TO BE THE SLAYER

The first episode in which we get to see Buffy as something other than the slayer is the episode called "Halloween" in the second season (Green 1997). The episode begins with Buffy missing her date with Angel, her vampire-with-a-soul potential boyfriend, as a result of her slaying duties. She remarks, "Dates are things normal girls have. Girls who have time to think about nail polish and facials. You know what I think about? Ambush tactics. Beheading. Not exactly the stuff dreams are made of." Buffy is very concerned about being romantically appealing to Angel and doesn't see how she could be as she doesn't have time to worry about stereotypical feminine things. Shortly thereafter, Xander hears another student speaking about Buffy in a derogatory manner and he proclaims, "I'm going to do what any man would do about it, something damn manly." Just as the much larger male student is about to beat him up, Buffy steps in and stands up for herself and Xander, which annoys Xander because "cowardice has an unlimited shelf life." Xander is worried that he will be made fun of or thought less of because a girl stood up for him. Within a couple minutes of the show starting, there are already nods to the societal norms associated with masculinity and femininity, as well as examples of them being broken. Both of these violations of social norms are viewed negatively by those who feel they do not fit the norm.

Later, as the Scooby Gang is searching for Halloween costumes, Buffy is enthralled by a pink eighteenth-century reproduction dress, which the shop owner makes her a very good deal on. Xander purchases some toy guns to carry and will wear his relative's military fatigues. It turns out the reason the shop owner was willing to give Buffy such a good deal is because he has enchanted all the items in his shop. Whatever costume one has on, as long as it was purchased at that shop, will become real when a spell to Janus is uttered. As a result, we see Buffy turn into an actual eighteenth-century woman who does not have any of the knowledge or power of the slayer and Xander becomes a soldier. Eighteenth-century Buffy leans hard into gender stereotypes that continued into the Victorian period, proclaiming, "I was brought up a proper lady. I wasn't meant to understand things—just meant to look pretty and then someone will marry me, possibly a Baron." With Buffy at her weakest, it is up to her friends to make sure she survives long enough for the spell to be broken. With the help of Xander, Willow, Angel, Giles (Buffy's Watcher), and even the local popular girl Cordelia, Buffy manages to survive long enough for the spell to be broken after which she quips "ya know, it's good to be me" before defeating the vampires threatening her.

Buffy's uselessness and terror are in stark contrast to her normal self. They remind the viewer of the stereotypical gothic heroine who is "fairly passive, finding her way out of one disastrous situation after another only because someone comes along to rescue her" (Heiland 2004, 28–29). It simultaneously harkens back to the narrative tradition in which *BtVS* styles itself and shows how far women have come since the eighteenth century. Even Cordelia, the stereotypical helpless popular girl of the 1990s is more capable than eighteenth-century Buffy. Problematically, the type of behavior that is shown in a positive light in this episode is very masculine. Angel refers to eighteenth-century women as "dull, simpering morons" and makes it clear its modern Buffy's ability to fight and her willingness to protect the vulnerable that he likes (Green 1997). Xander also receives closure by beating up the pirate version of the bully he was almost beaten up by earlier in the show. Xander's ability to successfully beat up a bully is viewed as positive, as is modern Buffy's ability to stand up for herself. Both of these actions revolve around the perpetuation of violence and behaving in a stereotypically masculine way. The episode allows that women can have power, but only if they do it in a masculine way. It does nothing to challenge the masculine/feminine binary, although it does allow that masculine traits can be found in a female and be positive. Feminine traits on the other hand are never portrayed as positive, regardless of whether they are found in a male or a female.

At the beginning of season 3 we see Buffy chose to leave behind her Slayer responsibilities in "Anne" (Whedon 1998). Buffy leaves Sunnydale after the event at the end of season 2. Her mother finds out she's the slayer and tells her not to come home, she has to kill Angel, the man she loves, because his evil alter-ego has opened a portal that will end the world and the only way to stop it is to kill him, and she is expelled from school. She feels she has nothing left in Sunnydale, so she goes to the city, starts calling herself Anne, and gets a job as a waitress. This is Buffy's idea of a 'normal' life in which she can hide from her responsibilities as a slayer. Notably, even though she has the ability to do something about it, she does not do anything when a male diner patron slaps her ass. This is an incredibly bleak view of what normal womanhood looks like. With all her power, Buffy still enacts 'normalcy' through allowing sexual harassment to happen. The reasons behind this are not discussed in the show—is she worried about losing her job, does she think that's what women allow, is she just trying not to rock the boat as she is hiding? The viewer is never sure, but the picture presented of non-slayer Buffy, through her own choices, is one of weakness and acquiescence.

Back in Sunnydale Giles and Joyce, Buffy's mother, are discussing Buffy's potential whereabouts after Giles goes on another failed excursion trying to find her. Giles refers to Buffy as "the most capable child [he's] ever known." This statement, paired with the scene of Buffy working, highlights her liminality. She is not considered an adult by society as she is under 18, but she is financially supporting herself, has her own apartment, and engaging in typical 'adult' activities. Following this statement Joyce blames Giles for pulling Buffy into the world of vampires and demons, and he replies "I didn't make her who she is." As both Giles and Joyce serve as parental figures in Buffy's life, this statement is a nod to the role Buffy plays in shaping her own life. She does not allow her parents, her fate, or her Watcher to determine who she is and what decisions she makes. It is a reminder that Buffy exerts control over her own life and rejects attempts to control her out of either necessity to save the world or desire to have a life of her own choosing.

Heading back to the city we see Buffy trying to avoid helping a woman, originally called Chanterelle, now calling herself Lilly, whose partner has gone missing. She's worried about him because he takes care of her, and she's not good at taking care of herself. Buffy had previously assisted her as Chanterelle, and she turns to Buffy saying "that's who you are—you help people and stuff." Buffy attempts to deny it, she's explicitly trying to get away from her slayer duties by heading to the city, but eventually agrees to help Chanterelle/Lilly because she doesn't know what to do or how to go about finding her boyfriend. Even when she doesn't want to, Buffy still does the right thing because it's who she is as a person, someone who helps. Even though she has turned her back on slaying she still cares about the people around her. Buffy then discovers that a demon pretending to be a local man, Ken, has been taking kids to a shelter and somehow prematurely aging them. She goes to the shelter and gets pulled into a hell dimension where humans are turned into slaves and forced to work until they are old at which time they are returned to the human dimension.

Upon arriving in the hell dimension, Buffy reminds Ken that he didn't choose her to come to the hell dimension. She is starting to reclaim her own agency in the story, rather than being involved against her will. She also refuses to allow the demons to strip her of her identity and proudly proclaims "I'm Buffy the vampire slayer—and you are?" This statement is followed by a fight with demons and demon Ken proclaims, "you don't fight back, that's not how this works." Ken then grabs Lilly and threatens to kill her if Buffy doesn't stop. While giving a big speech about how Buffy's behavior will not be tolerated, Ken forgets about Lilly, assuming she is too meek to pose a threat. That proves to be a mistake as Lilly pushes demon Ken off the platform he is standing on and seriously injures him. Lilly is inspired by Buffy standing up for all of them to stand up for herself and act to protect all the people who are trying to escape. Her action allows Buffy to keep moving, fighting off other demons, and get the escaping prisoners to safety. Chanterelle/Lilly shows the power of taking agency over one's own life. Her action saves not only her life, but the lives of the rest of the escaping prisoners. As Chanterelle/Lilly is self-described as not capable of taking care of herself, her actions are even more poignant. She didn't need any special powers to make a difference; she just had to take action. Once again, we see that the action taking place, pushing someone to their possible death, is violent, and might be more associated with masculinity. The audience sees a woman take control of a situation through violence. This reinforces the idea that women can wield power, but that the type of power they must wield to make a difference is masculine in nature. The episode ends with Buffy giving Chanterelle/Lilly the keys to her flat and informing her that her boss at the dinner is willing to give her Buffy's old job. Chanterelle/Lilly then asks if she can go by Anne. This is a stark reminder that we are what we present to the world. Chanterelle/Lilly sees Buffy/Anne as capable and wants that for herself. Buffy promises to call and check on her before returning to Sunnydale and hugging her mother. She is, in a short span of time, acting parental toward Chanterelle/Lilly and then being a child herself returning home, showing once again how Buffy defies categorization.

Later in the season, as Buffy approaches her eighteenth birthday, her slaying powers are once again removed without her consent. The episode, called "Helpless," starts with romantic music and the camera panning past a romantic meal until we see Buffy and Angel sparring (Contner 1999). This juxtaposition shows how different Buffy's life is. She is at her boyfriend's, had had a romantic meal and, instead of engaging in amorous activity, they are fighting and making uncomfortable statements about the fact that they can't have "satisfaction." Buffy then leaves Angel's home and goes on patrol where she is nearly killed by a vampire when her powers suddenly desert her. The following day Buffy learns that her father will not be able to make their annual father-daughter birthday plans—a trip to go see the Ice Capades. After telling Giles about her powers deserting her the night before, she tries to get him to accompany her to the ice-skating show instead. In an attempt to explain why it means so much to her she states "and ok, it's a big dumb girly thing, but I love it." Buffy clearly feels the need to justify her desire to go see the Ice Capades and qualifies her desire by recognizing that it is a dumb girl thing. This sends the message that stereotypical "girly" things need to be justified or excused, therefore casting them in a negative light.

Giles does not pick up on the hint and instead encourages Buffy to work on her slayer training with crystals. While staring at the crystal Buffy goes into a trance and Giles is shown injecting her with a compound, which we later learn is a combination of muscle relaxants and adrenaline suppressors designed to make her weak. This is part of a ritual, what van Gennep would consider the right of separation that all slayers face on the eighteenth birthday according to Watcher's tradition. According to the Head Watcher, this trial is meant to make the slayer realize that she is more than physical

strength, she must have intelligence and confidence as well. Giles is following his orders by injecting her but is clearly conflicted, knowing that Buffy
could die as a result of this rite of passage. Multiple times throughout the
episode he is shown arguing with the Head Watcher about whether this ritual
is really necessary. The rite of passage involves subduing the physical aspects of the slayer and sending her into a house with an insane vampire to see
if she can still figure out how to survive.

The following day Buffy tries to stand up for Cordelia who is being
harassed by a male student. Instead of being able to stop him, Buffy gets
swatted away and Cordelia starts yelling at him and engaging in stereotypical
"girl fight" behavior. As Buffy is normally the student who stands up for
others, this is an unusual twist. Back in the library she has the following
interaction with Giles:

> Buffy: "I have no strength, I have no coordination. I throw knives like . . ."
> Giles: "A girl?"
> Buffy: "Like I'm not the slayer."

This interaction showcases how far Buffy is outside what Giles would per-
ceive as the norm. Giles sees normative femininity as weak, uncoordinated
individuals who are not good at perpetrating violence. Buffy counters this by
saying she simply doesn't feel like the slayer, which suggests that, to her,
femininity can be inclusive of strength, coordination, and the ability to take
care of one's self. This loss of power is a source of concern for Buffy
throughout the episode. When talking to Angel about what not being the
slayer would mean, Buffy muses "I've seen too much, what if I can't fight it?
What if I just hid under my bed all scared and helpless, or what if I just
become pathetic?" Despite her earlier protestations that she will deal if she's
not the slayer and her own apparent belief that women are capable, she still
worries about whether she will have the courage and psychological strength
to face what's hiding in the dark without her powers. She also questions what
her identity is, who she is at her core. If she is not the slayer, what is she?

It turns out the slayer is more than mystical powers, it's who she is, a
point that she is first made aware of by Kendra in "What's My Line Part 2"
(Semel 1997). By this point in the show Buffy has accepted that the slayer is
part of who she is, but she still thinks of the slayer as being linked to the
demonic powers imbued in the first slayer and directed by the Watchers
Council. As Buffy is walking home, she is sexually harassed by two men on
the street, she almost turns around and then thinks better of it, knowing that
her strength has deserted her. The insane vampire manages to escape its
confines and tracks Buffy down after she is harassed on the street. He is just
about to catch her when Giles pulls up in his car and the two speed away.
Buffy laments "I can't be just a person. I can't be helpless like that." She is

fully questioning her identity as the slayer and views being physically frail as being helpless. Back at the school library, Giles tells Buffy about the drugs and the trial. She feels an immense amount of betrayal and does not want to hear any of the thin excuses Giles tries to make. Unfortunately, upon arriving at home she discovers that the insane vampire has kidnapped her mother. Missing physical strength or no, Buffy knows she must face the vampire if she wants to save her mother. It is her love of her mother and connection to the human world that propels her into conflict with the vampire. She chooses to act as the slayer, despite not having her physical strength, because it's who she is. Her entrance into the house with the vampire begins the rite of margin or liminality, she does not possess the physical strength of the slayer, but still must act as the slayer. She both is and is not the slayer at once.

In the house Buffy struggles to match the vampire without her physical powers. Several minutes are devoted to watching Buffy get her ass handed to her, watching her struggle to open locked doors (normally she would simply break the lock) and run away, and she is almost killed. She eventually discovers that the vampire she is currently facing is dependent on his pills, and she fills his glass with holy water. In his desperation to take the pills, the vampire drinks the holy water and then turns to dust. This showcases a different type of ability, one that still allows Buffy to defeat her enemy but is more straightforward. Buffy essentially poisons the vampire. She uses her wits to survive, but also engages in a style of violence which is more often ascribed to females. The message here is that without her physical strength Buffy must engage in more devious less straightforward means of achieving her aim. The long period she spends in distress also highlights the precarious nature of femininity without physical strength. A second vampire then tries to attack Buffy as she is untying her mother but is killed by Giles who has rushed to the house to try and protect her. The group returns to the library to find the Head Watcher waiting. He is angry with Giles for trying to help Buffy and for telling her about the rite of passage. Giles is fired because the Head Watcher views his affection for Buffy as getting in the way of his job as Watcher. He does not value Buffy's connection to the human world, he wants her to follow orders and defend the human world without having the human connections and experiences that make it worth saving. Buffy sees the Council for what it is and threatens to harm the Head Watcher if he does not leave town before her strength comes back. While a new Watcher is sent to guide Buffy, she never trusts him or the Council again. She has not fully completed the right of aggregation because, while she is still the Slayer, she is no longer under as much control of the watchers and, by the end of the season, refuses to listen to them anymore. Buffy is still the slayer, but she is going to do it her way. As she becomes less reliant on the Watchers Council for guidance and information, she becomes something different than previous slayers. Her guidance and information come more from her friends, including Giles who is still around, and she figures out what it is to be the slayer when not controlled by a patriarchal ancient order.

Buffy retains her slayer powers for the rest of the series, maybe. This brings us to the season 6 episode "Normal Again" (Rosenthal 2002). This episode is less Buffy loses her powers, and more did Buffy ever have slayer power or is she insane. While out patrolling one night, Buffy gets stabbed in the arm by a demon. When this happens, she is briefly transported to a mental ward. As the episode continues, the length of time Buffy spends in the mental institution increases. We learn that in this alternate reality Buffy never moved to Sunnydale and has been in a mental institution for six years. We see her parents come visit her and learn that her mother is still alive and still together with her father. While her parents discuss Buffy's prognosis with the doctor he says "In her mind, she's the central figure in a fantastic world beyond imagination . . . she thinks she's some sort of hero." This interlude suggests that Buffy being a hero is beyond imagination. The doctor focuses much more on her belief in herself and her ability to shape the world than her belief in vampires and demons as the reason for her stay in the mental institution. While it is not specified that this is beyond imagination because of her gender, that is the undertone. Her being a hero is somehow as worthy of placement in the psych ward as her belief in vampires and demons. Buffy's institutionalization for this brings to mind historical examples of women being institutionalized and diagnosed with hysteria for recognizing the injustices in the world and fighting against them.

Throughout the episode, Buffy goes back and forth over which versions of reality are real. The audience also learns that Buffy was institutionalized once before, when she first found out she was the slayer, and Buffy worries that she never actually left that institution. After having some unpleasant interactions with her friends and sister, and realizing how disconnected she feels from her own life, she decides through the episode that the mental institution is real. In order to fully embrace that reality, she is told she must give up the things that keep pulling her back to Sunnydale, her friends. Once again, we see Buffy's connection to her friends and human life in Sunnydale used to explain why she continues to slay. This time, the insinuation is that those ties are a negative. Her decision to follow through on this plan to rid herself of ties in Sunnydale results in her putting her friends in great danger and, briefly, refusing to protect them by not slaying. Buffy eventually decides that Sunnydale is real and protects her friends after her mother tells her to believe in herself in the alternative timeline. Joyce is trying to tell Buffy to believe in the mental institution timeline, instead Buffy believes that she is not crazy. Historically speaking, this is an interesting twist because being a strong-willed woman who believed in herself did get some women sent to asylums and it is Buffy's belief in herself that allows her to leave the asylum in her mind. She chooses the harder, more violent path because it's the one that she believes in and she is not willing to go back on her belief in herself. However, the episode ends with the doctor telling Buffy's parents that she has retreated into her mind. Her belief in herself and in Sunnydale means that she is viewed as unresponsive and insane in the alternate timeline. The last shot of the episode continues to call into question which reality is real. Is Buffy the slayer, or is she crazy?

DISCUSSION

There are several themes that thread themselves through these four episodes that deal particularly with gender. At the beginning of "Halloween," we see individuals who stray from their perceived gender role in a negative light, both as Xander is upset that Buffy defends him and Buffy is upset that she might not be girly enough for Angel. Both Xander and Buffy worry about their ability to fit in because they do not ascribe to heteronormative gender roles, and importantly, both want to be able to fit those roles. As the episode and series continue, we see masculine behavior and violence being shown in a more positive light. Xander and Angel's ability to protect eighteenth-century Buffy is good, Buffy's loss of physical ability in "Helpless" in incapacitating, and Chanterelle/Lilly's choice to shove a demon off a ledge allows the captured humans to escape. Positive things happen when people engage in violence, a trait more stereotypically associated with masculinity, and negative events occur when violence is not possible. While violence and power are seen in a positive view, heteronormative femininity is never seen as positive. Stereotypical women are portrayed as weak, silly and incapable. Eighteenth-century Buffy would have died if not for her friends, Chanterelle/Lilly would have been a slave to demons if Buffy wasn't there to inspire her to action, Buffy allows herself to be harassed when she is not physically strong, Xander is mocked for having a girl stand up for him, and Buffy almost dies when she loses her physical strength. The message this sends is that masculine behavior and violence is good wherever it is found, and feminine behavior is liable to get one killed, or at the very least harassed.

These episodes of *BtVS* do show women who can have power, but mainly if they wield that power in a masculine way—through violence which generally grants them authority and credibility. In "Halloween," Buffy's power is returned when the spell is broken, and she can chase off the vampires because of her physical strength. Chanterelle/Lilly comes to Buffy for help in "Anne" because she was previously able to look after a large group of humans and protect them from the vampires that wanted to kill them through violence. "Helpless" begins to paint a slightly different picture. At her physically weakest point Buffy still manages to protect her mother and kill the vampire, using cunning instead of strength. Being the Slayer is about more than being physically strong. Buffy has to use her knowledge of vampires and her knowledge of this particular vampire's weakness against him in order to save the day. She does manage to kill the vampire but is physically the worse for wear because of it. This episode also clarifies for her how deeply problematic the Watchers Council is and starts Buffy on the path of extracting herself from their influence and control. Despite being physically weak she is showing a mental toughness and belief in herself that belies her momentary physical limitations. She is formally beginning to redefine the role of slayer as she sees it, not as the Watcher's Council sees it.

Choice is fundamentally important in *BtVS* and these slayer/not-a-slayer episodes are no different. Buffy chooses to dress as an eighteenth-century woman for Halloween, she wants a fantasy, she does not consent to being turned into an eighteenth-century woman with no ability to protect herself. It is Giles, her Watcher, who actually manages to break the curse turning her and the other individuals who had shopped at Ethan's into their make-believe come-as-you-aren't Halloween counterparts. Giles recognizes that standing up for people who do no consent, even if you are not directly affected, is important. He does not let the social pressure of seeing an old friend, who is actually the one who did the spell to cause the transformation, to keep him from doing the right thing. The message here is profound—do right by your fellow humans, make the right choice not the easy one. It's a message that still resonates today. Outside of spells and betrayals Buffy does a good job of controlling her own destiny as well. She chooses to leave home at the end of season 2 and chooses to help Chanterelle/Lilly before returning to Sunnydale. She chooses to act as the slayer, even when her physical powers have been taken from her. Buffy's choices define who she is, and she is someone who helps people. Showcasing someone who exhibits so much control over her own life, even when fate would seemingly take a lot of choices away from her is valuable. It shows the audience that there are always choices, they may not be easy, they may be scary, but there are choices and one has the ability to steer their own life, even when outside forces try to influence you in one way or another. Chanterelle/Lilly shoving demon Ken off the ledge, and Buffy's rebuttal of the Watcher's Council are examples of women playing an active role in their own lives to better their own circumstances.

Buffy also has a fundamental choice to make in the episode "Normal Again"—which reality is real. This episode really undercuts any attempts to claim the show has an overarching feminist plotline because it calls into question, some might even say suggests as it end on that timeline, that Buffy is in a mental institution and all of her power is in her own head. If Buffy's belief in her own hero status, her power, authority and ability, is causing her to be locked up, that suggests that women who display those traits are crazy. The feminist claims of *BtVS* were already on shaky ground. Yes, Buffy is a strong woman who shapes her own destiny. Unfortunately, the type of power she wields is reflecting hegemonic norms that we see within society anyways, she does nothing to disrupt what type of actions are considered worthy of power, just shows that women can wield those forces. That in itself is a step in the right direction, but the viewpoint of femininity as undesirable or weak undermines a message of female empowerment. Buffy's ability to control her own destiny is also potentially inspiring, showing the audience that women can do what they want and build a world around them that suits their needs. The show cannot truly be called feminist because what it depicts is a woman owning male types of power, rather than utilizing new forms of power and calling into question why society associates power with stereotypical male displays. Furthermore, calling into question whether or not a woman exerting stereotypical male forms of power and engaging in violence is actually in a mental institution is devastating. It reveals the conservative undertones of the show and allows the viewer an easy out when grappling with any hard questions regarding the sex and gender systems under which our society operates.

BIBLIOGRAPHY

Berger, Roni. 2013. "Now I See It, Now I Don't: Researcher's Position and Reflexivity in Qualitative Research." *Qualitative Research* 15(2): 219–34.

Botting, Fred. 2008. *Limits of Horror: Technology, Bodies, Gothic*. Manchester: Manchester University Press.

Boutin, Alexis T. 2016. "Exploring the Social Construction of Disability: An Application of the Bioarchaeology of Personhood Model to a Pathological Skeleton from Ancient Bahrain." *International Journal of Paleopathology* 12: 17–28.

Butler, Judith. 1993. *Bodies that Matter: On the Discursive Limits of "Sex."* New York: Routledge.

Butler, Judith. 1995. "Conscience Doth Make Subjects of Us All." *Yale French Studies* 88: 6–26.

Butler, Judith. 2004. *Undoing Gender*. New York: Routledge.

Conkey, Margaret, and Joan M. Gero. 1997. "Programme to Practice: Gender and Feminism in Archaeology." *Annual Review of Anthropology* 26: 411–37.

Contner, James A, director. 1999. *Buffy the Vampire Slayer*. Season 3, episode 13, "Helpless." Aired January 19 on The WB.

Díaz-Andreu, Margarita. 2005. "Gender Identity." In *The Archaeology of Identity: Approaches to Gender, Age, Ethnicity, Status and Religion*, edited by Margarita Díaz-Andreu, Sam Lucy, Staša Babić, and David N. Edward, 13–42. London: Routledge.

Foucault, Michel. 1978. *History of Sexuality, Vol. I*. New York: Random House.

Geller, Pamela L. 2005. "Skeletal Analysis and Theoretical Complications." *World Archaeology* 37(4): 597–609.

Georgieva, Margarita. 2013. *The Gothic Child*. Houndmills: Palgrave Macmillan.

Gilchrist, Roberta. 1999. *Gender and Archaeology: Contesting the Past*. London: Routledge.

Gilmore, D. 2003. *Monsters, Evil Beings, Mythical Beasts, and All Manner of Imaginary Terrors*. Philadelphia: University of Pennsylvania Press.

Green, Bruce Seth, director. 1997. *Buffy the Vampire Slayer*. Season 2, episode 6, "Halloween." Aired October 27 on The WB.

Halberstam, Judith. 1998. *Female Masculinities*. Durham and London: Duke University Press.

Heiland, Donna. 2004. *Gothic and Gender: An Introduction*. Malden: Blackwell.

Henesy, Megan. 2020. "Leaving My Girlhood Behind: Woke Witches and Feminist Liminality in *Chilling Adventures of Sabrina.*" *Feminist Media Studies.* doi: 10.1080/1468077 7.2020.1791929.

Hirmer, Karin. 2013. "Female Empowerment: Buffy and Her Heiresses in Control." In *Images of the Modern Vampire: The Hip and the Atavistic*, edited by Barbara Brodman and James E. Doan, 71–84. Lanham: Fairleigh Dickinson University Press.

Horner, Avril. 2010. "Women, Power and Conflict: The Gothic Heroine and 'Chocolate-box Gothic.'" *Caliban* 27: 319–30.

Jones, Bethan. 2013. "Buffy vs Bella: Gender, Relationships, and the Modern Vampire." In *The Modern Vampire and Human Identity*, edited by Deborah Mutch, 37–54. New York: Palgrave MacMillan.

Joyce, Rosemary. 2017. "Sex, Gender and Anthropology: Moving Bioarchaeology Outside the Subdiscipline." In *Exploring Sex and Gender in Bioarchaeology*, edited by S. C. Agarwal and J.K. Wesp, 1–14. Albuquerque: University of New Mexico.

Madden, Victoria. 2017. "'We Found the Witch, May We Burn Her?': Suburban Gothic, Witch-Hunting, and Anxiety Induced Conformity in Stephen King's *Carrie.*" *The Journal of American Culture* 40(1): 7–21.

Magoulick, Mary. 2016. "Frustrating Female Heroism: Mixed Messages in *Xena, Nikita,* and *Buffy.*" *The Journal of Popular Culture* 39(5): 729–55.

Mitchell, Sally. 1995. *The New Girl: Girls' Culture in England, 1880–1915.* New York: Columbia University Press.

Modleski, Tania. 1982. *Loving With a Vengeance : Mass Produced Fantasies for Women.* New York: Routledge.

Pecheux, Michel. 1981. *Language, Semantics and Ideology.* London: Macmillan.

Petrie, Douglas, director. 2003. *Buffy the Vampire Slayer.* Season 7, episode 15, "Get It Done." Aired February 18 on UPN.

Price, Jessica. 2010. "The Role of Masculinity and Femininity in *Buffy the Vampire Slayer.*" In *Sexual Rhetoric in the Works of Joss Whedon: New Essays*, edited by Erin B. Waggoner, 215–25. Jefferson: McFarland and Company.

Rosenthal, Rick, director. 2002. *Buffy the Vampire Slayer.* Season 6, episode 17, "Normal Again." Aired March 12 on UPN.

Semel, David, director. 1997. *Buffy the Vampire Slayer.* Season 2, episode 10, "What's My Line: Part Two." Aired November 24 on The WB.

Smith, Charles Martin, director. 1997. *Buffy the Vampire Slayer.* Season 1, episode 1, "Welcome to the Hellmouth." Aired March 10 on The WB.

Smith, Michelle J., and Kristine Moruzi. 2018. "Vampires and Witches Go to School: Contemporary Young Adult Fiction, Gender, and the Gothic." *Children's Literature in Education* 49:6–18.

Solomon, David, director. 1997. *Buffy the Vampire Slayer.* Season 2, episode 9, "What's My Line: Part One." Aired November 17 on The WB.

Solomon, David, director. 1999. *Buffy the Vampire Slayer.* Season 3, episode 20, "The Prom." Aired May 11 on The WB.

Turner, Victor. 1987. "Betwixt and Between: The Liminal Period in Rites of Passage." In *Betwixt and Between: Patterns of Masculine and Feminine Initiation*, edited by Louise Carus Mahdi, Steven Foster and Meredith Little, 3–22. La Salle: Open Court Publishing Company.

Van Gennep, A., and D.I. Kertzer. 2019. *The Rites of Passage.* Translated by M.B. Vizedom and G.L. Caffee. London: University of Chicago Press.

Watt, Diane. 2007. "On Becoming a Qualitative Researcher: The Value of Reflexivity." *The Qualitative Report* 12(1): 82–101.

Wesp, Julie K. 2014. "Bodies of Work: Organization of Everyday Life Activities in Urban New Spain." PhD diss., University of California, Berkeley.

Whedon, Joss, director. 1998. *Buffy the Vampire Slayer.* Season 3, episode 1, "Anne." Aired September 29 on The WB.

Chapter Six

Fear Itself

The Vampire as Moral Panic

Holly Walters

Welcome to my house! Enter freely and of your own will!" He made no motion of stepping to meet me, but stood like a statue, as though his gesture of welcome had fixed him into stone. The instant, however, that I had stepped over the threshold, he moved impulsively forward, and holding out his hand grasped mine with a strength which made me wince, an effect which was not lessened by the fact that it seemed as cold as ice-more like the hand of a dead than a living man [15–16].

Thus, the vampire Dracula sets foot upon the literary stage in Bram Stoker's 1897 novel. Since then the vampire, and especially Dracula, has appeared in countless books, essays, articles, films, and plays to become one of the most popular cultural icons in history. Somewhere between a nightmare of immortal terror and an object of fascination and reverence, the vampire has been an enduring part of the mythologies of diverse cultures from around the world. He is the anti-hero, the tempting lover, the villain, the mysterious stranger, and the monster. Most people are familiar with vampires from books and movies, featuring a terrible yet compelling being rising from his grave to drink the blood of the hapless living. But the vampire did not originate in silent films nor in the dime store novels of the post-Industrial era. It has existed in almost every culture's folklore and mythology throughout history; from the night-roaming spirits of ancient Greece to the bloody masters of Romanian castles to the assorted myths and fictions of modern America. To be certain, the vampire has not always been called such, but every culture has proposed some manner of creature who cheats death by preying on the living; engaging in a fatal symbiosis by draining a vital essence (typically blood) and denied eternal rest for violating the mores and morality of the community; a scourge against established society.

The vampire is a powerful symbol to those who identify with it and a deeply intriguing metaphor for the collective fears and perspectives of the societies within which it dwells. But over the years, what began as a folktale of wandering spirits has accumulated a plethora of characteristics and interests which are now lumped together under the ubiquitous metaphor of the vampire. Yet the figure of the vampire and the ways in which we draw upon it have undergone many transformations over time. It is then these transformations that reveal something about our own relationships to impurity, danger, and death today. In other words, my aim here is not to address the symbol of the vampire as a relatively constant set of cross-cultural characteristics and meanings but to offer a reflection on the differences in symbolic expression over time as explained by changes in underlying social anxieties. Following the foundations of the Western concept of the vampire, from Classical Antiquity to Medieval Europe, is a complex process. But not only does the vampire symbolize the greatest fears a society has about itself, but it also embodies myriad regional beliefs concerning evil, death, and corruption. To wit, a kind of perpetual moral panic in iconic form.[1] It personifies the darkest aspects of life, the pain of disease and fear of mortality, questions of evil in nature, and struggles against spiritual failure; particularly as they relate to gender and sex. Following the institutionalization of Christianity across much of Europe in the Middle Ages, the vampire mytheme then metamorphosed through a set of profound changes to become the vampire we recognize today; though it yet remains the repository of our deepest collective fears.

AGE-OLD ANXIETIES AND THE SANGUISUGE

Although the vampire, by the modern definition of the word, does not occur outright in the writings or mythologies of ancient Greek or Roman authors, there are numerous mentions of various rituals, funeral ceremonies, and spiritual characteristics that demonstrate that the concept of vampirism was not unknown to the peoples of the Mediterranean. The majority of references regarding the vampire involve nocturnal spirits, or most usually demons,[2] which roam about and drain the blood or sexual essences of the living. These vampiric entities do not fall under the scope of ghosts, as by definition they were never living, but for those who were, they were considered little more than animate monsters whose souls had long left them (Wilson 1971). These spirits are called collectively *succubi* or *Lamia* for women and *incubi* for men and were believed to be the result of a body and soul's collective infection by evil or spiritual uncleanliness during life or shortly after death.

The taint, that which was the cause of vampirism, was often brought about by improper burial rites, disruption of the entombed ashes and bones, or anything that specifically disturbed the body from its purified state following the funeral rites. The Greek vampire also generally represents the cycle from birth to death and then rebirth, albeit in a false fashion, having been arrested in the state between life, death, and final burial; whereas the spirit and the body have not completely separated on their way to the next step. This was the genesis of the Western concept of the vampire and also of the definition of the vampire in respect to its existence as a semi-corporeal, night-dwelling, undead, being. Here also is the vampire's initial association with damnation and devilry (Sommers 1929; Frost 1989; Dundes 1998), later appropriated by Christianity during the Middle Ages.

In ancient Greece, many of the people who became candidates for vampirism after death were those who had died violent or tragic deaths, along with alcoholics, virgins, suicides, and heretics. One could also become a vampire if they were or had birthed a deformed child, were a prostitute, or a violent criminal. In other words, a person was in danger of becoming a vampire if they were a member of any particularly marginalized group considered "tainted" by the general population. The criteria, of course, tended to revolve around the latent hostilities of the "in-group," who feared and loathed the perceived differences of the individuals under suspicion (Rickels 1995) and projected onto them all manner of anxieties related to the corruption or pollution of proper society. This was somewhat in contrast to the later rise of Christianized versions of the vampire, where anyone viewed as an unrepentant sinner, a tainted "insider" in these cases, was liable to become vampiric. Because the Church found vampire lore particularly useful to its expansion, this then became the basis for the Church's doctrines regarding vampirism, which would be further popularized in the West beginning in Medieval Europe. The earliest Classical associations with demons and devils, however, must not be confused with the Christian concept of the Devil and his expression through the vampire. The demonic vampire of Catholic Europe was based on different principles than the Classic vampire of Greece or Rome, although the early classical writings were used as source material by the Church. Therefore, while the two concepts bear many characteristic similarities both in form as well as function, they are expressed differently within their respective contexts. I note this in particular as it relates to the issue of moral panic here because the shift in semiotic associations related to vampirism demonstrates how the vampire as a persistent folkloric and literary construct becomes broadly reflective of societally threatening evils: a "bad death" and aberrant "outsiderness" in the Classical world or proximity to sin and the Devil for the Medieval one. This, then, is how gender enters into the situation.

In Mesopotamia, the vampire was almost always female, though she shared the semi-corporeal demonic fate of her Mediterranean predecessors. The Mesopotamian vampire was also given the added benefit of deification. Here, the vampire is a god-like monster under the guises of *Khalk'ru the Feeder, Destructor of All* and the demonic *Ekimmu* (or Departed Spirits) which could only be subdued through the funereal sacrifice of blood (Frost 1989). In Babylonia, the earliest vampire on record is *Lilitu* the snake goddess, whose form is often shared among the Greek Empusae and the pagan Roman Lamia. Both the Empusae and the Lamia are characterized as naked, serpent-bodied, women whose aim is to seduce men and gain immortal power by stealing their bodily humors. In later Hebrew texts that were derived directly from these mythical characters, Lilitu and the characteristics of the Empusae and the Lamia would be incorporated into the biblical story of Adam and Eve where both the serpent and the demonic vampire play the role of adversary to Man and, once again, where women will be viewed as the ultimate downfall for the morally civilizing pursuits of men.

The vampire's association with blood and the consuming of blood also begins in Greek and Roman legend and was one of the primary characteristics that has remained a driving force throughout vampire folklore and literature over time. In pagan and earth-based religions, blood was regarded as having great magical properties which could be stolen by the drinker (similar to Frazer's principle of contagion). It is therefore within the classical mythologies of Greece, Rome, and the Fertile Crescent that the vampire concept starts to reflect an attitude regarding sex and to a greater degree, men's sexual perceptions of women (and their menstrual blood) as perilous or polluting. The triumvirate associations of blood, sex, and women have then continued into the modern era as the fundamentals behind the vampire as a symbol, particularly in regard to its expression as a form of false redemption; a reversal to the Christian Eucharist. The fear, and more specifically the vampiric and witch-based moral panics,[3] that followed among the populace, and became attached to the mythos overall, was then brought about through faith in the religious traditions that contained the vampire as a character. This fear is also later exacerbated through a tradition adopted by writers of the first stories containing the literary vampire, which was to claim that their stories were based on real events (Cohen 1971; Frost 1989). Ultimately, as Thomas Johansson notes, "moral panics are primarily about upholding boundaries between various groups of people and maintaining moral conceptions" (2000, 24). When such distinctions of collective identity are then threatened by the perception of a hidden danger, an evil outsider, or a secret world of internal corruption, the response is one of moral panic which then predicates the need to defend the imperiled boundary (see also: Radford 2019). In these cases, such boundaries were that which delineated men from women, good from evil, authority from subordination, and socially productive sex from destructive sex.

It is difficult to pinpoint the exact moment that the vampire entered European thought or, particularly, literature. One of the earliest European vampires is recorded in the Icelandic and Teutonic Sagas and in an obscure eleventh-century Anglo-Saxon poem called *A Vampyre of the Fens*. After a humble start, the vampire is almost all but forgotten in literature until the fifteenth-century publication of *Le Morte D'Arthur* by Sir Thomas Malory (Frost 1989). These early references to vampirism stemmed from the prevalence of pagan worship in Europe at the time, which took many of its beliefs from the classic stories of the vampire of a more ancient era. Here then is the binding thread from ancient times to the modern vampire concept. After Christianity had fully taken hold of Europe beginning mainly in the twelfth century AD, the Church could do little to dispel the deeply rooted regional myths of the vampire that existed among local cultures. Instead of trying to scour these myths out and possibly lose its dogmatic battle with local pagan traditions, it adopted them and began to perpetuate them as icons and parables. Thus, the contemporary vampire was born.

At this time, the vampire still maintained much of the same form as it had in ancient Greece and Rome but more importantly was still functioning in the same ways. The vampire remained the symbol of society's greatest fears about itself by assuming the social-psychological role of a needed encapsulation of whatever societal fears existed in that particular era. Unsurprisingly then, as Europe progressed into the Dark Ages, the vampire underwent a series of more Catholic transformations. At this point, the vampire was still usually female but the association with sex was not as important as the association with night, which in early Catholicism was presumed to be the time when the Devil was at his most powerful (a point which will also become important in understanding the relationship between gender and vampirism afterwards). It was also strongly associated with the Christian concept of Sin. Those who became vampires were those who had led lives of sin without salvation at the time of death or who were denied burial on holy ground. Such people were drunkards, suicides, perpetrators of incest, unwed mothers, or children born with teeth or cauls (a flap of skin over the face) who would rise at night to kill family or friends by biting them and draining their blood (Dundes 1998). As a result, it was not uncommon in eastern European countries to dig up corpses suspected of being vampires and burn or mutilate the body to save the rest of the town. There are hundreds of accounts of various local traditions and methods of destroying a vampire, but the most popular methods are the most familiar to us today. The methods of burning, binding with holy incantations, and staking through the heart or staking the body to the bottom of the coffin with a sharpened wooden implement were thought to undo the vampire permanently. Later on, burning became increasingly more popular with the onset of the Black Plague.

In the latter half of the fourteenth century, the vampire became better known as a harbinger of disease and the walking embodiment of the spread of the Plague. The vampire was still a soulless monster with no hope of salvation but now it had also taken on the purview of an even greater fear. No longer did a person have to die and then through immorality and damnation become a vampire. Even the innocent were now at risk, especially any family or close friends of the individual who died under notably unholy circumstances. The taint of the vampire now had the capacity to spread unwittingly much as the Plague itself did. The only way to save them, naturally, was to exhume the vampire's body and usually to burn it. The town elders would hear rumors about the exploits of a vampire from certain symptoms suffered by residents of the town and then troop down to the graveyard to dig up the body and check for signs of decay.

Proper decay was seen as a sign of holiness and because the mortal body was inherently sinful, it must be seen to decompose in order to demonstrate the departure of the purifying presence of a soul. The decay thus also demonstrated the acceptance of the soul by God. If the corpse was not decayed enough, officials would then either cut the body up or drag it into the center of town where a funeral pyre would be built. The body thought to be the vampire usually was fresh-looking, having rosy skin, lengthened nails and hair, and fresh or recently congealed blood around its mouth or eyes. It also was often found in a different position than the one in which it had been buried. Unfortunately, this was not unheard of in the era of the Plague because little was known at the time about the stages of normal decomposition (which can cause a body to move around) and it was also not uncommon for victims to be mistakenly buried alive only to die later of suffocation or dehydration in their graves. In any case, the townsfolk would then burn the corpse within the presence of a priest to ensure the dispelling of evil or devilish magic. Poignantly, this practice did work to stop the spread of the plague through the destruction of infected bodies but also, ironically, continued the belief in the vampire.

Once the body was ashes the night terrors and symptoms typically ended; the town returned to a state of calm through the ritualistic "final death" of the vampire and the purging of evil through fire (Dundes 1998; Rickels 1995; Sommers 1929).[4] To note, this was the same method that was used to 'purify' witches around the same time. With the spread of the witch-cult hysteria during this same period, social norms and expectations toward women were changing and the mythos of the vampire was not immune. Although women were very often likely to be the vampire, they were also seen as being particularly vulnerable to the vampire's seductions. This was part of the religious view of women as spiritually weak and metaphysically inferior in regard to men and most notably susceptible to the trickery of the Christian Devil. This was in direct correlation with the biblical story of the Fall of Man in the book of Genesis, where the serpentine Devil seduces Eve who then seduces Adam. Women fell to the wiles of the Devil and men fell to the wiles of women. Women, therefore, required strict rules and guardianship in order to be sure that they would not be seduced or coerced by the Devil or his ever-present minion, the vampire. As a result, the gendered vampiric moral panics of previous eras have much to tell us about similar moral panics now. Dangerous female sexuality, uncontrolled reproduction, the permeable nature of the female body to sex standing in for the permeable nature of the soul to evil, and the fear of women's individual rebellion against proper social and familial behavior remain.

The vampire symbol would endure in this state for much of the thirteenth through the seventeenth centuries, changing only slightly within local contexts across Europe. For example, in Russia it was common that, when a young girl died, she was to be dressed in wedding attire and accompanied to the grave by a young man. This young man was from thenceforth considered a widower in order that she would not rise again from the grave having been seduced by the promise of betrothal to the Devil. Yet again, traditions regarding the vampire bear remarkable similarities with tales of witches. The distinction of the vampire, however, was the ability to steal spiritual essences from people or objects and thereby sustain itself or its supernatural abilities through time. Some vampires could control the weather while others could command animals and certain characteristics of people. But in many cases, the vampire was still commonly female with power to fundamentally corrupt the home, fields, and children. Following the spread of Christianity this began to change however, and as time passed, more and more often, the vampire became male. For example, an Irish tale of a marauding vampire called the *Dearg-dhul*, meaning 'red-blood drinker' in Gaelic, appeared in the folktales of the peasantry beginning in the seventh century. In this tale, the vampire was a druidess in life, but, by the latter half of the thirteenth century, the *Dearg-dhul* had become not only male but a former Catholic priest as well (Sommers 1929). This shift was gradual and the changes in the vampire symbol were primarily localized, related to the incorporation of pagan beliefs into newly established Christian practices, until the coming of the eighteenth century and the debut of *Dracula*. No longer just the dangerous females of folklore, but the truly monstrous males of literature.

DRACULA THE UN-REAL

Beginning in the eighteenth century, there was a veritable vampire epidemic in literature. The vampire went from the frightening undead demon stalking the night to the seductive and mysterious gentleman of the evening. He was also no longer a strictly religious entity, instead becoming the idol of the Romantic movement and an icon for the hidden and generally forbidden desires (and fears) of the Western Victorian world. For example, through her repeated encounters with Dracula, Lucy transforms from an innocent, empty-headed girl to a powerfully erotic woman. This interpretation, of course, involves Lucy undergoing the culturally compliant woman's encounter with her own sexuality; an encounter Victorian society feared as evil (Johnson 1992). But perhaps the most important revolution in the vampire mythos at this time was that, for the first time in history, the vampire had also gained something of a human soul. The undead monster was not gone but the man inside the vampire had begun to emerge with all his emotions and desires. Much of this transformation was due to the flowering of modern science, particularly medicine and psychology, as well as a harsh de-emphasis on the power and teachings of the once all-powerful Catholic Church (a dichotomy well represented in the characters of both Dracula himself and his nemesis, Abraham Van Helsing). The Age of Reason took its toll on the magics and myths of Europe by exalting the critical mind and tearing down much of the religious superstition of the educated classes. But the vampire was not vanquished. Instead, the vampire symbol was once again transformed to fit the society in which it existed, now as a literary character, remaining the staid portrait of the dark depths the human soul was keen to reach as well as continuing to represent the latest moral panics about the containment of female sexuality and concerns over foreign male interlopers. But no character so changed the very face of the vampire in all of history than Bram Stoker's *Dracula*.

Published in 1897, *Dracula* was instantly popular. It was not the first vampire story of its kind; following close on the heels of such works as 1819's *Vampyre* by Dr. John Polidori under the tutelage of Lord Byron and James Malcolm Rymer's (alternatively attributed to Thomas Preskett Prest) *Varney the Vampyre* of 1847 (Cohen 1971). Dracula, however, was destined to become the most famous vampire in literary history. As popular opinion holds, Stoker's Dracula character was based on an actual person. The "real" Dracula was a fifteenth-century Romanian warlord named Vlad Tepes, born in 1431 in the fortified town of Strassburg (now Sighisoara), Romania. He became famous in his own time not for being a "vampire," but for his exploits as a wartime general against the Ottoman Turks and his reign as Prince of Wallachia and Transylvania, an area near the Carpathian Mountains. His favorite method of execution and torture was of impaling his captured enemies—and occasionally his own nobles—on long wooden spikes and drinking their blood with his dinner. At the time, however, this had much less to do with vampirism as it did with psychological warfare (Florescu and McNally 1989). Vlad Tepes, or Vlad the Impaler as he was later called, bore the family crest of the Order of the Dragon, called *dracul* in Romanian. This is likely where Stoker takes the name for his vampiric villain, if not much of his iconography. *Dracul* can mean either "dragon" or "devil": the association between the two most likely coming from the biblical Revelations of John where the devil is referred to as the "ancient serpent" or the "great dragon" (Beal 2002). It is important to note, though, that the actual specifics of Stoker's story appear to be based far more on Irish and Icelandic folklore than on the actual life of Vlad Tepes.

Stoker also used early vampire "case studies" written by clergymen of the Medieval period to set the Catholic associations with the vampire into the minds of his audience. Dracula was afraid of Christian crosses, holy water, and sacred ground and held sway with unholy animals and vermin. To what degree Bram Stoker researched Vlad Tepes himself or was aware of the history of the Wallachian Prince is highly debated (McNally and Florescu 1989 and 1994; Stoicescu 1978; Miller 1997 and 1999) but for my purposes here, it is important to understand that within a few years, the vampire villain of Stoker's novel came to represent all vampires as a whole. Therefore, the name and essence of Stoker's frightening creature identifies him not only with the legendary ruler and his reign but also with a long line of literary and religious symbols popular at the time. As *Dracula* became ever more popular, it then laid the foundation for all of the vampires that would follow as the epitome of collective modern fears.

VAMPIRES TODAY

The character of the modern vampire is easily observed eliciting an annoyed groan from one only to induce swooning in another. The plastic fangs, black cape, and cartoonish accent, once donned, are enough to spark the recognition of even the youngest Westerner. As a matter of fact, the vampire concept is so commonplace in modern American and European culture that vampires have done everything from advertising cereal to performing on children's television. The modern vampire is a conglomeration and continuation of virtually all the vampire myths and metaphors that have come before it and yet lacks the respect once due to a devilish and fearsome night-dweller. Today, the vampire is a fictional character straight from the literary traditions of the earlier eighteenth and nineteenth centuries with little of its former historic past in tow (Carter 1989). It is as popular as space aliens and angels and no more real in the minds of the populace than fairies and ghosts. The modern vampire is also, of course, the child of Bram Stoker's *Dracula*; the supernatural free from the bonds of religion and science, and an icon of dark sexuality for the young and rebellious. This contemporary vampire has undergone a variety of transformations in response to ongoing shifts in popular culture and the political mise-en-scene but the encapsulation of the moral panic remains. Increasingly, the vampire's religious associations, while not absent, are weakened and replaced primarily by sexual associations, just as Western culture has also become secularized and sexualized. The fear here then is one of disobedient youth, unsanctioned and freely available sex, the impenetrable rise of technology, and the fragility of the dominant Euro-American social order.

The fascination with the vampire is evident in the popularity of vampire films and books, such as Anne Rice's *Vampire Chronicles*, TV's *True Blood, Buffy the Vampire Slayer*, and *Supernatural,* and the oft-maligned *Twilight* series. The mid-1990s and 2000s also saw a great upswing in the popularity of vampire role-playing games such as *Vampire: The Masquerade* by Mark Rein-Hagen and White Wolf publishing, where, for a moment in time, the mantle of the vampire is assumed and played out. Furthermore, the vampire remains popular in Goth and Punk subcultures and in music, like *Concrete Blonde, Siouxsie and the Banshees*, and *Vampire Weekend*, where it parades its mysterious and elegant self and winds its way through society on wings made of the proliferation of fantasy and horror. The vampire has, however, become an ambiguous figure as of late. While tales of the dark side and the cautionary stories about sexuality remain, the vampire has become a story about human nature in a time when people are no longer sure what the nature of humanity is (Day 2002; Carter 1989). Better yet, the modern vampire has become a template by which our own humanity can be defined. Even the most sinful or subversive vampire is a statement on the humanity within which it lives and from which it came. The vampire was, after all, once human. What has given the vampire particular force now are the questions that it faces people with. Where does our humanity lie? Is it in our ability to control our needs and desires, our ethical and logical nature, or in our liberation from our baser natures? Is the vampire human or something wholly different (Day 2002; Holte 2002); a return to a state of nature, as it were, or deviance from it? For these reasons, the vampire metaphor not only remains strong within modern contexts but is still performing much the same role as it did in earlier times. The vampire remains the embodiment of the collective fears that society holds onto regarding itself, only gaining a new form of expression and a much larger audience. It has gone from the country dweller of folktales and superstitions to the stalker of the urban masses (Day 2002; Holte 2002; Gordon and Hollinger 1997). Today, the vampire is everywhere.

With the coming of film, the vampire concept gained mass exposure in the medium of the moving picture. For the first time in history, the vampire was actually seen and experienced; his presence on the screen so profound that he remains there today. Entire genres of movies have been made with the vampire as everything from hero to anti-hero to villain. The vampire is also no longer the feral monster of old religions; instead he is exotic and powerful, extravagant and alluring, gentlemanly, deferential, and wholly malignant. A monster still, but one with a rather pleasant veneer. But contrary to the vampire of nineteenth-century literature, he has gained a human soul. He now has motivations and emotions that could be identified with and has emerged with a personality all his own that is likeable, if not desirable. The first vampire movies; such as *Dracula* (1931), *Nosferatu* (1922), *Vampyre* (1932), and the "B-movies" of the infamous Hammer Studios, were not yet completely a change from the famous literary vampire. They were a chance to indulge in the perversions of the night and imaginatively experiment with the dangerous and forbidden. These films sensationalized the primal and the frightening with terrifying and lurid images of stakes, blood, fangs, and violence. They terrified and excited by conjuring up the sexual taboos of the times and moral panics regarding promiscuous women, Satanic ritual abuse, and psychedelic drug-taking; the violent imagery once contained only in books; and invoking the powerful physiological "fight or flight" response that makes horror popular (Day 2002; Toufic 1993). It was the movies that first brought this kind of imagination to sense experience and for this reason the vampire became more tangible. And with it, so did the fear.

The case of the vampire in the late twentieth century followed suit. The vampire became an escape into the realms of disenchantment with reality, realms of magic and supernaturalism, and is filled with romanticism and the promise of freedom and desire. He invites his audience to reject society and community and be, once again, redeemed. But this escape does also have a negative side. Demystification can lead to disillusionment as value and meaning are traded for fact, and magic is dismissed as childish musing (Day 2002; Gordon and Hollinger 1997). Lately, however, the stories of the vampire are much more about sensationalistic sexuality. The bite has become a kiss, what was painful is now pleasurable, and death is now the ultimate, if fatalistic, expression of love. The vampire as moral panic thus culminates in later representations in a somewhat more straightforward sense. He partakes of the forbidden, is damned for it, and now spends his days luring in the ignorant, the innocent, and the hapless who stand to be rescued only by the intervention of the morally upright and socially empowered.

In the 1980s and into the early 1990s the vampire concept took on yet another brief but poignant trait reminiscent of the Plague vampire of the late 1300s. In vampire movies such as *Pale Blood* (1992), the *Subspecies* trilogy (1991–1993), and *The Lost Boys* (1987), the vampire is a thinly disguised warning against sexual promiscuity and disease. For this particular period of time, one might assume that the disease in question is almost certainly AIDS. The vampire imposed his undead state on another through the bite, which took on a virulent, contagion-like, quality and he had no compunction about inflicting his "kiss" on a member of the same sex. Since the vampire portrayed was almost always male in these cases, and the bite was likened to a forbidden sexual act, the association becomes easy (Gordon and Hollinger 1997). This vampire was the vampire of the homophobic "gay panic."[5] For these purposes the vampire's sexuality was best when it was portrayed as an ambiguous suggestion of what otherwise could not be acted out, even if the suggestion was less than ambiguous. The concept of the "queer goth" and the vampire as an outlet for homosexual tensions has long been gaining popularity in contemporary times. In fact, a wide collection of literature devoted to this topic has been slowly accumulating as the vampire comes to stand in as an icon of forbidden sexuality (often coded as queer). Most of this literature can be found in fan fiction, in short-story compilations, and in anthologies of various subjects but films and television shows in particular have grown increasingly more comfortable with the theme especially within the last ten years. The sexuality then became explicit (in a society which now embraces expressions of sex to a certain degree) and the charisma of the vampire figure erotically disarming. In other words, this part of the modern vampire concept is no longer the "great secret" of the literary nineteenth century but merely another fact about it (Day 2002; Toufic 1993; Silver and Ursini 1993), though the moral panic remains safely embodied in a monstrous state.[6]

The modern vampire is also a creature born of violence on both a social and an individual level. The vampire is at war with himself, his anachronistic nature, and with those around him. Numerous modern vampire movies (see for example *Vampire Hunter D* (1985 and 2000), *Blade* (1998), *Blood: The Last Vampire* (2000), and *To Die For* (1989)) focus on the violent aspects of the vampire. In the television series *Forever Knight* (Cohen and Parriott 1992–1996), the enigmatic vampire LaCroix exhorts his companion Nicholas, a vampire attempting to regain his human state, to "feel the animal inside of you." More especially he goes on to encourage raw pleasure without the burden of ethics and killing without conscience. Here, the central theme of the new vampire mythos is the transformation from sex to violence (Day 2002; Rickels 1999). More specifically, the focus shifts from the controlling of sexual instincts to controlling the predatory ones, which arguably remains one of the defining problems of Western civilization in to the twenty-first century.

The vampire today is not only the metaphor for uninhibited sexuality, but it is also the warning of what happens when those urges are not kept in check or expressed in a suitable social manner. Ironically, in an age where the status of women is generally more equalized than it has ever been, the vampire is still usually male and his victims typically female. This vampire represents pervasive male social domination over women and, in many cases, the act of "feeding" takes on an equally sexual meaning. The vampire is a sexual predator and often his target is a woman who has no chance of defending herself and who ends up in a situation that takes another male, usually another lover of hers, to rescue her from. This is a large part of the character and story that is Stoker's *Dracula* and what is accepted as the quintessential vampire concept dating back to the gendered moral panics of Medieval times. The woman is portrayed as in the vampire's thrall and spiritually unable to resist. Very similar in many aspects to the older folk tales of vampires regarding women's spiritual weakness toward anything unwholesome, the vampire demonstrated here only adds the characteristic of being overtly sexual. The human man in the situation is therefore called upon to be the hero and save the women in distress (or be consumed by them if he can't). The vampire is rape or the theft of virginity, the vampire is violence and murder, the vampire is power over another, and most especially the vampire, although a monster in the dark, is us. As the writer Nina Auerbach says, regarding malleability: "Every age embraces the vampire it needs" (1997, 145).

In exploring the modern vampire concept, Dracula remains a central figure. Whether it is a retelling or a complete reinvention of Stoker's character, movies like *Bram Stoker's Dracula* (1992), *Dracula* (1931), *Dracula 2000* (2000), *Dracula Untold* (2014), and his appearance in a recent BBC drama and Netflix series, let us know that he is still the quintessential vampire concept. In contemporary media, interpretations of Dracula change in relation to the mythos within which he resides. In Dracula's first transformation, about 60 years after the publication of Bram Stoker's novel, he becomes the protagonist ready to be freed from the constraints of an outmoded, repressive, Christian-imaged past (Day 2002; Toufic 1993); taking on a collective fear about the abandonment of faith and tradition. He is still anachronistic, but the lure of modern city life is enough to break the cycle in which he often finds himself. In a second transformation he becomes the romantic gentleman vampire, first made popular in the 1930s and then resurrected in the 1970s where he takes on the moral panics of rebellious sexuality, women's liberation, drugs, and civil unrest. In this incarnation Dracula is also a creature of need and desire where the more animalistic and bestial natures of the vampire are drawn out. In the third and most recent transformation, Dracula has joined a growing rank and file of vampire characters and has become integrated into the greater scheme of the modern vampire mythos at large that still speaks to widespread fears of sexual deviance (and the societal breakdown such terms imply), gendered sexual agency, violence against marginal communities, and queer visibility.

At last, the postmodern vampire arrives. No longer a kind of escapism as much as a form of expression, the vampire is once again changing to fit the moral panics of the current times. In truth, postmodern is a difficult label with which to bind the vampire mythos, since postmodern is still a term which is being used to identify literature and art as it is becoming, and not as it is. This shift in the popular thinking and style of modern America has led and currently is leading to the vampire concept as it will be. The vampire of today, like many monsters in modern fiction, is no longer the outsider but begins his narrative from the inside. His is a collective fear that starts within ourselves rather than derived from an external evil. The traditional perspectives of the fantasy/horror genre in which the vampire currently resides are also changing. Many recent works involving the vampire mythos are breaking down the traditional binary thinking of vampire and human (Day 2002) and moving further and further into contemporary fears regarding humanity itself as a scourge to the planet, as unsustainable consumers, and as the cause of our own societal downfall. In short, that we are the ones sucking our world dry in a desperate bid to attain immortality and always were.

The vampire concept is also beginning to lose its clear-cut distinctions between good and evil. In its former role as the "other," it guaranteed the presence of good, but this is no longer necessarily the case. Evil is not simple and neither, now, is the vampire and since it is no longer clearly demarcated as evil, it is not so easy to simply destroy it (Holte 2002). In fact, in anthologies like McNally's *A Clutch of Vampires* (1974), Anne Rice's *Vampire Chronicles* (1975–1995) series, and Christopher Frayling's *Vampyres* (1991), the very existence of Evil itself is questioned. The vampire is still in between something however (almost liminal in a sense), but the audience is no longer certain exactly what the vampire is in between. In this way, the concept retains the aspects of false rebirth and renewal into a different existence even if the aspect of being "damned" is much less emphasized. Here, the vampire steps out into the future, still the reflection of our times and the representation of our fears and repressed urges. But as our fears and compunctions change the vampire will remain as our collective metaphor for them and will be, as always, whatever scares us all the most.

NOTES

1. I am using the term "moral panic" in the sociological sense. As in, fear spread among a large number of people that some evil threatens the well-being of society as a whole or as "the process of arousing social concern over an issue—usually the work of moral entrepreneurs and the mass media." See Scott, John, ed., 2014. "M: Moral panic." A Dictionary of Sociology. Oxford New York: Oxford University Press, p. 492 and Cohen, Stanley. 1972 [2011]. Folk Devils and Moral Panics: The Creation of Mods and Rockers. Routledge.

2. Though, not "demon" yet in the Christian sense. Rather, "demons" (daemon) in the Ancient Greek and Roman sense meant lesser deities, spirits, or other quasi-divine beings who occasionally caused problems for living mortals.

3. For example, Roman gossip claiming that Christians were actually cannibals (for partaking in the "body and blood of Christ"), accusations of Jewish blood libel and human sacrifice, fears of underground demonic orgies and debauchery involving young women or children, various theological schisms and fears about both pagan and Christian heretics, and, of course, witch hunts.See also: Cohn, Norman. 2001. *Europe's Inner Demons: The Demonization of Christians in Medieval Christendom*. University of Chicago Press.

4. See also: Tucker, Abagail. 2012. "The Great New England Vampire Panic." *Smithsonian Magazine*. (https://www.smithsonianmag.com/history/the-great-new-england-vampire-panic-36482 878/)

5. Chuang, H. T. and Addington, D. 1988. "Homosexual Panic: A Review of Its Concept." *The Canadian Journal of Psychiatry*. 33(7): 613–17; and Worthen M. 2020. *Queers, Bis, and Straight Lies: An Intersectional Examination of LGBTQ Stigma*. New York: Routledge.

6. See, for example, "queer baiting" and the queer-coding of villains in animated film.

BIBLIOGRAPHY

Ashida, Toyoo, dir. 1985. *Vampire Hunter D*. Ashi Productions Company, Japan.

Auerbach, Nina. 1997. *Our Vampires, Ourselves*. Chicago: University of Chicago Press.

Beal, Timothy K. *Religion and its Monsters*. New York: Routledge, 2002.

Browning, Tod, and Karl Freund, dirs. 1931. *Dracula*. Universal Studios Backlots, Universal City, CA.

Carter, Margaret L. ed. 1989. *The Vampire in Literature: A Critical Bibliography*. Ann Arbor: UMI Research Press.

Cohen, Barney and James D. Parriott, writers. 1992–1996. *Forever Knight*. Toronto, Ontario, CA.

Cohen, Daniel. 1971. *A Natural History of Unnatural Things*. New York: The McCall Publishing Co.

Cohen, Stanley. 1972/2011. *Folk Devils and Moral Panics: The Creation of Mods and Rockers*. New York: Routledge.

Coppola, Francis Ford, dir. 1992. *Bram Stoker's Dracula*. American Zoetrope, Los Angeles, CA.

Day, Patrick Willian. 2002. *Vampire Legends in Contemporary American Culture*. Lexington: The University of Kentucky Press.

Dreyer, Carl Theodor, dir. 1932. *Vampyr*. Tobis Filmkunst, Germany.

Dundes, Alan. 1998. *The Vampire: A Casebook*. Madison: The University of Wisconsin Press.

Florescu, Radu and Raymond T. McNally. 1994. *In Search of Dracula: The History of Dracula and Vampires*. New York: Houghton Mifflin Company.

Florescu, Radu and Raymond T. McNally. 1989. *Dracula: Prince of Many Faces*. Boston: Little Brown and Co.

Frayling, Christopher. 1978. *Vampyres: Lord Byron to Count Dracula*. London: Faber and Faber.

Frost, Brian J. 1989. *The Monster with a Thousand Faces: Guises of the Vampire in Myth and Literature*. Bowling Green: Bowling Green State University Popular Press.

Gordon, Joan and Veronica Hollinger, eds. 1997. *Blood Read: The Vampire as Metaphor in Contemporary Culture*. Philadelphia: University of Pennsylvania Press.

Heldreth, Leonard G. and Mary Pharr, eds. 1999. *The Blood Is The Life: Vampires in Literature*. Bowling Green: Bowling Green State University Popular Press.

Holte, James Craig. Ed. 2002. *The Fantastic Vampire: Studies in the Children of the Night*. Westport: Greenwood Press.

Hsu, V.V. Dachin, and Michael W. Leighton, dirs. 1990. *Pale Blood*. Noble Entertainment Group, Los Angeles, CA.

Johansson, Thomas. 2000. "Moral Panics Revisited." *Young* 8(1): 22–35.

Johnson, Robert L. 1992. *Vampire, The Archetype*. Lecture to the Jungian Society of Jacksonville, Florida.

Kawajiri, Yoshiaki, dir. 2000. *Vampire Hunter D: Bloodlust*. BMG Funhouse, Japan.

Kitakubo, Hiroyuki, dir. 2000. *Blood: The Last Vampire*. Aniplex, Japan/USA.

Lussier, Patrick, dir. 2000. *Dracula 2000*. Dimension Films, Showline Studios, Toronto, Ontario, CA.

McNally, Raymond T. 1974. *A Clutch of Vampires*. Greenwich (CT): New York Graphic Society.

Meyer, Stephanie. 2006. *Twilight* (The Twilight Saga). Boston: Little Brown Books for Young Readers.

Miller, Elizabeth. 1999. "Back to the Basics: Re-Examining Stoker's Sources for Dracula." *Journal of the Fantastic in the Arts* 10(2): 187–96.

———. 1997. "Dracula: The History of Myth and the Myth of History." *Journal of the Dark* No. 9 (Spring 1997).

Murnau, Friedrich Wilhelm, dir. 1922. *Nosferatu.* Jofa-Atelier Berlin-Johannisthal, Orava Castle, Germany.

Newman, Kim. 1992. *Anno Dracula.* New York: Simon and Schuster.

Nicolaou, Ted, dir. 1991. *Subspecies.* Castel Film Studio, Romania.

Norrington, Stephen, dir. 1998. *Blade.* Amen Ra Films, Long Beach, CA.

Radford, Benjamin. 2020. "The 'Momo Challenge' and the 'Blue Whale Game': Online Suicide Game Conspiracies." *Skeptical Inquirer.* February 28, 2019. Retrieved June 1, 2020.

Rice, Anne. 1976. *Interview with the Vampire.* New York: Ballantine Books.

Rice, Anne. 1985. *The Vampire Lestat.* New York: Ballantine Books.

Rice, Anne. 1988. *The Queen of the Damned.* New York: Ballantine Books.

Rice, Anne. 1992. *The Tale of the Body Thief.* New York: Ballantine Books.

Rice, Anne. 1995. *Memnoch the Devil.* New York: Ballantine Books.

Rice, Anne. 1998. *Pandora.* New York: Ballantine Books.

Rice, Anne. 1998. *The Vampire Armand.* New York: Alfred A. Knopf.

Rice, Anne. 1999. *Vittorio the Vampire.* New York: Alfred A. Knopf.

Rickels, Laurence A. 1999. *The Vampire Lectures.* Minneapolis: University of Minnesota Press.

Sarafian, Deran, dir. 1988. *To Die For.* Arrowhead Productions, CA.

Schumacher, Joel, dir. 1987. *The Lost Boys.* Warner Bros., Palos Verdes, CA.

Senf, Carol. 1988. *The Vampire in Nineteenth-Century English Literature.* Popular Press 1.

Shephard, Leslie. ed. 1977. *Dracula Book of Classic Vampire Stories.* New York: The Citadel Press.

Sherman, Aubrey. 2014. *Vampires: The Myths, Legends, and Lore.* Holbrook: Adams Media.

Shore, Gary, dir. 2014. *Dracula Untold.* Universal Pictures, Northern Ireland, UK.

Silver, Alain and James Ursini. 1993. *The Vampire Film.* New York: Limelight Editions.

Sommers, Montague. 1929. *The Vampire in Europe.* London: Kegan Paul, Trench, Trubner & Co.

Stoicescu, Nicholae. 1978. *Vlad Tepes: Prince of Wallachia.* Editura Academiei Republicii Socialiste Romania.

Stoker, Bram. 1897/1981. *Dracula.* New York: Reprinted by Bantam Books.

Toufic, Jalal. 1993. *Vampires: An Uneasy Essay on the Undead in Film.* Barrytown: Station Hill.

Twitchell, James B. 1981. The *Living Dead: A Study of the Vampire in Romantic Literature.* Durham: Duke University Press.

Wilson, Colin. 1971. *The Occult.* New York: Random House.

Chapter Seven

Gay Bloodsucker or Post-Soviet Buzzkill?

Vampiric Possibilities in Sektor Gaza

Lev Nikulin

Vampires are a global phenomenon, as is gay attraction, and blood is sexy in any vampiric context. But to what extent does cultural specificity alter the possibilities that vampires carve out for queerness in their particular settings? In this chapter, I interrogate the extent to which there is such an entity as a "Slavic vampire" or *upyr'* in Russian popular culture, using as a case study the work of scandalous post-Soviet punk/metal band Sektor Gaza. Are the *upyri* that plague Russia different from the vampires of Western Europe and the United States—the regions whose traditions of vampirism have closely co-evolved with those of Russophone cultural production? If so, what queer encounters can they facilitate or inhibit?

UPYRI, VAMPIRY, AND OTHER CRITTERS

In modern Russian, vampires are commonly referred to as *vampiry* (vahm-PEER-y, singular *vampir*). However, several alternate terms exist, most prominently *upyr'* (oo-PYR,' plural *upyri*). These words are often used interchangeably but differ in connotation: the *vampir* refers to vampires generally, but also specifically to the alluring vampire found in the Western European Gothic tradition. The stylish vamp in the 1997 Russian song "The Tender Vampire (Nezhnyi vampir)"[1] by Nautilius Pompilius and Boris Grebenshchikov exemplifies this type:

I am a mysterious guest in a silvery cape

And you know why I have come to you
To give you strength, to give you power,
To kiss your neck, to kiss you to my heart's content [Nautilus Pompilius 1997].

Meanwhile, the *upyr'* and the *vurdalak* are associated with Slavic traditions of the undead and are often portrayed as ugly and disgusting, more zombie-like than fashionably vampiric (*upyr'* is sometimes translated as "ghoul").[2] Alexander Pushkin features a famous *upyr'* in a poem of his folkloric cycle *Songs of the Western Slavs*, in which a frightened man mistakes a dog for a vampire: "Someone is gnawing a bone, grumbling [. . .]. Oh God!—thinks the poor man / It must surely be a red-lipped *vurdalak* / gnawing on bones" (Pushkin 1959, 410). The term *vurdalak* (voor-dah-LAHK, plural *vurdalaki*) was introduced by Pushkin and is, along with *upyr,'* associated with Slavic vampires (Ivanov 1987, 31).

The *upyr'*/*vampir* distinction is not, however, reflective of any stark cultural division between discrete vampire types; in folklore as in literature, the overall picture is rather one of complex cultural interactions and borrowings. Russian literature took up Gothic production soon after Western European writers began writing about castles, ghosts, and secrets in the late eighteenth century.[3] In turn, Western European writers drew on both Eastern European myths and mythologized ideas of Eastern Europe to write their own stories.[4] In Russian popular culture, the image of the vampire is more immediately indebted to Gothic and Romantic retellings of vampire myths than to folklore. Even supposedly "authentic" instances should be treated with caution; Pushkin's "Western Slavic" cycle referenced above was based on a source later revealed to be a mystification concocted by French writer Prosper Mérimée (Wachtel 2012, 279–80).

In short, no "authentic," pre-Western Slavic vampire may be reliably located in Russian cultural production in the wake of Gothic literature and of Romanticism. However, the *idea* of such a distinction exists palpably for Russian creators. Sometimes it is addressed explicitly; in the 1841 novella *Upyr'* by Aleksei Tolstoy, a character alerting the protagonist to the presence of vampires immediately switches topic to expound on the superiority of the term *upyr'* over *vampir*. The character claims that *upyr'* is the vampires' "real Russian name" and that the word *vampir* is a result of a linguistic mangling by "Hungarian monks": "'*Vampir, vampir!*'—he repeated with disdain,—just imagine if we, Russians, were to say 'phantom' or 'revenant' instead of ghost [prividenie]" (Tolstoy 2019)! This aside points to an anxiety over excessive borrowing (linguistic, literary, and cultural) from Western Europe and is reminiscent of the objections of some of Tolstoy's contemporaries who feared that Russian culture would be forever in Europe's shadow; in this light, Tolstoy's fear about the disappearance of authentically Russian monsters points to a larger fear about the influence of Western Europe over Russia in the broader context of European nationalism.[5] When it came to the vampire, the concern was not unfounded: over the course of the nineteenth century, the *upyr'* began to change, dropping its penchant for consuming corpses whole and taking on the title *vampir*.

PERESTROIKA GHOULS

Artificial as the *upyr'/vampir* divide is, it is highly relevant when it comes to questions of gender and aesthetics, because the two categories have almost opposing relationships to gender. Where *vampiry* are gendered (even hyper-gendered) creatures, feminized/effeminate and alluring, *upyri* are genderless (but also masculine) and repulsive. Substantial scholarship exists on vampires and sexuality, and much of it is applicable to *vampiry*. As for *upyri*, we also do not have to start from scratch: the similarity between *upyri* and zombies (corpse-eating, repulsiveness, reanimation) is readily apparent, and many insights into zombies apply to *upyri* as well. Whereas vampires are highly gendered and often linked with effeminacy and camp (Gelder 1994; Mennel 2012), zombies lack gender: "given the lack of social construction which makes gender and constructs gendered difference, the zombie remains merely Other" (Lanzendörfer 2018, 129). This opposition between gendered *vampiry* and genderless *upyri* would come into play in the chaotic decade of the 1990s, during which aesthetic as well as gender norms experienced significant upheaval in the wake of the Soviet collapse.

Horror was severely constrained in the USSR; perhaps the most obvious evidence of this is the dearth of Soviet horror films, a condition that persisted until the 1980s, when aesthetic possibilities became more malleable.[6] The vampire in particular staged a comeback, and preference was given to highly aestheticized *vampiry* in films such as *The Wild Hunt of King Stach* (1979), *Master Designer* (1987), and *Drinkers of Blood* (1991) (based on Tolstoy's novella *Upyr',* referenced above). The 1990s witnessed the importation of alternative styles of all kinds, fueling the popularity of vampires in the mainstream; the normally exuberant pop singer Filip Kirkorov impersonated a morose Goth in the music video for the song "Bat" (1999), and rock auteurs Vyacheslav Butusov and Boris Grebenshchikov posed with ornamental canes, cravats, and eyeliner in the video for "Tender Vampire" (referenced above). The experiments in gender and sexuality made possible by the *vampir* fit well with the no-holds-barred atmosphere of the 1990s, when limits on post-Soviet queerness had not yet been established. Among the feast of alluring *vampiry*, a significant outlier stands out: the hypermasculine, filthy, vulgar vampires featured in the music of punk/metal band Sektor Gaza.

FLESH AND BLOOD OF THE PEOPLE

Sektor Gaza attained scandalous popularity in the 1990s with their some-times humorously vulgar, sometimes performatively naïve music. "Sektor Gaza" (which bears no relation to the Gaza strip) means "gas sector" and is the nickname of a factory district in Voronezh home to Iurii "Khoi" Klins-kikh (Klinskikh 2000), the unique and charismatic frontman and songwriter. Sektor Gaza (hereafter SG) started playing in Voronezh punk clubs in the late 1980s and achieved enormous success in the early 1990s with their use of profanity (a still-novel phenomenon in music at the time), their hard-hitting and raw sound ranging from punk to rap metal, Klinskikh's distinctive piercing, nasal voice, and the humorous and grotesque depictions of then-shocking subject matter (Tikhomirov 2001).

Klinskikh sang about sex and sex work, drinking, drug use, violence, police corruption, poverty, and the ugly prejudices of post-Soviet Russian society, as well as witches, devils, and supernatural horror of all kinds. His songs evoked a gritty, unglamorous rural identity far removed from the nor-mative optimism of official Soviet depictions of rural life; he coined the phrase "Kolkhoz punk" in a song of the same name and drew on rural as well as broadly working-class markers, tapping into the confusion swirling around class demarcations in the 1990s. This direction is present in the music of other punk groups of the time, who saw their music—correctly or not—as an expression of something more homegrown, authentic, and raw than what could be found in other genres: "Punk [in Russia] came from drunk guys [muzhiks] who wanted to play the guitar and yell about the pain in their soul" (Interview with Svetlana Elchaninova, Aksiutina 1999).

SG were highly successful but consistently critically panned—hardly sur-prising, considering their intentional stance as provocateurs. They fit as poor-ly with the glitzy Russian pop superstars of the 1990s as they did with the "intellectual" tradition of Russian underground music exemplified by musi-cians such as Boris Grebenshchikov, who emphasized complex texts dense with literary and cultural references sung in an often contemplative, bookish style (see Steinholt 2003). SG were closest in style to the abrasive punk tradition, which included such groups as Avtomaticheskie udovletvoriteli ("Automatic Satisfiers"), Distemper, and Kretinicheskie Dni, all of whom used profanity; with rare exceptions, however, none of these groups attained anything like the success of SG.[7] The exclusion of SG from consideration in the phenomenon of punk is evident from existing volumes on the subject (see, for example, Herbert 2019; Aksiutina 1999).

Negative reviews tended to treat SG as a mystifying and singular phe-nomenon of post-Soviet music, attributing their success to their edgy "bad boy" appeal and also, significantly, to the poor taste of the masses:

Television channels don't like to show them, respectable publications turn their noses in distaste, but [. . .] despite everything, their fame continues to build. Here we see the effect of the "bad boys" who attract well-behaved girls [. . .]. Sektor Gaza is the true flesh and blood of the people [istinnaia plot' ot ploti naroda] [Kruglov 1997].

The term used for "people," *narod*, carries connotations of a monolithic mass of humanity which decides its desires and tastes on the basis of a naturalized ethnic character. *Narod* is not composed of individuals but is an undifferentiated mass which cannot critically consider its musical tastes or consumption patterns. Thus, the phenomenon of SG's popularity is explained away through an appeal to class stereotypes by critics who rhetorically distance themselves from the phenomenon they describe. Undoubtedly, the truth is more complex, even if SG's contrarian self-fashioning invites this sort of response.

SG has left behind a cult following, but vanishingly little scholarship; this is a gap worth addressing, not least because Klinskikh's use of anti-aesthetic, anti-intellectual, ugly vampires creates unique possibilities and unique dangers for queer vampirism.

"DUMBASS OF THE NIGHT": THE *UPYR'* AS CONDUIT FOR UGLINESS

Horror themes are prominent in Klinskikh's songwriting. Sektor Gaza recorded eleven albums (excluding rereleases, remixes, and the like) between 1989 and 2000, when Klinskikh died. All but one album (*Gazovaia ataka* (*Gas Attack*) (1996)) featured supernatural horror songs. In total, SG recorded between twenty-three and twenty-nine horror songs and two horror-themed albums: *Zloveshchie mertvetsy* (*Ominous Corpses*) (1990) and *Voss-tavshyi iz ada* (*Hellraiser*) (2000), which was released after Klinskikh's death.[8] The twenty-three indisputable horror songs feature supernatural creatures such as zombies ("Love Beyond the Grave"), witches ("Walpurgis Night"), and the undead broadly speaking ("The Night Before Christmas"); vampires are especially common, appearing in many songs—for example, "The Crazy Corpse" and "Vampire Destroyers."

As is characteristic for Klinskikh's work more broadly, serious, sometimes plaintive, emotion is combined in these songs with grotesque humor. A meditatively morbid song from *The Ominous Dead* fuses these elements seamlessly:

Who came up to me so suddenly and imperceptibly?
It's my death
Who's lying on top of me and pressing on my chest?

It's my death
Who wears a black tie and black gloves?
It's my death [. . .]
Who let them practice on my corpse?
It's my death [. . .]
You can't run away from her, you can't breathe
I'll start up my moped and head off for the afterlife
Well, I'm off [SG, "Moia smert' (My Death)," *Zloveshchie mertvetsy*].

A somber meditation and simultaneously a joke, this song finds the protagonist contemplating the unsparing realities of death while switching between pathos and humor. He describes the terror and loss of bodily autonomy which accompanies the process of dying; however, he is conducted to the afterlife not through lofty means, but via that least sublime of vehicles, the moped. Death, referred to as "she" (the Russian *smert'* is feminine in grammatical gender) at first appears properly mysterious, wearing classic black and acting as the answer and refrain, as though reluctant, to the repeated question "Who . . . ?" but is also personified and participates in the details of dying. The casual "Well, I'm off"—a phrase one would expect of someone going out for an errand rather than confronting death—punctuates the song, cementing the relationship between death and humor.

The dimensions of ugliness and gruesomeness—even disgust—are key to Klinskikh's engagement with horror motifs. His songs feature no glamorous vamps; instead, he sings about ugly, bestial corpse-eaters, well-suited to SG's harsh, distorted sound as well as the harsh post-Soviet realities reflected in the texts. Simultaneously masculine and genderless/sexless, the *upyr'* is shut off from the glamour and sex appeal of the *vampir* and instead speaks to the poverty and hardship of post-Soviet life as reflected in SG's music.

Perhaps the strongest expression of gruesome vampirism in SG is the song "Chernyi vurdalak (The Black Vurdalak)" (SG, *Vosstavshyi iz ada*), the lyrics of which appear to have been partially plagiarized from *Reek of Putrefaction*, the 1988 debut album of the British goregrind band Carcass.[9] An example of SG's later rap-metal style, the song provides an equally gruesome and comically absurd portrait of a vampire and self-described "dumbass of the night (nochnoi mudak)," born from the union of a "she-*upyr'* [upyrikha]" and a "necrophile," happily consuming dead bodies. Its upbeat, driving sound complete with characteristically simplistic riffs belies the gruesome anatomical details of the necro-cannibalism being performed, as Klinskikh cheerfully raps: "Chyme, bile, pus, and blood bubble in the grave [. . .]. I hawk up a mixture of phlegm, slime, and bile/And deliciously gnaw sweet human bones." In song after song, Klinskikh cements the connection between vampires and disgust, often in conjunction with an unexpectedly playful approach.

WHAT ARE OUR BOYS MADE OF?

SG's song "What [Are They Made Of] [Iz chego zhe]?" (1994) darkly reimagines a Soviet-era song of the same name.[10] The Soviet version combines utopian optimism with gender stereotyping, asking, "what are our girls/boys made of?," and answering that "our" (that is, Soviet) boys are made of "freckles," "rulers" and "batteries," while Soviet girls are made of "little flowers," "glances," and "secrets" (Chichkov 1988). This anthem of banal sexism was popular as a children's song in Soviet times and even attained some notoriety recently when it was reworked for a pop-feminist ad by Nike Russia (2017).[11]

SG's version borrows the formula of the previous song but shifts its meaning away from a sanitized grade-school version of gender essentialism to a decidedly adult one. It begins with a piano playing the familiar Soviet melody; this is then replaced by a harsh punk sound with intentionally simplistic, hard-driving percussion over a distorted guitar line. Klinskikh sings, with characteristic abrasiveness:

> What, what, what
> Are our boys made out of?
> Out of knives and brass knuckles
> Out of sawn-offs and guns
> Are our boys made [SG, "Iz chego zhe," *Tantsy posle poreva* (*Dances After Sex*)].

The simplicity of the call-and-response format throws this expression of gender pessimism into sharp relief, additionally opening the door to irony. The same is true of the crass misogyny invoked in the second verse concerning "our girls," who are defined through "the clap and bras, [. . .] coke and blowjobs."

The intentional and overt simplicity of the song belies its interpretive challenge: what collective group is being referred to as "us"—Russians, post-Soviet people, punks? Implicitly, this nebulous collective is at least in part defined through class markers, which were prominent if chaotically understood in the mid-1990s. The references to drugs, alcohol, addiction, sex, and STIs—realities which had been unacknowledged in Soviet times and became ever more tangible and talked-about in the perestroika period and the 1990s—establish a link between gender and poverty. *Other* girls/boys might be defined through other (perhaps loftier) attributes, but not *ours*. The invocation of the Soviet song additionally makes "What [Are They Made Of]?" into an anthem of the disappointed and disoriented post-Soviet subject witnessing the failure of the Soviet state along with its promises. Listeners may be tempted to distance themselves from the doctrine of gender described in the song, but in doing so are put into a position where this distancing also becomes a rejection of class markers and potentially a claim to class super-iority. At any rate, the pronoun "we" encompasses SG themselves—this is evident from the final verse, which asks, with an air of inevitability, what Sektor Gaza themselves are made of and answering, "needles, dope [*khanka*, specifically raw opium], and weed,/Bottles and glasses." The band positions itself not as above or apart from the "us" under scrutiny, but as part of that imagined collective.

Men as a group, according to this song, are defined through violence and substance use—they are, in fact, very much like *upyri*, who substitute claws and fangs for weapons and blood for liquor and drugs. This association between *upyri* and the working class recalls another insight made by scholars of the zombie—that zombies are "peculiarly egalitarian" (Lanzendörfer 2018, 130) in comparison to aristocratic vampires. This is true of *upyri*, the supernatural creature of choice in SG's world of class disenfranchisement. They are ugly and violent monsters, Klinskikh challenges, but they are *our* monsters.

VAMP4VAMP? HOMOPHOBIA VS. THE EROTIC POSSIBILITIES OF THE *UPYR'*

Nothing in Sektor Gaza's anthem of gender essentialism leaves any space for queer encounters to take place, and all could remain solidly heterosexual in the dealings of their violent *upyri*. However, vampiric categories are rarely so stark, and Klinskikh's ghouls, cadaverous though they may be, cannot be exclusively understood through the category of the *upyr.'* Their desire for blood in particular is keenly relevant to the possibilities of queerness which may or may not exist in Klinskikh's music. This is due in part to the wide range of cultural references used in his work, including both Soviet and U.S. influences: Klinskikh reported drawing inspiration both from Hollywood horror and from *Vyi* (1967), one of very few significant Soviet horror films (Tikhomirov 2001). It is unsurprising that the theme of sexuality bleeds over into SG's lyrics—and since the hypermasculine world of his *upyri* contains almost no women, men become its outlet. [12]

The collision of *upyr,' vampir*, sexuality, and death is palpably present in "Dirty Blood (Griaznaia krov')," a darkly comic horror song from *Hellraiser*, SG's last album. The narrator of "Dirty Blood" is attacked by a bestial "bloody old vampire" while drunkenly walking home through a graveyard; however, his blood has been tainted by a lifetime of alcohol consumption, rendering it "dirty," and the vampire becomes poisoned and dies. He even suffers the extremely human symptom of prolonged vomiting—the narrator wryly remarks that, "medically speaking, it was pretty bad."

The motif of "dirty blood" would seem to set class and sexuality in opposition to each other: a potentially erotic encounter—a vampire's bite—is transformed into a grotesque scene due to the protagonist's toxic blood, made impure by a lifetime of implicit class disenfranchisement (he reports drinking cough syrup and moonshine as a child), rendering him an unpalatable victim. Klinskikh raps the verses but sings the refrain mournfully over a distorted wall of sound:

> Blood, blood, my dirty blood
> If a mosquito drinks it, it dies
> Dirty blood—and how could it be clean?
> I've been wasted every night for forty years [SG, "Griaznaia krov," *Vosstav-shyii iz ada*].

The blood that marks him as an alcoholic is the focus of the deeply tragic refrain, but the scenario of the song is engineered to render that quality useful to him. The "dirty" nature of the protagonist's blood allows him to traverse the cemetery without fear ("If I'd been sober, I would have lost my shit (ohuel)") and to emerge as the triumphant plucky hero for whom this incident is not even particularly notable: the song ends with him drinking a toast to the dead *upyr'* ("one vampire less / I drank a toast to him") and running off to bed. He even expresses slight remorse: "If I'd known, I wouldn't have given him a drop."

Even in this quotidian, anti-aesthetic treatment, however, the eroticism of blood cannot be ignored, and Klinskikh's blatant, direct approach strengthens the erotic implication rather than downplaying it. The vampire's attack is rendered as a joke about oral sex:

> That vampire thirsted for my warm blood
> He even let out his fangs in anticipation
> But as soon as he'd sucked me off a little—
> Sucked my blood, that is—
> He fell right into the grave [lit. "cunt into the grave [v mogilu pizdyk]"]

The first three lines are overtly sexual and represent bloodlust as lust, as is classic for aestheticized *vampiry*—however, this is severely undercut by the comic last line. One way to parse this is that the vampire is suffering from a confusion of genre categories; he behaves as a *vampir*, attempting a genre-appropriate sexualized bite, but because he is in fact in the hyper-masculine world of "our boys," he is instead poisoned and dies. However, the possibility itself of a gay interaction between men in Klinskikh's universe is startling.

It is worth noting that Klinskikh wrote a handful of songs which explicitly courted homophobia by drawing on overt stereotypes; while doing so, he placed himself into the "gay" role in the song, even in those containing the most overtly homophobic lyrics. For example, in "Evil Night," three closeted characters are outed through fortune-telling during an "evil night": a woman outed as lesbian, a man outed as gay (referred to as *pidoras,* a slur used against gay men), and the narrator himself, who is "outed" as a "dumbass [mudak]"—although it is implied in his rebuttal ("But I'm normal!") that that, too, stands for queerness. After this twist, the narrator opportunistically rejects the results of the fortune-telling: "Evil night, none of us believe in you!" Here as in "What [Are They Made Of]?" Klinskikh places himself into the implicated, reviled category, with odd results.

Blood, of course, is erotic, all the more so due to the connotation of risk it brings. Blood signifies interpenetration on a deeper level than (vanilla) sex, magnified under the fear of contamination and death. Writing about blood, fluids, desire, and alterity, Elliot Evans describes "the desire, the need, for an 'experience of unfettered intimacy' [. . .] erotic encounters with alterity are often bruising and bloody, tearing apart the subject while leaving otherness intact" (2019, 109–11). This logic of interpenetration, desire, and danger is palpable here. Klinskikh was aware of HIV and AIDS and referenced them in other songs (SG, "Ia mraz' [I'm scum])," and that specter cannot be ignored; on a simpler level, a sexual encounter with a man is liable to "contaminate" the protagonist of "Dirty Blood" with gayness. He might become Other— vampiric, queer, disgusting. But the risk is also bidirectional: in the end, the vampire, the stand-in for gay men, is killed by the "poison" of the narrator, who hangs on to his straightness and his (literally) toxic masculinity. He returns to the life of drinking described in the refrain, seemingly unaffected by the encounter.

This is not a narrative of explosive queer possibility in the ruins of the Soviet empire—there is nothing so optimistic to be gleaned from Klinskikh's discography, where brutal, violent masculinity reasserts itself time and again. However, I argue that dismissing the queer possibilities of the *upyr'* outright in favor of those of the *vampir* is a mistake. Rather, both models have something to offer, and both are frustratingly limited. The limits of the *upyr'* are obvious, those of the *vampir* often euphemistically veiled. It is thrilling to see men in eyeliner in Russian music videos in the 1990s, although the bar cleared in such an instance is low—but phenomena like these are easily negated once the political climate shifts. This is one of the benefits of euphemism, in fact—it offers protection for queer subjects through plausible deniability. Cruising is relevant in this context as well, relying as it does on coded subtlety born of necessity. But euphemism may also be used as an excuse for leaving queer possibilities unexplored, especially by those with the power to tell queer stories—and all too often, implication is all we are left with once the specters dissipate. Armand and Louis are beautiful in *Interview with the*

Vampire (1994), but their lips never touch; consumption of "queer-coded" media is riddled with such disappointments.

Klinskikh, meanwhile, is seemingly allergic to euphemism: everything he raises is placed squarely on the table. The possibility of oral sex between a vampire and his victim in "Dirty Blood" may be joked away, and queerness punished (as it so often is even in the most euphemistic of narratives), but the subtle vampire, rarely allowed to broach explicitly the possibility of gay sex or acknowledge that blood-sucking is a sex act, might stand to learn something about honesty from the unsubtle vulgarity of the *upyr.'*

NOTES

1. Unless otherwise noted, all translations are the author's.

2. The Russian *vampir* is a recent borrowing from French (*vampire*) or German (*Vampir*); *upyr'* is related to *vampir*, perhaps through common Slavic origin (Wilson 1985).

3. The first known Russian Gothic work, Nikolai Karamzin's "The Island of Bornholm," dates to 1793. The early decades of the nineteenth century saw a boom of Gothic readership, then Gothic authorship, in Russia. For histories of this phenomenon, see Vatsuro 2002 and Cornwell 1999.

4. See, for example, Gelder 1994, 1–23.

5. The antagonists in this debate within Russian nineteenth-century literary and critical circles would become known as the Slavophiles and the Westernizers; the former sought to forge a Russian culture distinct from that of Europe, while the latter saw themselves as champions of progressive European ideas. See, for example, Edling 2006.

6. Horror film production is almost nonexistent in the USSR, with *Viy*—sanctioned through its connection to Nikolai Gogol, the author of the 1835 novella of the same name—as the only exception prior to the late 1970s.

7. One partial exception is Egor Letov and his punk group Grazhdanskaia Oborona ("Civil Defense"), whose music can be imagined to be a bridge between the abrasive punk tradition and that of "intellectual" rock. Letov often employed a simplistic, low-tech sound as well as profanity, but relied equally on complex lyrics and philosophical concept albums.

8. Klinskikh's horror songs are on the whole sharply distinct from his other themes and are thus easy to classify; they contain explicit supernatural monsters and threats in conflict with humans and rely on familiar horror figures such as vampires and witches. The six "borderline" songs deviate from this in one way or another: for example, "Good night, little ones" is a meditation on fear based on a sinister children's lullaby but contains no explicit supernatural elements.

9. The borrowing or plagiarism from Carcass has been proposed on SG fan forums (besedka.sektorgaza.ru 2014) and is fairly unmistakable with a side-by-side comparison with the Carcass songs "Fermenting Innards" and "Feast on Dismembered Carnage" (Carcass 1988).

10. "Iz chego zhe" was popular in the 1970s.

11. "Iz chego zhe sdelany nashi devchonki," Nike Russia, 2017.

12. All of Klinskikh's vampires are men but one: the vampire in "Vurdalak" who is, however, as disgusting as the male *upyri*.

BIBLIOGRAPHY

Aksiutina, Olga. 1999. *Pank-virus v Rossii*. Moscow: LEAN.

besedka.sektorgaza.ru. 2014. "Rassuzhdenie ob albome "Vosstavshyi is ada." Accessed July 10, 2020.

Carcass. 1988. *Reek of Putrefaction*. Birmingham: Rich Bitch Studios.

Chichkov, Iu. 1988. *Izbrannye pesni dlia detei.* Moskva: Sovetskii kompozitor.

Cornwell, Neil, ed. *The Gothic-Fantastic in Nineteenth-Century Russian Literature.* Amsterdam: Rodopi, 1999.

Edling, Susanna Rabow. 2006. *Slavophile Thought and the Politics of Cultural Nationalism,* Albany: SUNY Press.

Evans, Elliot. 2019. "'Your Blood Dazzles m/e': Reading Blood, Sex, and Intimacy in Monique Wittig and Patrick Califia." In *Raw: PrEP, Pedagogy, and the Politics of Barebacking,* edited by Ricky Varghese. Regina: University of Regina Press.

Gelder, Ken. 1994. *Reading the Vampire.* London and New York: Routledge.

Herbert, Alexander. 2019. *What About Tomorrow? An Oral History of Russian Punk From the Soviet Era to Pussy Riot.* Portland, OR: Microcosm Publishing.

Ivanov, Viach. Vs. 1997. "Ob izomorfizme dvukh stikhotvorenii Pushkina." *Lotmanovskii sbornik 2.* Moscow: OGI.

Klinskikh, Yurii. 2000. Introductory note included with *Hellraiser.* Moscow: Gala Records.

Kruglov, Semyon. 1997. "Khoi—eksperimentator." *Gazeta Ekstra-M.* No. 24. p. 261.

Lanzendörfer, Tim. 2018. *Books of the Dead: Reading the Zombie in Contemporary Literature.* Jackson: University Press of Mississippi.

Mennel, Barbara. 2012. *Queer Cinema: Schoolgirls, Vampires, and Gay Cowboys.* New York: Columbia University Press.

Nautilus Pompilius. 1997. "Nezhnyi vampir." *Iablokitai.* Moscow: DANA Music.

Pushkin, A. S. 1959–1962. *Polnoe sobranie sochinenii v desiati tomakh Vol. 2.* Moscow: GIKhL.

Sektor Gaza. 1994. *Zloveshchie mertvetsy.* Moscow: S.B.A./Gala Records.

———. 1994. *Tantsy posle poreva.* Moscow: Gala Records.

———. 2000. *Vosstavshyi iz ada.* Moscow: Gala Records.

Steinholt, Yngvar B. 2003. "You Can't Rid a Song of Its Words: Notes on the Hegemony of Lyrics in Russian Rock Songs." *Popular Music* 22(1): 89–108.

Tikhomirov, Vladimir. 2001. *Khoi! Epitafia rok-razdolbaiu.* Moscow: Antao.

Tolstoy, Alexei. 2019. *Upyr.'* St. Petersburg: Arkadia.

Wachtel, Michael. 2012. *A Commentary to Pushkin's Lyric Poetry, 1826–1836.* Madison: University of Wisconsin Press.

Wilson, Katharina M. 1985. "The History of the Word Vampire." *Journal of the History of Ideas* 46(4): 577–83.

Vatsuro, Vadim. 2002. *Goticheskii roman v Rossii.* Moscow: NLO.

Chapter Eight

From Femme Fatale to Fatal Female

Vampiric Power as Coded Female in A Girl Walks Home Alone at Night *and* Only Lovers Left Alive

Rebecca Gibson

The first cinematic vampire was not female—Nosferatu (Murnau 1922), drawing heavy inspiration from Bram Stoker's novel *Dracula* (1897), gave an androgynous look to the vampiric presence, but that androgyny leaned more heavily toward male appearance than female. In the century since the lurking, swooping, creepy presence first dominated the silent screen, we have seen most vampire movies trend male as well, from multiple interpretations and reinterpretations of Dracula, to the adaptations of Anne Rice's Vampire Chronicles. Due to the pressures of Hollywood and the overt misogyny of the film industry, among other reasons, even films where the lead role is ostensibly female (and the movie is not a spoof or a comedy) often end up focusing on the male characters (Łuksza 2015; Mukheria 2011). This can be seen in *Queen of the Damned* (Rymer 2002), the second and final Vampire Chronicles film, where Akasha—the aforementioned Queen, is a parody of her book representation, and the movie focused on Stuart Townsend's interpretation of Lestat. That particular movie did not do very well at the box office, and plans for continuation of the series were scrapped (in part due to the death of the singer Aaliyah, who played Akasha). It can also be seen in the Underworld movie franchise, where the main character, Selene, is female, but displays all the stereotypical male vampire traits.

However, two recent films are heavily female focused, with vampiric power, emotional and physical strength, and rationality all seated in the main female characters. Directed by Ana Lily Amirpour, an Iranian-American, British born writer/director, and starring Sheila Vand (an Iranian-American

113

of Persian descent), the movie *A Girl Walks Home Alone at Night* (2014) held the tagline "The first Iranian Vampire Western." Though it was shot in California—echoing the long history of "Westerns" being shot on California backlots—the setting is a fictive Iranian ghost-town called "Bad City," and this city is ruled by vice. Enter, The Girl. Over the course of the movie, she cleans up the city, terrorizing and eventually eating a junkie and a pimp, and using her strength and her fangs to pressure those she designates as redeemable into doing the right thing. The Girl does fall in love, and she has a distinct personality, but she's no femme fatale; she is, instead, the personification of a fatal female.

Contrast the titular character, The Girl, with the gentle care expressed by the female vampire, from the 2013 joint Germany/United Kingdom film *Only Lovers Left Alive* (Jarmusch). While The Girl is dark bloody vengeance, Eve is motherly, fun-loving, and happy. This film has Tilda Swinton's Eve in the main role, played against her lover Adam (Tom Hiddleston) and while Adam is morose, broody, suicidal, and short-tempered, Eve demonstrates foresight, an even temper, planning skills, and optimism in the face of multiple crises. Many of these crises are tipped off by the movie's emotional foil—Eve's annoying brat of a younger sister, Ava (Mia Wasikowska). The lovers do depend on each other for emotional support, but it is Adam who is the weakest link, and who ends up being taken care of by the strong, caring, dependable Eve. Eve's love is very nurturing, as befits the woman wearing the name of the originator of human life, and she is in this vampiric life for the long haul, as both mother-figure and fatal female.

In this chapter I will use these two examples to interrogate changing ideas about the representation of vampires as female, and death as female, in a gender-theory based structure, contrasting them against other cinematic vampires. While strong, rational, and deadly, both characters are undeniably feminine in their own ways, and occupy the liminal space between day and night, light and darkness, and life and death, epitomizing vampiric power as coded female.

PERCEPTIONS OF GENDER: VAMPIRES ON THE SILVER SCREEN

There is something about a cinematic vampire that mingles sexiness with blood and death (Łuksza 2015; Mukheria 2011; Franuik and Scherr 2013). We are not meant to be purely scared of the death that comes in the night, wanting to drink our blood—we are also meant to be entranced, enthralled, desirous of them, desperate for them to take our essence into theirs, to use us, to turn us into one of them. This "turn" comes by way of penetration; their fangs penetrate the victims' bodies, a small violation with a large consequence. Here we can already see how vampires are coded male. In sex, it is traditionally, though thankfully not exclusively anymore, the male body that is seen as doing the penetrating. Also, in conceiving a child, it was long believed that the sperm, likewise, did the penetrating—chemically tunneling its way through a resisting egg. This, it turns out, is a scientific fallacy, which has since been debunked (Martin 1991), yet it can still be seen in textbooks and illustrations of the process of conception. It is "common knowledge," which casts the male in the active role, and the female in the passive, whether receiving penetration from a penis, or from a sperm, or from a pair of fangs. In order to get to the point where we can begin to discuss non-passive, but also non-masculine female vampires, we need to look at the stereotype first.

When we see many cinematic vampires, what we are seeing is the penetrative, aggressive, sexual behavior, coded male/masculine, regardless of which sex is wearing the fangs. Two examples of this are Akasha from *Queen of the Damned* (Aaliyah), and Selene from the 2003 *Underworld* franchise (Kate Beckinsale). While both are hyper-feminine in appearance, with curvy bodies, soft-featured faces, female-coded hair styles, and skin-baring or skin-tight clothing, they remain stereotypically masculine in behavior (for discussions of gender-coded clothing/artifactual representation, see: Barthes, 1967; Berg and Lie 1995; Conkey 2007; Entwistle 2000; and Gero and Conkey 1997). Waking from hundreds of years of slumber, Akasha seeks to take over the world with her immense vampiric power, enslaving both humans and vampires alike. While she and Lestat (played by Stuart Townsend in this version, rather than Tom Cruise who originally brought the character to film) mutually feed on each other, she is the power and physical strength in the relationship, burning, destroying, and penetrating. Her power comes from her immense age and is enough to sweep over the whole world, laying waste to it. It is harsh and violent and cares not for puny mortal lives.

Selene's power is more human-scaled—she is a relatively high-ranking vampire in service to a progenitor of the vampire race, who one day stumbles on a nice guy who just happens to become a vampire/werewolf hybrid, and saves him from being hunted by the two factions, during which she falls in love with him. Here we might have the makings for an atypically feminine vampire, but no—Selene's role is to be the violent, penetrative protector, a hyper-masculine role.

While we see her lover, Michael (played by Scott Speedman), using his fangs on her on occasion, Selene's penetration is more direct, and of the kind often seen in action/adventure movies: she shoots, slices, and stabs her way to dominance over her enemies, once using a sword so quickly that her opponent has a chance to give her a shocked look before one part of his head separates from the other. She has nurturing aspects (they eventually have a daughter together), but at least in the first two films (Wiseman 2003; 2006), those aspects are aimed at ensuring that Michael does not do something fatally stupid before he fully settles into his developing powers. He, unfortunately for all involved, attempts many things that would be fatally stupid, such as fighting full-power ancient werewolves and vampires with only his fists, or eating human food.

Here I must pause for a moment to distinguish sex and gender and gender expression—note, I am not saying that Akasha and Selene are male vampires, merely that they are female vampires onto whom masculine or stereotypically male traits, attitudes, and behaviors have been mapped, due to the nature of the cinematic vampire. We can address this by understanding more about the concepts of sex, gender, and gender expression, and by examining the cinematic vampire more closely.

Sex refers to the physical configuration of biological features with which one is born, or which one acquires by surgery, and (in most Western cultures) is divided into male, female, and intersex, which becomes a catch-all category to encompass the many and varied people who do not strictly adhere to the main binary. Most people are assigned male or female at birth, based on an examination of and determination from their external genitalia—if the doctor sees a penis and scrotum, the child is declared a boy, and if they see a vulva and clitoris, the child is declared a girl. If the external genitalia is ambiguous in any way, then they are declared intersex, and often the parents will elect for surgery to alter the existing structures into a recognizable penis or clitoris—this surgery is now beginning to be seen as harmful to children, and is thankfully on the decline, as more parents opt to allow the child to decide on surgery or not as they get older. These determinations are not always accurate or absolute, but are often treated as though they determine gender, which they do not.

Gender refers to internalized feelings in regard to behaviors, attitudes, and choices which various cultures have determined should be held and performed by males, females, or intersex people. Gender and sex do not necessarily match up, but the cultural expectations placed upon people often proscribe them from deviating from their sex's expected gender. Thus, having assigned a female body to Selene, the screenwriters assigned male gender behaviors to her, even though her gender is almost undoubtedly female. She is not identifying with a male gender, per se, but merely behaving counter to the way that society thinks women should behave.

Gender expression, on the other hand, is the outward expression of the internal gender state. Gender expression is the way we move through society, conforming or nonconforming to the expected norms of our gender. Gender can be expressed through clothing, hair styles, the use or lack of use of makeup, shaving/not shaving, the pitch and pattern of our speech, and many other visible and "readable" traits (for gender-expression theory, see Geller 2009; Ortner 1974; and Perry, Turner, and Sterk 1992). In this way, we control (or attempt to control) people's perceptions of our gender. To return to Selene, although her actions are coded masculine (counter-gender), her dress, hair, mannerisms, makeup, and overall presentation is uber-feminine. She reads as both female and as the feminine gender expression, despite her masculine behavior.

That masculine behavior traces back to the shared history of cinematic vampires, beginning with Nosferatu, moving to most of the screen adaptations of Dracula, and continuing with non-Dracula vampires, whose power is violent and penetrative (Douglas 1966/2001; Fairclough 2003; and Freud 1893/1952). Tropes, once established, seem to be difficult to put aside, despite myriad real-life examples of different types of power, love, sexual activity, and gender expression. To see the epitome of the masculine vampire trope in action, one need look no further than the 1992 film *Bram Stoker's Dracula* (Coppola).

The Internet Movie Database (IMDB) lists two-hundred visual works (feature length movies, shorts, and TV episodes) with the word "Dracula" or a derivation thereof in the title, and an additional two-hundred with "vampire" (and these may be truncated lists), demonstrating how completely the idea has gripped visual media.[1] *Bram Stoker's Dracula*, starring Gary Oldman as the titular vampire, Winona Ryder as his thrall Mina Harker (née Murray), and Sadie Frost as the wanton Lucy Westenra, is a remarkable visual journey from the Westenra mansion in the countryside, to the streets of London, to the wilds of Transylvania. It is worth a watch for the costuming alone, which is overtly beautiful, and packed with subtle nods toward the personalities expressed by the characters (Riberio 1986/2003; Coppola and Ishioka 1992).

With performances ranging from haunting (Oldman, chameleonic as ever, and Ryder, despite her failed attempt at a British accent) to hilarious (Anthony Hopkins chews the scenery and hams it up as Dr. Van Helsing) to regrettable (Keanu Reeves' wooden take on Jonathan Harker is really quite bad, and having Monica Bellucci as one of the Brides is an epically tragic misuse of Monica Bellucci and her immense talents), this movie gives us everything we expect to see in a vampire movie, and sticks remarkably close to the epistolary style and frantic tone of the book.

Three of the characters (as they originated in the novel but expressed in this movie) give us our male/female vampire tropes, into which almost all cinematic representations, both prior to 1992 and afterward, fall—Oldman's Dracula, Ryder's Mina, and Frost's Lucy. Oldman's Dracula is exquisite. He is fang-tastic, erudite, charming before his violent nature is exposed, but then very, very violent, sending wolves, rats, snakes, winds, and the threat of his own penetrating fangs after our heroes. While he first bites Lucy, wishing to turn her into another Bride, he soon fixates on Mina as a replacement for his dead wife, Elisabeta. As in the novel, Dracula is based on an historic person—Vlad III Dracula, the Voivode of Wallachia, also known as Vlad Țepeș, also known as Vlad the Impaler. The moniker of "the Impaler" was earned by his vicious and violent treatment of the Ottoman Turks against which he fought many times during his life, and also against anyone who crossed him or who displeased him in any way (Florescu and McNally 1994). He was said to have his enemies impaled on stakes, and left to die, or to have banquets amidst his impaled victims (ibid). As rumors are wont to do, his cruelty grew into legend, leading to his actions inspiring Stoker's vampire—it is not a far leap from impaling someone to drinking their blood.

We must also note here that impaling is a penetrative act, by its nature. When we are looking at Vlad the Impaler, in this case in the form of Old-man's Dracula, we are seeing fangs and stakes as phallic representations. No more so than in his treatment of Lucy and Mina. Lucy begins the movie by trying to choose between three suitors—Dr. Jack Seward (Richard E. Grant), Quincy P. Morris (Billy Campbell), and Lord Arthur Holmwood (Cary Elwes). While she wants to be married, and is waiting for a proposal, she flirts with and kisses all of them. Her flirtation is highly sexualized, filled with innuendo and insinuation and lewdness.

After accepting Lord Holmwood's proposal, Lucy is first bitten by Dracula, though he visits her more than once. Her transformation begins, and her lustful nature and sexualized portrayal intensify, with her writhing in various places (her bed, the gardens) and slinking sinuously in other places (the gardens, and eventually, her tomb). As a newly made vampire Bride (not a full vampire, because Dracula never gave her his blood), she displays only residual intellect. She recognizes Holmwood when the men come to her tomb to dispatch her from her undeath, but she barely clocks any of the others present until they attack her. She feeds on children, because she's not a female/feminine vampire, nor is she a fully masculine vampire, she's an unwomanly, unmotherly, wanton thrall of Dracula—practically a vampiric non-entity, like the other Brides seen in the film who also feed on babies.

In contrast, the character of Mina loses her womanliness during her transformation, becoming more masculine, more violent, more aggressive, and more penetrative as she grows closer to changing. While Mina's character pre-transformation is kind and gentle, even to the revolting, fly eating, mad character Renfield, and she redirects the aggressively masculine young version of Dracula with charm and wit before succumbing to his glamour, her liminal state during which she transforms renders her angry and aggressive, verbally striking out at those she loves, and attacking Van Helsing when he comes too close, before eventually impaling Dracula with an enormous knife and chopping his head off. It is in this liminality where we find our answers about what cinematic vampirism does to female characters—it is the transformation that drains them of their feminine gender aspects, and they reawaken with masculine behaviors in female bodies (for the theory of embodied gender, see: Geller 2009; and Haraway 1991). And, in fact, only the masculine can beat the masculine in many of these movies—vampires of any gender are only killable by two methods (though they can often die by others, such as the sun): cut off their head, and stake or remove their hearts. Violent penetration is the answer to the vampiric condition, whether in the form of blood drinking, the transformative penetrating bite, or the eventual final death of the vampire. Now that we understand the cinematic vampire, we can look at examples that confound the trope and restore the feminine aspect to the transformed vampire—Eve from *Only Lovers Left Alive,* and The Girl, from *A Girl Walks Home Alone at Night.*

While the focus of most vampire movies is the vampires being vampires, the focus of the two which the rest of this chapter will discuss is very different: it is on the vampires' humanity. Through *Dracula,* through *Queen of the Damned,* and through the Underworld movies, we see vampires that have lost the ability to exist as though they were mortal. We see vampires so wrapped up in their own (masculine, violent, penetrative) power that they almost aggressively fail to blend in. The only appreciations of beauty come from soliloquies about blood or the desirability of their next meal/conquest/ partner. The only long-term planning has to do with inter-vampire strife or besting the humans upon which they feed. They are out of touch, and often do not have personalities beyond that of their vampiric natures. Not so for The Girl and Eve, whom I will address in sequential sections below.

THE GIRL: BAD CITY'S CONSCIENCE

In most vampire movies, the viewer understands that there are other vampires, even if they are not shown or mentioned. Lestat has Akasha. Selene has the rest of her clan. Dracula has the Brides. Eve has Adam, Marlowe, and her sister. But The Girl in *A Girl Walks Home Alone at Night* is singular. The inhabitants of Bad City are also singular—one pimp, one junkie, one prostitute, one boy, one love interest. There is a party (thrown by the one princess) with more people, but it mostly serves to move the love interest into view of The Girl. The rest of the movie is very focused on one-on-one interactions. In addition to the fact that the movie is shot in black and white, this singularity creates a feeling of unreality, of simulacrum where the world is represented in microcosm. If part of a watching a movie is suspending disbelief, then this, conversely to how it might seem, helps the viewer do that, as we are free to concentrate on the personalities involved.

And that is one of the first things we notice about The Girl; she has a personality. Living alone in a small apartment, she covers her walls with posters of bands. She dances to American rock music, her bobbed hair waving across her face. She wears a striped shirt beneath her black chador, the body length robe and veil worn by some Iranian women. She often wears the chador open, showing the striped shirt underneath. Despite this nod to tradition and modesty (Rajasakran, et al. 2015; and Ribeiro 1986/2003), The Girl wears what she wears for two reasons: because she wants to, and to lure her prey closer so that they may experience her judgement.

While that judgement often ends at the points of her fangs, and she does have the vampiric traits of speed, strength, stamina, and bloodlust, she moves more toward the feminine side of the spectrum not because she fails to bite (violently, penetratingly) but because she tries to reform her victims before eating them. Almost every person she encounters is given the chance to do the right thing, to live a moral life, before falling to her thirst. If she finds them redeemable, they live. If not, then she is on a mission to clean up Bad City, and nothing gets in her way.

Her first victim is Saeed "The Pimp" (Dominic Rains). A hilariously exaggerated caricature, The Pimp picks her up on the street as she is walking home and invites her back to his place. He seems to enjoy the challenge of seducing her, or possibly he wants to line her up to be his next prostitute, but regardless of his motivations, she goes with him. At his crib, his first action is to snort a line of coke and turn on music with a heavy tuneless beat. Her subsequent eye roll tells us all we need to know about his eventual fate: this man is unredeemable. However, she lets him continue—sometimes she likes to play with her food.

In rapid succession, The Pimp: counts money; snorts more coke; turns the music up; lifts weights while staring at her; dances at her and opens his shirt; offers her coke; and snorts even more coke. The Pimp is hyper-masculine, from his music and weightlifting to his aggressive dancing, and would never let himself be seen to be intimidated, particularly not by a little girl, even once she shows her true nature.

He strokes her hijab, and then the side of her face and her lips. She opens her lips, and he seems pleased . . . until her fangs descend with a "schnick" sound. He steps back in surprise, but quickly regains his bearing as she reaches for his hand and brings it to her face. In a deliberately and aggressively sexual gesture, she sucks his finger into her mouth. Therefore, the first physical action we see The Girl take toward another character is receptive, not penetrative. And The Pimp momentarily believes that he once again has the upper hand—his hyper-masculinity allows him to disregard the warning of the fangs, and selectively accept the sexual action as what he deserves. His belief is unfounded. She bites off the penetrating finger and spits it out at him, chases him across the room, uses the bloodied dismembered finger to caress his mouth, and then eats him to death and steals his music and jewelry (for theory on male dismemberment, see: Rajasakran, et al. 2015).

Although this may seem counter to my argument of her femininity, the use of her fangs to penetrate and drain him were her last resort, used only when the person is unrepentantly bad and will not work to redeem them-selves—we see as the movie continues that everyone gets a chance to demonstrate their true nature before she decides to remove them entirely. Had The Pimp invited her up to his crib to have tea and discuss music, we feel, perhaps he might have been spared. In her next encounter, she does spare the mortal, but she scares him thoroughly first.

Walking alone, she comes across The Street Urchin (Milad Eghbali). A small child who begs from the love interest, and whose character may be leaning toward the bad side of things, The Street Urchin carries a skateboard and acts tough, emulating certain attitudes of The Pimp, but stops short when The Girl stands in front of him, not allowing him to pass. She asks:

> G: Are you a good boy? Answer me. Are you a good boy or not?
> U: Yes. **he is clearly terrified, and lying**
> G. Don't lie. Are you a good boy?
> U: Yes.
> G: I'll ask you one more time. Tell the truth. Are you a good boy? **hisses at him and bares her fangs, and her voice drops a full register** I can take your eyes out of your skull and give them to dogs to eat. Till the end of your life, I'll be watching you. Understand?
> U: Yes.
> G: Be a good boy [Amirpour 2014].

He runs away, leaving the skateboard behind. She skates off down the middle of the road, her chador flowing out behind her like a cape, giving a visual throwback to traditional vampire movies.

Here we see her motherly side. Not a kind mother, nor a gentle caring person, like Eve, but a great and terrible mother who enforces good behavior with the fear she instills in her children. The Street Urchin is redeemable—not yet too bad, not yet devoted to the life of Bad City, he lives and will be a good boy. She recognizes potential, a theme which shall be returned to when we discuss the love interest. However, first, her final two encounters—The Prostitute and The Junkie.

Atti "The Prostitute" (Mozhan Marnò) is older and rough around the edges; she occasionally does drugs, and in general is sad and desperate. As the movie is set in Iran, we might read the implication that sex itself is taboo or wrong, but Amirpour is not showing us the stereotypical viewpoint of a preconceived Western notion of a religious country, she's showing us that exploitation and greed are wrong, and that in cleaning up Bad City, The Girl is also attempting to stamp out the exploitation and self-exploitation of its inhabitants.

As she meets The Prostitute and follows her, we begin to see her evaluation of her victims as a pattern, rather than singular incidents. She waits to see how they will react, what they will do, before she either lets them live, or takes their lives. The Prostitute asks:

P: Why are you following me around? What do you want?

G: **holds out her hands full of the jewelry stolen from The Pimp**

P: **puts her arm around The Girl and hurries her back to The Prostitute's rooms**

P: Where did you get this? Girl, where did you get this? **offers The Girl a dish of plums** Have one. They're sweet.

G: **takes a plum**

P: What are you following me around for? Are you religious or something?

G: No.

P: Look who found her tongue. You want to do what I do? It's not easy. If that's why you're following me around, I'm not a teacher.

G: You don't like what you do.

P: You're watching me?

G: At night.

P: So . . . what did you see all this time watching me?

G: You're sad. You don't remember what you want. You don't remember wanting. It passed long ago. And nothing ever changes.

P: Idiots and rich people are the only ones who think things can change.

G: You're saving your money. For what?

P: Are you a thief?

G: No.

P: So what are you? [Amirpour 2014]

The Girl never answers that question, nor addresses that we have already seen her steal from people twice in the narrative—once at The Pimp's crib, and the skateboard from The Street Urchin. So, what is she?

She is Bad City's mother, its conscience, its moral center. If we look at her actions, she does not punish bad things done for good reasons. She believes that The Prostitute wants change, and wants to leave, so she lets her live. She believes that The Street Urchin will grow up better now that she has terrified him, so he lives as well. She sees how widely The Pimp's influence has affected Bad City (he not only pimps out The Prostitute, but he steals the love interest's car, supplies drugs to The Junkie, and generally abuses anyone he comes into contact with), so he must die. And what about The Junkie?

She has already encountered him, briefly mirroring his actions as they walk along the same street, terrifying him. However, you cannot terrify someone out of an addiction, and on top of being an addict, Hossein 'The Junkie' is just not a great person. He is the love interest's father, and sometimes client of The Prostitute, and considers his own life to be worthless. While the love interest loves him, The Junkie is indeed pretty worthless, and when The Prostitute fulfills The Girl's expectations of her—tries to change and refuses The Junkie's advances—The Junkie tries to rape The Prostitute. However, The Girl comes to the rescue, dragging him off of The Prostitute and eating him. After this, it is obvious that The Girl must leave Bad City.

The City is too small for her now, and her clean-up work is done. It is here where we must examine her relationship with the love interest.

The love interest, Arash (Arash Marandi), is a young man who knows what he likes and what he wants but who also has trouble getting those things because he lives and works in Bad City. He likes rock music, shy girls, lasting tender relationships, his car, and his cat. He wants stability, freedom from the burdens of his dad, The Junkie, who he must care for, and of The Pimp, who beats him up and steals his car. While he is collateral damage in much of The Girl's clean-up efforts, her actions benefit him in the end—they find love, he is no longer beholden to The Junkie or The Pimp, and when they leave town, they take the cat with them in his car, which he has recovered.

It is in their interactions where we see the sweet, girlish side of The Girl. She first spots him when he is returning from a party thrown by Shaydah "The Princess." He is drunk and dressed as Dracula. Rather than menacing him or eating him, The Girl takes him back to her apartment, and puts on music as he sobers up. She ends up embracing him, and eyes his neck, but instead, puts her head on his chest and listens to his heartbeat. Here she has spotted a pure person—he has done bad things but done them in the service of good. They meet up the next night, near the power plant. He brings her a hamburger, but she doesn't eat it:

> A: You don't like hamburgers? I've never met someone who didn't like hamburgers. I don't even know your name.
> G: You don't know me.
> A: Obviously. We just met. What was the last song you listened to?
> G: "Hello Hello," Lionel Richie.
> A: Sad. Sad songs hit the spot, don't they? **he turns on the stereo** I know something else about you. Your ears aren't pierced. **he gives her diamond flower earrings that he stole from The Princess**
> G: They're pretty.
> A: They're for you. Too bad you can't wear them.
> G: **unhooks a safety pin from her chador and holds it out to him**
> A: Seriously? **he sterilizes the pin with his Zippo** Are you sure?
> G: **nods**
> A: **he pierces the first ear, and she turns away and gasps, baring her fangs briefly** Did it hurt?
> G: **bares the other ear*
> A: You don't have to.
> G: Do the other one.
> A: Forget it.
> G: Do it.
> A: **pierces her other ear** It's done. What lucky earrings. **he leans in to kiss her, she pulls away**
> G: I've done bad things. I'm bad.
> A: Obviously.
> G: You don't know the things I've done.

A: And you don't know the things I've done.
G: **shakes her head and starts to leave**
A: If there was a storm coming right now, a big storm from behind those mountains, would it matter? Would it change anything? [Amirpour 2014].

So, where is her femininity and what signifies it? Her femininity and her humanity go hand in hand—the remorse she feels for having done bad things, the way she wants her ears pierced, the way she wears her chador, and the affection and curiosity she feels about Arash, whom she eventually trusts with her life, as they both flee Bad City. Hers is, as calling her The Girl indicates, a young and promising femininity, but with both motherly and avenging overtones. Contrast this youth with the weight of the ages, shown in Eve, from *Only Lovers Left Alive* (Jarmusch 2013).

EVE: THE WORLDLY CURIOUS NURTURER

Almost the first thing the viewer notices about Eve is her ease and comfort with herself and her surroundings. The movie begins in Tangier, where Eve (blonde, and dressed in white) walks through the dark city to a café. Street toughs try to hassle her, but she calmly continues on, demonstrating the self-possession of centuries of unlife. This is not a vampire that fears the mortals around her, nor one at war with other vampires, this is a calm, collected person, set on her destination. That destination brings her into contact with an old friend, Christopher Marlowe (played by John Hurt), who supplies her with fresh, clean blood. That's right—supplies. Here we spot another difference between *Only Lovers Left Alive* and most vampire films: these vampires prefer to avoid feeding on humans directly.

There are several reasons for this made clear in the movie, from disease and drugs, to the covertness of making deals with doctors rather than indiscriminately feeding on non-consenting people, to their preference for O-, which can more easily be accommodated by donated blood, but what it adds to the lore is extraordinary: the vampires are no longer enacting penetrative violence in order to survive. Penetration occurs, of course—there's no way to extract blood without it—but it is done non-violently, by the clean, safe, and consensual practice of donation via a phlebotomist. The humans are doing the penetrating, while the vampires are doing the drinking. The vampires pay (cash, of course) for their blood, and our first blood drinking scene involves Eve, Marlowe, and Adam, in three separate locations, reverently drinking one aperitif glass full of blood each, and finding bliss from it. They are not gluttonous, nor violent, nor penetrative, nor hateful or harmful to the humans on whom they feed.

To return to Eve, however, we must see all that she does and is in this movie is in relation to Adam. Adam is younger than her by far, and they appear to have lost and found each other over and over again through the centuries. Where Eve is lightness, he is darkness. Where Eve has hope, he has despair. The central emotional quandary of the movie is Adam's suicidal ideation. Blissful on blood, Eve calls Adam and picks up on his mood, asking him to come to her, to shake up his routine a bit. He silently refuses, so she decides to go to him.

Though we have already seen her caring nature in interactions with Marlowe (she kisses his cheek in the café, an action that may garner some consternation in Tangier due to cultural and religious conventions about male/female interactions), we see the nurturing, loving, generous side of her in her relationship with Adam. Their initial greeting, on the path to his house in Detroit after a cab drops her off, is passionate, but not sexual. They embrace tightly, and kiss tenderly. Their intimacy with each other, with the way they feel against one another, the sound of each other's voices, their scent, that familiarity that comes with deep, abiding love, is obvious to the viewer in every second of screen time they share. And, to be clear, this is love and intimacy, not sex or not sex alone, that the actors are portraying, though sex is in there too.

These vampires place a lot of importance on touching hands—when Eve gets out of the taxi, her driver offers to shake hands and she swerves, avoiding his touch even though she has gloves on. When Adam has taken her bags indoors, and invited her in formally, she asks permission to remove her gloves. He does it for her, passionately kissing her palm, in a gesture that reinforces their intimate bond. In the majority of the scenes where they are together, they are touching in some way—draped on each other, hands in each other's hair, leaning on each other, kissing, or holding hands. Their first day of slumber at Adam's house is shown with both vampires nude on a backdrop of black sheets, their hands resting on each other's arms. Their bodies are in proximity to each other, legs touching gently, but there is space between them as well—it is an intimacy that recognizes their individuality.

This contrasts sharply with the nudity we have seen in other vampire movies. Where Lucy Westenra was partially nude during her transformation, as was Mina Harker, those scenes were played as something forbidden and scandalous, and not merely because of the time period in which *Bram Stoker's Dracula* was set. We were not seeing the director's interpretation of Victorian moral standards, but rather the idea that female vampiric sexuality was unnatural—that the femininity of their characters was being stripped away by their transformation, and the (sharp, penetrative, violent) masculine vampire nature was being revealed, just as their skin was being revealed. Akasha from *Queen of the Damned* is most often seen in an ab and leg baring metal bikini, which looks extremely uncomfortable, and not at all in keeping with ancient Egyptian day-ware, so I conclude we are seeing the cinematic "male gaze," more than we are seeing anything about the vampire herself.

And with Selene, we barely see any skin at all, but we do see her body shape, as she is dressed in covering, encompassing, skin-tight leather or a leather substitute. This indicates more "male gaze," but also the functional, practical, masculine need for movement, speed, and protection from penetration.

With Swinton's Eve, what we see is her own vibrant but ethereal femininity, unique, not curvaceous like Selene or Akasha, but earthy and unpolished and real. Both Hiddleston and Swinton are incredibly talented, and objectively also incredibly attractive, yet it is Swinton's casting that brings uniqueness to the vampiric world built in this movie. Tilda Swinton, though female, has embraced her androgynous appearance, and spoken openly about moving androgyny to a more feminine aspect through her choices of dress and hair style. Having vampires marked as visually androgynous is nothing new—recall, Nosferatu was male-androgynous—however, female vampires are often coded hyper-feminine, despite their masculine personality traits. When naked, Swinton's Eve looks female, but a very different female than Lucy, Mina, Selene, or Akasha.

She is incredibly thin, rather than voluptuous or curvaceous, and at the age of fifty-three (in 2013), and after having children, Swinton's body, though exquisite, is not that of a young woman or a hyper-feminine woman. Her breasts are not huge, full, or rounded but pointed, soft, and on the small side. Her ribs can be seen. Her upper abdomen is not smooth. Her hands are weathered and show her age. She is, in short, very human, with the body of an adult human woman, more androgynous than femme, who has experienced fifty-three years of life. A deliberate casting choice was made to create this character, Eve, as a person, rather than as a projection of perceived male fantasy or the masculine vampire traits mapped onto a female body. As such, Swinton's casting is perfect, and her performance, combined with her appearance, delivers on that premise in several ways—her nurturing as discussed above, her curiosity, and her ability to calmly and efficiently deal with problems that come up, from the mundane to the catastrophic.

Her curiosity is limitless, ranging from nature, to outer space, to facts about music (Adam is a musician), to things about Adam himself. When Eve spots various living creatures, she talks to them, calling them by their binomial nomenclature—a skunk is addressed as *Mephitis mephitis*, a grapevine as *Vitis vinifera*, a mushroom as *Amanita muscaria*, and she loves all of these things, for the pure beauty of them. She has cultivated (or developed) the power to identify most things by sight or touch, and when Adam asks her how old one of his guitars is, reaches behind her head to stroke it gently and without looking at it she replies "Oh. She's a pretty one. A Gibson. 1905," (Jarmusch 2013). Surrounding herself with books, Eve uses the centuries of her life to become a walking font of knowledge about her world.

She uses this curiosity to tease Adam out of his mood . . . and to distract him away from the game of chess that they play. She takes his queen, and when he tries to concentrate, she asks:

E: Did you play chess with Lord Byron?
A: . . . Eve, please.
E: No, I want to know. You love telling me these things, and I love to hear them. So what was he like?
A: . . . frankly, he was a pompous ass.
E: Why am I not surprised. What about Mary? What was Mary Wollstonecraft like? [Ed. note: I think she's talking about Mary Wollstonecraft Shelley, based on the context of Lord Byron, who was only associated with the Godwin/ Wollstonecraft/Shelley entourage after Mary Wollstonecraft's death.]
A: **sighs and shrugs**
E: Come on, tell me, what was she like?
A: . . . she was delicious.
E: **laughs** I'll bet she was. **takes his king** Checkmate, my darling.
A: Eve, you're ruthless. You're brutal.
E: I'm a survivor, baby, [ibid].

Eve wants to know everything, but she also wants to get Adam laughing and happy again. She has made him blood popsicles, and helps him fix the electricity, and marvels at the music he creates, and adores him, but you cannot adore someone out of suicidal ideation. His problem is finally revealed in its full intensity when she finds a gun, with a bullet he has specifically commissioned and had made out of hard wood, hard enough to destroy a vampire's heart or head.

He returns from replenishing their blood supply to find her holding the gun. She confronts him:

E: Just tell me that you're having trouble with one of the others. Please tell me that.
A: I don't see any others. Ever.
E: Okay. **lightning quick she chambers the bullet and aims it at her heart; they fight over the gun, with Adam victorious**
A: Don't *ever* fuck around like that.
E: Just playing a part in your story . . . [J]ust tell me what's so not frightened about that? **she gestures to the gun** How can you have lived for so long and still not get it? This self-obsession, it's a waste of living that could be spent on surviving things, appreciating nature, nurturing kindness and friendship. And dancing. . . . you've been pretty lucky in love, though. If I may say so [ibid].

This dialogue speaks not only to her wholeness as a person, but to the femininity denied to other female vampires. Kindness, friendship, love, and a connection to the natural world, are all coded feminine, and are only seen in the other examples when they fulfill a part of the cinematic vampire trope. Dracula (and therefore Lucy and Mina) has an affinity for certain animals, but all those animals are masculine and penetratively violent (wolves, snakes, bats, and rats). Selene does love Michael, but he doesn't actively have that much of a personality either, and their plotline feels like it was there to show that her loyalties are not with her progenitors, but with the future, and to give her someone to protect.

In contrast, Eve does not protect Adam. She instead shows him that he needs to take agency and responsibility for protecting himself, and rather than standing in front of him to shield him from events, she stands beside him, a true partner asking for his cooperation and participation in their part-nership. That they are partners, a true family, can be seen by their collective reaction to Eve's sister.

The tension builds by the occurrence of prophetic dreams. Adam men-tions that he has had a dream about the sister. Somewhat later, Eve says that Marlowe had dreamed of her too. Eve believes that her sister Ava (played by Mia Wasikowska), is looking for them:

> A: Fuck!
> E: Well, I mean, it's been quite some time.
> A: Yeah, not long enough. Shouldn't she be sleeping in a fucking coffin somewhere anyway? Preferably with a wooden stake shoved in?
> E: Adam, she's my sister.
> A: Is she now?
> E: Well, we are related by blood [ibid].

When one first watches this scene, it feels eerie. We have the expectations of dozens of other vampire movies influencing our reactions, and despite how much this one has already stepped out of the various tropes, we cannot put aside those expectations so lightly. The effect is that eerie feel—they must be dreading Ava's arrival and talking about her being staked because she is powerful and fearsome and some sort of vampire queen, like Akasha, right?

Wrong. Although Ava shares several traits with the masculinized versions of female vampires, she inhabits them in a very feminine way: a bratty, spoiled, juvenile feminine way. Considerably younger than Eve or Adam, Ava is full of energy, gorges herself on blood, uses her fangs on one of Adam's mortal contacts, and destroys part of his house. She is a one-woman whirlwind of chaos and destruction, but she also brings life and liveliness into the situation. Yet, as fond of her as Eve is, the last straw is the assault on the mortal within Adam's house. After she drains him, fails to turn him (which would at least make him useful), and behaves completely unrepen-tantly, Eve and Adam are in agreement—Ava must go. They kick her out, throwing her luggage into the street and ensuring that she acknowledges that she is no longer welcome, and then turn to the task of disposing of the body.

In the disposal task, they are finally working as partners. Adam has been shocked into realizing that he actively wants to live, and he finds a "water-way" to dump the body in. You can tell as they prepare to throw the body that they have done this same maneuver, together, probably multiple times before. Overall, their normal blood drinking habits are much more civilized, yet before the advent of modern phlebotomy, they must have killed before, whether accidentally or on purpose. The "water" eats away the flesh in moments, clearing up Ava's indiscretions, but the jig is up—others saw them with the human while out at a bar with Ava the previous night—and they must flee the city. Eve books them tickets to Tangier.

In fleeing, we see Eve's capability, born from her hundreds of years of existence, in matching fake identities, arranging flights that will both take off and land at night, ensuring they can take as much with them as possible (though, not all, of course) and in covering their tracks. She remains unflappable, even though booking problems and a lack of blood make this flight precarious. She also solves the rest of their problems, finding them a new couple of mortals to enthrall or turn, and buying Adam a beautiful musical instrument.

While Eve has the typical vampiric traits of strength, speed, stamina, blood-lust, sun intolerance, and nocturnality, she uses them in feminine ways, and they are not the focus of her characterization. She is a whole, female person, and while we never lose sight of the fact that she is a vampire (how could we, with "O negative. On a stick" [Jarmusch 2013]?) her humanity and femininity shine to the fore much more strongly.

WHAT HAPPENS TO GENDER WHEN
BECOMING A CINEMATIC VAMPIRE?

The traits we attach to masculinity and femininity are not immutable—they change from culture to culture, from time period to time period. In the time period where vampire stories have influenced cinema, and in the Western cultures in which most of those stories are created, masculinity is often portrayed as being violent, penetrative, and full of the power of brutality and weaponry (whether fangs or blades or guns). Male cinematic vampires most often have taken their cues from Dracula, and the Dracula derivatives, which show vampires with these masculine traits (Florescu and McNally 1994; Franiuk and Scherr 2013; Łuksza 2015; and Mukheriea 2011). When female vampires began getting their own movies, whether related or unrelated to the Dracula mythos, they were often spoofs—like *Vamps,* comedies—like the *Lesbian Vampires* movies, or had the traits of male vampires mapped onto female bodies—like we see in *Queen of the Damned* and the *Underworld* movies. Were we to go by these tropes, and the stereotypical examples discussed in this chapter, the answer to the question "what happens to gender when becoming a cinematic vampire?" would be that the entire gender spectrum gets flattened to male/masculine.

There appear to be two main reasons for this, based on the above examples and observations from a lifetime of watching vampire films: the massive influence of Dracula, and the difficulty many screenwriters have dealing with characters, specifically female characters, as whole people. Dracula, and those influenced by him, does not need to be a whole and complex person (though the book does a much better job of his characterization). We are not here for Dracula's motivations; we are here to see the effects of his actions. We are here to watch good banish evil, to watch vampires drink blood and be sexy at each other, and to see that penetrating masculine coded violence. And there's nothing wrong with that. There's nothing wrong with wanting to sit in front of a movie and know the eventual outcome and how it will most likely make you feel. Yet the weight of that influence is so overarching that even when a female protagonist is put forward by the movie, the genre keeps pulling her back to the masculine, like Selene, Akasha, and Mina.

The wrongness comes when the genre becomes proscriptive, when we cannot name more than a handful of vampires, male or female, who break out of that mold. When all that we see is the masculine part of humanity, and the violent masculine at that, represented on the screen. Anne Rice's Vampire Chronicles had a softer male vampire, Louis, and a female child vampire, Claudia, but they were secondary characters in both the books and the movie *Interview with the Vampire* (Jordan 1994), and even though Louis narrated the movie, the focus was on Lestat—angry, vindictive, violent Lestat. Indeed, Claudia was praised by Lestat even after she was responsible for his downfall, because she was also angry, vindictive, violent, and penetrative— slashing his throat with scissors.

What happens to gender in vampiric transformation and undeath has the capacity to change, however, if given room in the genre and quality screenwriting. We see this in *A Girl Walks Home Alone at Night* (Amirpour 2014) and in *Only Lovers Left Alive* (Jarmusch 2013). We see two fully formed women, The Girl—Bad City's conscience, and Eve—the caring nurturing curious world traveler, who are written with personalities, and likes, and the ability to grow and change and form friendships, and dance. We also see a non-Western perspective in both films, represented by the intense male/male bonds of the love interest with his father, The Junkie (Amirpour 2014), and between Marlowe and the café owner (Jarmusch 2013)—the cultures of both Iran and Morocco understand the softer masculinity expressed in same-sex friendship and sociality (Raiasakran, et al. 2015). With time, perhaps these movies and others like them will influence the genre to a more realistic and nuanced take on the gender spectrum, as well as incorporating a less

Western-/Euro-centric take on masculinity, regardless of the sex of the person wearing the fangs.

NOTES

1. Internet Movie Database, https://www.imdb.com.

BIBLIOGRAPHY

Amirpour, Ana Lily. 2014. *A Girl Walks Home Alone at Night.* Say Ahh Productions, Taft, CA.

Barthes, Roland. 1967. *The Fashion System*, trans. Ward and Howard, Berkeley: The University of California Press.

Berg, Anne-Jorunn, and Merete Lie. 1995. Feminism and Constructivism: Do Artifacts Have Gender? in *Science, Technology, and Human Values* 20, no. 3: 332–51.

Comaroff, Jean. 1985. Bodily Reform as Historical Practice: The Semantics of Resistance in Modern South Africa, in *International Journal of Psychology*, 20: 541–67.

Conkey, Margaret W. 2007. Questioning Theory: Is There a Gender of Theory in Archaeology? in *Journal of Archaeological Method and Theory* 14, no. 3: 285–310.

Coppola, Francis Ford. 1992. *Bram Stoker's Dracula.* American Zoetrope, Los Angeles, CA.

Coppola, Francis Ford and Eiko Ishioka. 1992. *Coppola and Eiko on Bram Stoker's Dracula.* San Francisco: Collins Publishers San Francisco.

Douglas, Mary. 1966/2001. *Purity and Danger: An Analysis of Concepts of Pollution and Taboo.* New York: Routledge.

Entwistle, Joanne. 2000. *The Fashioned Body.* Malden: Blackwell Publishers.

Fairclough, Norman. 2003. *Analyzing Discourse: Textual Analysis for Social Research.* New York: Routledge Publishers.

Florescu, Radu and Raymond T. McNally. 1994. *In Search of Dracula: The History of Dracula and Vampires.* Houghton Mifflin Company New York and Boston.

Freud, Sigmund. 1893/1952. *Selected Papers on Hysteria*, in Great Books of the Western World, Vol. 54. Freud. Chicago: The University of Chicago Press/Encyclopedia Britannica, Inc.

Franiuk, Renae, and Samantha Scherr. 2013. "The Lion Fell in Love with the Lamb": Gender, Violence, and Vampires, in *Feminist Media Studies,* 13, no. 1: 14–28.

Geller, Pamela. 2009. Bodyscapes, Biology, and Heteronormativity, in *American Anthropologist*, 111, no. 4: 504–16.

Gero, Joan, and Margaret W. Conkey. 1997. Programme to Practice: Gender and Feminism in Archaeology, in the *Annual Review of Anthropology*, 26: 411–37.

Haraway, Donna. 1991. A Cyborg Manifesto, in *Simians, Cyborgs and Women: The Reinvention of Nature*, New York: Routledge.

Internet Movie Database. https://www.imdb.com/.

Jarmusch, Jim. 2013. *Only Lovers Left Alive.* Recorded Picture Company, Detroit, MI.

Jordan, Neil. 1994. *Interview with the Vampire.* Geffen Pictures, CA.

Łuksza, Agata. 2015. Sleeping with a Vampire: Empowerment, Submission and Female Desire in Contemporary Vampire Fiction, in *Feminist Media Studies*, 15, no. 3: 429–43.

Martin, Emily. 1991. The Egg and the Sperm: How Science Has Constructed a Romance Based on Stereotypical Male-Female Roles, in *Signs*, 16, no. 3: 485–501.

Mukherjea, Ananya. 2011. My Vampire Boyfriend: Postfeminism, "Perfect" Masculinity, and the Contemporary Appeal of Paranormal Romance, in *Studies in Popular Culture*, 33, no. 2: 1–20.

Murnau, Friedrich Wilhelm. 1922. *Nosferatu.* Jofa-Atelier Berlin-Johannisthal, Orava Castle, Germany.

Ortner, Sherry. 1974. Is Female to Male as Nature is to Culture? in *Women, Culture and Society,* Michelle Ronaldo ed. Stanford: Stanford University Press.

Perry, Linda A. M., Lynn H. Turner, and Helen M. Sterk, eds. 1992. *Constructing and Recon-structing Gender: The Links Among Communication, Language, and Gender*. Albany: The State University of New York Press.

Rajasakran, Thanaseelen, Santhidran Sinnappan, Thinavan Periyayya, and Sridevi Balakrish-nan. 2015. Muslim Male Segmentation: The Male Gaze and Girl Power in Malaysian Vam-pire Movies, in *The Journal of Islamic Marketing*, 8, no. 1: 95–106.

Ribeiro, Aileen. 1986/2003. *Dress and Morality*. London: Berg.

Rymer, Michael. 2002. *Queen of the Damned*. Warner Bros., Hollywood, CA.

Wiseman, Len. 2003. *Underworld.* Lakeshore Entertainment, Hungary.

———. 2006. *Underworld: Evolution*. Screen Gems, Britannia Beach, British Columbia, Can-ada.

Part IV

Reanimation with Sentience

It's ALIVE . . . or is it? Not quite, but sentient all the same.
As we all know, (Victor) Frankenstein was the monster, and the creature, no matter the version, was tragically misunderstood.

Chapter Nine

Masculinity, and Not Femininity, as Gendered "Nature" in Cinematic Adaptations of Mary Shelley's *Frankenstein*

Devi Snively and Agustín Fuentes

Author Virginia Woolf (1929) is often credited with the phrase "For most of history, Anonymous was a woman," and Mary Shelley is a prime example of such a reality. *Frankenstein* was first published anonymously and with good reason. The material was controversial enough coming from a man, much less a woman, much less a woman like Mary Shelley, who was a figure of controversy even before she penned her infamous opus (Hunt-Botting 2018).

As such, it's perplexing it took academics until the 1970s to recognize Frankenstein not only as a significant work of literature but also as a significant feminist work—the primary reason often noted for this oversight being that the women characters in Shelley's novel do not play major roles in the story, nor do those who do appear have any real agency. What these same scholars failed to recognize, however, is that it is precisely due to the detrimental results of the absence of female agency—emerging from societal expectations/roles of the era—that leads not only to the women's victimization with the untimely deaths of Justine and Elizabeth, but also to the downfall of the men, primarily Victor and his creature, men who willfully ignore the sage advice of the women that in all likelihood would have prevented the "manmade" catastrophes that ensue. In short, the women in Shelley's novel say little but speak volumes.

At the same time, the theme exploring *what is at the core of human being, and human becoming*, is central to the novel, especially in the context of what it means to be male. In Shelley's novel, the creature is male but not always typically masculine. As he becomes "civilized" through increased contact with human society, the reader witnesses him move through a range of emotions, starting with confusion and fear, compassion and a yearning to be loved, and ending with anger and the emergence of a lethal vengeance. He is both a "brute" and a savant. He is a complex being, a composite of many dead men's bodies and thus born into life as a form of "everyman" who navigates the process of becoming human. Shelley contrasts this complex creaturely maleness with the classic early nineteenth-century masculinity of Victor: selfish, egotistical and prone to fits of anger and depression when all does not easily turn his way. Victor and the creature provide diametrically opposed paths to manhood, and yet end up mirroring one another in their revenge-fueled battle. Both achieving a paralleled form of toxic, kamikaze masculinity. Mary Shelley offers us a critique, through the journeys of Victor and the Creature, of both the concept of an immutable or fixed human nature and a particular notion of what it means to be masculine.

There's already an abundance of scholarly literature available on Mary Shelley's novel in the context of feminisms and the role of the creature as a mirror for "human nature" (Ginn 2013; Hoeveler 2004), so we don't want to rehash other scholars' work. Rather, here we engage how male-centric views of the *Frankenstein* novel, and of human nature, have translated into almost exclusively sexist film adaptions of this feminist novel, and in doing so further a false notion of "naturalness" of a particular form of masculinity.

DESPERATELY SEEKING MASCULINITY IN 'HUMAN NATURE'

What we think of as human nature, however defined, configures how we see the world. And, there is no doubt that Mary Shelley provides a particular view of what it means to be, and become, human, in her novel. The film versions, however, present a somewhat different view of human nature (Ginn 2013) than the novel. Shelley's version involves considerably more depth than the mere science of creation or a faulty brain, the driving forces of the "nature" of the creature in the films, and herein lies the disconnect. To clarify that what one actually means when referring to a "human nature" is never a truly scientific, empirical notion. Rather, it is a dynamic construct involving various normative, conceptual and even metaphysical aspects and assumptions (Fuentes and Visala 2017; Hannon and Lewens 2018). This is what Shelley presents, grounding her tome in the realms of anthropology, philosophy and a multitude of other fields of study.

Scholars in said fields have long sought to identify both universal and distinct features across human cultures. While acknowledging a great range of diversity in the human experience, there often lies the assumption of a core "way of being" that underlies it. This core has been explained via genetic, theological and philosophical arguments, among others (Fuentes and Vislala 2016), often coming down to an explication of why humans are the way they are as related to sex/gender (Guttman 2019). Of all the assumptions about what a "human nature" might entail, among the most solidly entrenched as a "natural" feature is that which we term "masculinity." This usually assumes a form of aggressive, violent, and sexually driven basal nature and is where many of the filmic versions arrive. However, interpretations of what it means to be human based in this assumption inevitably fail as they oversimplify what sex/gender actually is and means (Hyde et al. 2018).

To clarify, "sex" in humans is generally connected to 23rd chromosomal status, the outcomes of specific functioning in a set of genomic sequences on the X and Y chromosomes, and a set of specific reproductive capacities. In biological reality, nonetheless, defining sex as a physiological category is a much more complex and multivariate process (Fausto-Sterling 2000; Hyde et al. 2018). XY and XX binary classification does not always correlate with the physical and behavioral patterns we associate with male and female. Intersexed individuals and biological variation that muddles the clear distinction between dichotomously defined biological "male" and "female" are fairly common in humans (Fausto-Sterling 2000; Hyde et al. 2018). Human biological sex is a dynamic system of development that produces, on average, patterned physiological and developmental outcomes associated with functional reproductive processes.

"Gender" emerges from the entanglement between physiological and developmental processes and societal perceptions of what males and females are and the roles they are expected to play. "Gender refers to the social, cultural and psychological constructions that are imposed on the biological differences of sex" (Nanda 2000). Wood and Eagly (2002) highlight that it is "the formation of gender roles, by which people of each sex are expected to have psychological characteristics that equip them for the tasks that their sex typically performs." While gender is not simply a social construct, gendered behaviors cannot always be functionally mapped to patterned physiological or morphological differences. The gender/sex reality for humans is complex and not simply dichotomous, either as nature/culture or as feminine/masculine (Fausto-Sterling 2000; Hyde et al. 2018). In the novel, Shelley's creature confounds simplistic masculinist notions of sex/gender. But, as we show below, this is not the case in filmic versions.

The anthropological toolkit allows us to understand humans both as a single species with a diverse and largely overlapping range of bodies and physiologies (with some patterned differences), and simultaneously living in many cultures, ecologies and geographies, exhibiting many ways to successfully be human. Anthropological investigation leads to the recognition that humans all share much in common, and yet remain remarkably diverse behaviorally and culturally. A critical aspect of that diversity comes in the range of gendered realities, and specifically those behaviors that fall under the rubric of what is termed "masculinity." And in the novel, Mary Shelley takes such an anthropological view in narrating the development, the becoming, of the creature.

There certainly is some substance to what we call "masculinity," and it is much more than simply the possession of the qualities traditionally associated with men (Gutmann et al. 2021; Gutmann 2019). More often than not, this "masculinity" is intrinsically linked with violence. It is important to point out that not all males are violent, but most humans who commit the most injurious acts of physical violence are males rather than females. This is a complex and very important social reality, one that begs an interdisciplinary and deep examination and explication (Gutmann 2019). But that is not what it usually receives. Rather, many argue for such violence as inherent in the outcomes of being a male of the species: a masculine evolved proclivity to violence (e.g., Pinker 2012; Wrangham and Peterson 1997; Wrangham 2019). And this is how the creature is often presented in films.

In the final scenes in *Frankenstein* the novel, the actions taken by both Victor and the Creature, appear to fall into this realm of "natural" masculinity. But, their journey to that end is much richer and more nuanced, especially for the creature, than merely a reflection of what it means to be male. While made of male parts, Shelley's creature is not *created* masculine but rather *becomes*, across the length of the novel, a kind of reactionary masculinity in response to (or in interaction with) the various individuals, contexts and circumstances he encounters. Therein lies Shelley's deft, and feminist, critique of a particular masculinist trope of *human nature*.

Shelley accurately predicted the body of research from across anthropology, biology and psychology, demonstrating that facile unidimensional representations of men, maleness and violence are not supported by data (Ferguson 2021; Fuentes 2021; Gutmann et al. 2021). Yes, more violent acts are committed by males, but most males are not violent across time and space. The view of humans as having a naturally violent masculinity is overly simplistic and does a disservice to the range of gendered behaviors, histories and futures in our species (Gutmman 2019; Gutmann et al 2021). However, this myopic view of a "nature" for masculinity and violence remains in spite of centuries of scientific and literary challenges to its veracity. Why? Because it is created and promulgated by cultural mores, expectations and assertions of what it means to be male in the contemporary moment, especially in settler colonial societies and their places of origin (for example the United Kingdom, United States, and Australia, see Smith 2021). One central way in which this trope is maintained and ingrained in the twentieth and twenty-first centuries is through the venue of media and popular culture. During the twentieth-century film, horror films have been especially adept at gauging and reinforcing cultural stereotypes and expectations of masculinity. And few have done more to do so than the male-interpreted versions of Mary Shelley's *Frankenstein*.

MAKING THE MASCULINE, OBSCURING THE FEMININE: FRANKENSTEIN AT THE MOVIES

From Edison's first cinematic adaptation of *Frankenstein* in 1910, well over one-hundred films that borrow the basic premise and ideas from Shelley's *Frankenstein* have been produced. While one imagines there must be at least a couple out there written and/or directed by women, few to none come across in any survey of the films. Viewing more than sixty *Frankenstein*-themed films to date and perusing the more than 126 IMDB[1] movie titles linked with the *Frankenstein* mythos reveals primarily male-directed and male-written films. The authors encountered only a paltry number of entries coauthored by females, always with their names listed second.[2]

Of course, a film need not be written and directed by a woman to feature a feminist perspective—in theory, at least. Lamentably, in practice, it seems to be the exception and not the rule—especially in the case of *Frankenstein* adaptations. With but few exceptions, to date, the female characters in these cinematic reimaginings of the story are represented as either damsels in distress and/or sexual objects whom, for the most part, have little to contribute to the narrative save for their sexual allure and/or ability to be threatened and/or saved by a man.

The role of women, feminism and masculinity in Frankenstein films is a significant topic for exploration in regards to the crafting and maintaining of assumptions about "human nature" because one can say the name "Frankenstein" pretty much anywhere in the world and many, if not most, people will demonstrate at least some familiarity with the story. The title itself influences perceptions globally ("Frankenstein economics," "Frankenfood," "Frankenscience," etc.). However, and importantly, most of those expressing familiarity with Frankenstein will not have actually read Shelley's novel, basing their perspectives solely on one or more cinematic interpretations. For instance, a majority of people will recall the Creature as an inarticulate brute a la Boris Karloff rather than Shelley's far more complex, intellectual individual on a journey to discover what it means to be human.

In order to demonstrate the specific importance of male cinematic interpretations of Shelley's novel in regards to the construction and promulgation of a particular mode of "natural masculinity," we offer a brief overview of some of the better known *Frankenstein* films and review the sole production we found that takes any real feminist perspective.

Thomas Edison's *Frankenstein* from 1910 is basically a fourteen-minute man-of-science-opening-a-Pandora's-Box story. The female role, Victor's fiancée, presents her as her intended's nurturer who becomes his damsel in distress when the Creature comes after her, which in turn allows Victor to become the masculine hero by saving her through physical feats of bravery. Thereafter, her loving ways cure him of his brief bout of PTSD. This short reflects a huge departure from Shelley's tale and radically recenters the male, and decenters the female, relative to Shelley's arguably more nuanced and complex feminist take. It also sets the stage for the famous feature films to come.

The Universal *Frankenstein* franchise begins with James Whale's films in the 1930s (*Frankenstein* and *Bride of Frankenstein*). Once again, these are male-dominated films and often, it's suggested, with homoerotic subtext[3] (Benshoff 2004). In these films both the Creature and the scientists are men in violent conflict with one another over women and over the right to be "master." The Creature, himself, does show some glimpses of caring and even frailty, usually childlike in content, but ultimately resorts to physical violence once frustrated and seems hellbent on getting a woman (human or creaturely) as his goal. The classic masculine "nature" of the creature is impossible to miss, violent, sex-driven and quick to physical anger—he is Mr. Hyde to other men's Dr. Jekyll—the uber-masculine beast within.

In contrast to the males, the women characters in these films are submissive, playing victim to both the creature and the male scientists who put them in danger. They also occasionally serve as sexual objects. These roles reify the male-female split and place the violent version of masculinity front and center as the pivotal, driving force of the narrative.

The exceptions to the passive female motif are two roles in *Bride of Frankenstein* both played by Elsa Lanchester.[4] First appearing as Mary Shelley herself at the onset of the film, she sits on a sofa doing needlepoint while Lord Byron and Percy Shelley tease her for being girlishly afraid of the thunderstorm.

> Byron: Look at her, Shelley. Can you believe that bland and lovely brow conceived of *Frankenstein*, a monster created from cadavers out of rifled graves? Isn't it astonishing?
>
> Mary: I don't know why you should think so. What do you expect? Such an audience needs something stronger than a pretty little love story. So why shouldn't I write of monsters? [1935]

The female takes the stage of creator and narrator, asserting that woman can (and did) conceive of the monstrous better than man. However, so as not to be *too* feminist and risk overshadowing the male centered perspective of the film, at this point Lanchester as Shelley pricks her finger and frets over the sight of blood.

Lanchester later appears as the intended, created, mate for the creature who, in straying from Shelley's tale, is indeed brought to life. She rejects the creature's all too masculine advances, which demonstrates a certain indication of free will. But in doing so, alas, she is more animal than human, hissing and jerking in fear, thus prompting her immediate destruction without ever uttering a word. While not as sexist as many interpretations, one does not come away from these films remembering strong feminist icons.

The Hammer Films' *Frankenstein* franchise, commencing in 1957, is another of the more famous entries in the *Frankenstein* cinematic cannon. However, anyone familiar with Hammer films knows that their basic formula was to portray men in hero and villain roles and the women in low-cut dresses, revealing as much nudity as the censors would allow. The goal with these films, however, was never about capturing Shelley's work but, rather, to make a profit from two "name brands"—Hammer and *Frankenstein*—stemming more from the popularity of Universal Films than Shelley's work. Thus, their agendas, that is, financial success, relied on conveying a particularly violent and masculine presentation of the creature and scientists by having the women attacked (Creature), saved (scientists) and desired (both). Again, Shelley's original nuance within the Creature's journey, the women's roles and the fight against a simplistic basal nature for men is completely ignored.

A worse offender, given our argument here, nonetheless, is found in the most problematic of the filmic interpretations: Kenneth Branagh's 1994 adaptation of Shelley's novel. In creating this film Branagh specifically said he aimed to, "use as much of Mary Shelley as had not been seen on film before" and "to take things out that earlier films had invented" (Kooyman 2013). Yet wholly unlike Shelley, Branagh's tale paints Victor as a tragic hero driven by grief of his mother's death rather than a scientist hellbent on, to paraphrase Shelley, "creating a new species, which would see him as its benefactor." For Branagh, Victor is depicted as more of a romantic character. In fact, in Branagh's version Justine is in love with Victor, which likewise weakens Justine's role and further diminishes her agency.

In the novel Justine is a martyr figure highlighting Victor's reckless selfishness. He alone has the power to save her from wrongful execution yet lets her die so as to avoid confessing his own crimes and facing the punishment himself. Branagh softens Victor's culpability by placing him as a helpless bystander as a mob drags a screaming Justine away to be hanged—a far cry from the Justine in the novel who, rather than shrieking like a banshee, calmly states: "I do not fear to die, that pang is past. God raises my weakness and gives me courage to endure the worst" (Shelley 1818/1831).

Furthermore, in Branagh's misplaced 'homage' to Shelley, we lose one of Elizabeth's strongest feminist moments in the novel. Though Shelley presents a society where women are not permitted to be outspoken, Elizabeth does indeed speak out at Justine's hearing with an impassioned speech on her friend's behalf, saying: "It may . . . be judged indecent in me to come forward on this occasion: but when I see a fellow creature about to perish through the cowardice of her pretended friends, I wish to be allowed to speak that I may say what I know of her character" (1818/1831)—which she proceeds to do at considerable length.

This is a powerful moment of a woman, sheltered by Victor from the truth, who finds the courage to do what she *believes* is right, when Victor, who has evidence to back up what he *knows* to be true, hides behind his own cowardice. Branagh robs Elizabeth of this strength and simultaneously enables us to pardon Victor.

And yet, Branagh argued he felt it was crucial in a modern movie—especially of a novel by a great woman writer and the daughter of a very important feminist—to make sure that Elizabeth is represented by someone who isn't just a "love interest" and stating that, contrary to Shelley's story, he was aiming to create a more *equal* partnership in the relationship between Victor and Elizabeth. While it is clear Shelley did not make Victor and Elizabeth equals, contrary to Branagh's interpretation, we would argue Shelley makes both Elizabeth and Justine far stronger than Victor in both character and courage. So, in effect, Branagh has reduced the feminist components of Shelley's novel but hides his own toxic masculinity under the guise of his warped notion of "feminism"—one that, given the actual behavior and actions of the males in the movie, reflects a perspective much more in line with previous cinematic masculinizations of Shelley's tale.

In Branagh's film, Elizabeth ultimately leaves Victor for his recklessness and demonstrates more agency overall throughout the story, but therein lies the problem. This is a period piece and this characterization is not representative of Shelley's time or intent. It's Shelley's demonstration of the *absence* of women's power, despite their voices of reason, that offers a more realistic feminist perspective. That Branagh and others fail to recognize this oversight, illustrates their own limitations in understanding of the context and intent of Shelley's feminist actions. This pattern of obfuscation of Shelley's words and scenarios is a critical factor in enabling masculinist interpretations that reify a particular notion of 'nature' and ignore the complexity and nuance that could have been brought to the fore.

While there are a multitude of other movies worthy of examination in this discussion, in the interest of space, we'll mention but two more that are particularly noteworthy in their relative departures from the norm.

The first is *Young Frankenstein*. One should not go so far as to label this film feminist in as much that women are portrayed as silly and reliant on men for sex and approval. However, since their male counterparts are likewise silly and beholden to their sexual appetites toward women, at least males and females are presented to some degree as intellectual equals, which is a big step up from most other cinematic interpretations—with the exception of one scene in which the creature does, in effect, rape Elizabeth who says "no" when he climbs on top of her but comes to enjoy the resultant nonconsensual sex, thus supporting the idea that "no" does indeed mean "yes" and that a particular aggressive masculine "nature" is what both males and females see as ideal at heart. As such, *Young Frankenstein* doesn't line up with the famous Mary Shelley quote: "I don't wish women to have power over men; but over themselves."

This leaves us with Frank Henenlotter's *Frankenhooker*, which, surprisingly, given its B-movie, raunchy sex-comedy cult status, is the one film portrayal of *Frankenstein* that suggests the writer/director not only read Shelley's novel but understood it in a way few other filmmakers demonstrate.

The Victor character is named Jeffery and his dialogue is absurdly on-the-nose subtext from Shelley's book:

> Something's happening to me that I just don't understand. I can't think straight anymore. It's like my reasoning is all, uh, twisted and distorted, you know? I seem to be disassociating myself from reality more and more each day. I'm anti-social. I'm becoming dangerously amoral. I-I've lost the ability to distinguish between right from wrong, good from bad . . . [Henenlotter 1990]

Yet, though Jeffery presents this internal conflict that we likewise experience with Victor in Shelley's novel, also in accordance with Shelley, Henenlotter does not let this character off the hook, nor excuse his irresponsible behavior.

The one huge difference between the scientists is that Jeffery, unlike Victor, is not building his creature to become a God or mother substitute of sorts but rather to resurrect his girlfriend whose death is the direct result of one of his other creations gone wrong (a self-mowing lawn-mower, which she inadvertently causes to run over herself). Nevertheless, Henenlotter finds other ways to work in more contemporary hypocrisies that uphold Shelley's feminist lens. For one, Jeffery has only Elizabeth's head and brain to work with so he must find additional body parts to bring her back as a whole woman. Given that Elizabeth's own body was considered 'overweight' by strict contemporary beauty standards, Jeffery narrows down his choices to sexy airline stewardesses and prostitutes, finally opting for the latter as they'll be easier to control given that he can buy them, and they are less likely to be missed.

As the film delves into "crack whore" parties with ample nudity and sex acts, one does not expect the story to take a feminist turn, but it does. Early on, Jeffery watches a talk show on TV where a sex worker speaks on the importance of legalizing prostitution to give women power and safety. It even delves into race/racism as well as women's issues within the context of crack cocaine and how men with power use it to enslave women, people of color and the disenfranchised in general. Though heavy-handed, Henenlotter strives to demonstrate the lack of agency women suffer due to societal structures and structural violence. This reality is wholly in-line with key elements in Shelley's novel.

Pointedly, in this vein, after Jeffery has created his perfect version of Elizabeth with hand-picked parts from a slew of dead hookers, she rejects him because he doesn't have any money: he wanted a hooker, he got one. Henenlotter's Elizabeth follows not only her own instincts but those of the voices in her head that belong to the women whose parts comprise the new her. This is an extraordinary story twist because, in short, Henenlotter is saying, "Women are more than just body parts. They have thoughts and feelings and drives of their own." Elizabeth as Frankenhooker controls men, uses her sexuality on her own terms and even kills the abusive pimp that once terrorized the women whose parts she now possesses.

The final elements may challenge our assertion of continuity with Shelley but do offer some component of counter narrative to a masculinist hegemony in cinematic recreations of the novel. In a showdown with the antagonist pimp, Jeffery is killed and Frankenhooker brings Jeffery back to life using his own research notes. However, his reanimation serum is an estrogen-based female-only formula and, of course, she only has the leftover dead hooker parts with which to rebuild him. So, she reanimates Jeffery, but now with a body almost identical to her own—with breasts and a vagina and so forth. When Elizabeth reveals Jeffrey's nude body to him, he screams in horror:

> Jeffrey: No! Where's my Johnson? What did you do to me, Elizabeth?
> Elizabeth: Granted, what I did may have been a bit unorthodox. But, hey, you look great, and you're alive. And you're back with me, and I love you . . .
> He screams in horror. [Henenlotter 1990].

We find it interesting that *Young Frankenstein* and *Frankenhooker*, the two *Frankenstein* films that do not present females as submissive or otherwise inferior to their male counterparts, each take a tongue in cheek approach to the material. Dark comedy, as opposed to straight horror, in this case seems to be an avenue for the expression of greater connectivity to Shelley's thematic intent.

We end the filmic review with one of our own. Arising from the frustrating quest to find a film that takes a more serious approach that addresses the inherent feminism in Shelley's story, one of us (Snively) decided to make one herself.

Bride of Frankie is a nineteen-minute *Frankenstein*-themed film that deals with the subject matter in a darkly comedic, yet serious and dramatic context at turns. We mention this to offer an anecdote that happened during the auditions to shed additional light on the themes and examples we've offered up in this chapter.

For the majority of *Bride of Frankie*, the Victor character is absent, and the focus is on his female counterpart, Frankie, whose role wavers between ambitious scientist, mother/nurturer and, to her surprise, suitor and eventually lover. She's a complex character, and we were certain actresses in their late thirties and forties would be starved for such a role. We were in for a big surprise.

Employing a casting agent in Chicago, we saw highly pedigreed actors straight from the prestigious Steppenwolf Theater, along with many boasting equally prestigious thespian credits. Yet, in attempting to play the role of "a woman in a *Frankenstein* film," the vast majority confined their interpretations to one of two stereotypes: a kindergarten teacher or a Mel Brooks's dominatrix.

Snively tried every last trick in her directing toolbox, and yet most could not get past these preconceived notions of 'the female' in *Frankenstein*. The one woman who came in and performed the role perfectly, unabashedly in a Shelleyian note without any direction whatsoever, was a woman who had not seen a single one of the film adaptations but had read Shelley's novel. We found this turn of events very telling and key to the argument we are making here. The popular perception that what "is" is shaped and molded by what we are told and shown "is." For the majority of the public, *Frankenstein* "is" a movie about the violent nature of masculinity and the lack of agency in femininity. This is NOT what Mary Shelley writes in her novel, and it is not what we hope the readers of this essay will blindly accept on future viewing of the *Frankenstein* narrative.

PARTING THOUGHTS

Despite the focus on masculinity laid out here, we are not simply arguing against a fixed nature for masculinity or that one mode of envisioning it is better than another. Rather, we are trying to highlight that the assumptions about the nature of masculinity and its representation in cinematic versions of *Frankenstein* are obfuscating or masking the feminist voice and perspective, and all of the gender variants and interpretations that accompany it, in the popular perception of *Frankenstein*. It's important to understand that diverse perspectives on masculinity, particularly feminist ones, offer a greater bandwidth for engaging the reality of human gender diversity and Shelley's novel along with its many reinterpretations is a fabulous text to explore this subject.

Simone De Beauvoir said: "Man is defined as a human being and woman as a female—whenever she behaves as a human being she is said to imitate the male" (1949). Lamentably, too many contemporary storytellers fall into this trap, promulgating hegemonic tropes about gender, masculinity, and femininity, especially in the various cinematic versions of *Frankenstein*. But Shelley did not initiate this problematic trend in her novel. Rather, she masterfully demonstrated a particularly feminist perspective and interpretation not defined against or via the masculinist gaze. Shelley doesn't beat us over the head with Charlize Theron-type characters kicking men's asses in the reboot of *Mad Max*, nor does she show us historical scenarios where women unrealistically overcome the obstacles that plague them in that era's particular oppressive society. Instead, she depicts her key female characters as strong-willed individuals who act admirably, yet realistically, in the context of their situation. It is up to the reader to understand how this feminist gaze offers alternatives to dominant tropes, how context matters and how *human nature* is a more nuanced and dynamic reality than most versions of the Creature and Victor lead us to believe.

NOTES

1. Internet Movie Database, https://www.imdb.com/.
2. This varies as one expands the search into short films and a wider range of independent filmic products. Case in point: one of the authors (Snively) both wrote and directed a Frankenstein-genre film.
3. This too has a whole range of implications for themes and views of masculinity, ones that arguably introduce some very subaltern theory and manipulation into this whole theme . . . but that is the topic of various other essays. This particular view also creates whole new lens for interpreting the motives for creating life without the need of women.
4. Elsa Lanchester herself challenged much in the stereotypes of gender in her day and today, making these small pushes against normativity especially potent (e.g., https://www.popmatters.com/elsa-lanchester-herself-2614904290.html?rebelltitem=2#rebelltitem2)

BIBLIOGRAPHY

Benshoff, Harry M. 2004. "The Monster and the Homosexual." In *Queer Cinema: The Film Reader*, edited by Harry Benshoff and Sean Griffin, 63–74. New York: Routledge.

Branagh, Kenneth, director. 1994. *Mary Shelley's Frankenstein*. TriStar Pictures.

Brooks, Mel, director. 1974. *Young Frankenstein*. Gruskoff/Venture Films.

De Beauvoir, Simone. 1949. *The Second Sex*. New York: Knopf Doubleday.

Fausto-Sterling, Anne. 2000. *Sexing the Body: Gender Politics and the Construction of Sexuality* New York: Basic Books.

Ferguson, Brian. (in press). "Masculinity and War." *Current Anthropology*

Fisher, Terrance, director. 1957. *The Curse of Frankenstein*. Hammer Films.

Fuentes, Agustín. 2021. "Searching for the 'Roots' of Masculinity in Primates and the Human Evolutionary Past." *Current Anthropology*. DOI: https://doi.org/10.1086/711582.

Fuentes, Agustín and Aku Visala. 2016. *Conversations on Human Nature*. Walnut Creek: Left Coast Press/Routledge.

Ginn, Sheryl R. 2013. "Mary Shelley's *Frankenstein:* Exploring Neuroscience, Nature, and Nurture in the Novel and the Films." *Progress in Brain Research* 204: 169–90.

Griffin, Gail. 2018. "Monstrous Masculinity: Frankenstein at Two Hundred." *Ploughshares*. Accessed October 10, 2019. http://blog.pshares.org/index.php/monstrous-masculinity-frankenstein-at-two-hundred/

Gutmann, Matthew. 2019. *Are Men Animals? How Modern Masculinity Sells Men Short.* New York: Basic Books.

Gutmann, Matthew, Robin Nelson, and Agustín Fuentes. (in press). "Epidemic Errors in Understanding Masculinity, Maleness, and Violence." *Current Anthropology*

Hannon, Elizabeth and Tim Lewens. 2018. *Why We Disagree About Human Nature.* Oxford: Oxford University Press.

Henenlotter, Frank, director. 1990. *Frankenhooker.* Levins-Henenlotter.

Hoeveler, Diane. 2004. "Frankenstein, Feminism, and Literary Theory." In *The Cambridge Companion to Mary Shelley*, edited by Esther Schor, 45–62. Cambridge: Cambridge University Press.

Hunt Botting, Eileen. 2018. *Mary Shelley and the Rights of the Child: Political Philosophy in Frankenstein.* Philadelphia: University of Pennsylvania Press.

Hyde, Janet Shibley, Rebecca S. Bigler, Daphna Joel, Charlotte Chucky Tate, and Sari M. van Anders. 2019. "The Future of Sex and Gender in Psychology: Five Challenges to the Gender Binary." *American Psychologist* 74(2): 171–93.

Kooyman, Ben. 2013. "The Pedagogical Value of Mary Shelley's *Frankenstein* in Teaching Adaptation Studies." In *In Fear and Learning: Essays of the Pedagogy of Horror*, edited by Aalya Ahmad and Shawn Moreland, 245–64. Jefferson: McFarland & Company.

Nanda, Serena. 2000. *Gender Diversity: Cross Cultural Variations.* Long Grove: Waveland Press.

Pinker, Stephen. 2012. *The Better Angels of Our Nature: Why Violence Has Declined.* New York: Penguin.

Shelley, Mary Wollstonecraft. 1818/1831. *Frankenstein; or, The Modern Prometheus.* London: Lackington, Hughes, Harding, Mavor, & Jones.

Snively, Devi, director. 2017. *Bride of Frankie.* Deviant Pictures Production.

Whale, James, director. 1931. *Frankenstein.* Universal Pictures.

Whale, James, director. 1935. *Bride of Frankenstein.* Universal Pictures.

Wood, Wendy and Alice H. Eagly. 2002. "A Cross-Cultural Analysis of the Behavior of Women and Men: Implications for the Origins of Sex Differences." *Psychological Bulletin* 128(5): 699–727.

Woolf, Virginia. 1929. *A Room of One's Own.* London: Hogarth Press.

Wrangham, Richard and Dale Peterson. 1997. *Demonic Males: Apes and the Origins of Human Violence.* New York: Mariner Books.

Wrangham, Richard. 2019. *The Goodness Paradox: The Strange Relationship Between Virtue and Violence in Human Evolution.* New York: Pantheon Books.

Chapter Ten

The Animated Dead

Reimagining the Beautiful Corpse in Tim Burton's Corpse Bride

Gillian Wittstock

Historically, colliding representations between death and femininity within Western horror cinema have produced problematic imagery of the female form, rendering women as either passive erotic objects, or alternately, as the monstrously abject. Although this exploration is evident across various genres and media of literature, the objectification of female bodies has found particular purchase within Western horror cinema. Scholars such as Julia Kristeva (1982), Carol Clover (1987), Barbra Creed (2002) and Sarah Arnold (2013) have located and disputed the problematic male gaze in horror films. Kristeva's influential "Powers of Horror: An Essay on Abjection" (1982) centralized the feminine body as a site of the monstrous within horror film, which was later critiqued and repositioned by Clover's influential article "Her Body, Himself. Gender in the Slasher Film" (1987). Here, Clover situated male ego as the predominant gaze of the camera lens in horror film. As a result, horror literature has extensively exploited the female body as terrain to explore, and on which to impart ideological conventions of femininity within a patriarchal sexual economy. However, there are rare feminine figures, within this prolific canon of problematic feminine representation, whose construction not only disturbs the conventional horror representation of women but simultaneously seeks to reimage it.

This chapter offers a reading of the ways in which the character Emily, from Tim Burton's *Corpse Bride* (2005), reimagines historical horror clichés by adopting, subverting, and undermining problematic imagery associated with the beautiful corpse. I argue that Emily's representational practices collapse the binary between the beautiful dead and the monstrous abject by renegotiating the beautiful corpse's codes and conventions. As a result, Emily's construction produces a self-reflective lens through which iconography associated with the beautiful corpse is both embraced and undercut. Therefore, Burton's reflections offer subtle commentary on feminine representation in horror films by actively destabilizing and reimagining the beautiful corpse's iconography within a camp horror animation. I propose that this is realized through two particular aspects which are exploited within the genre of camp horror animation. These aspects are (1) representational practices constructed through character design and (2) the employment of grotesque humour within a camp horror genre framework. The intersection between these aspects creates a fruitful landscape in which Burton navigates previous historical representations of the beautiful corpse by offering a complex reimagining of this trope as a liminal and ambiguous figure.

In order to explore Emily's subversive construction of feminine horror codes and conventions, it is important to briefly reflect on conventional representations of women in horror films. Historically, women have been represented as threatening and terrifying within a patriarchal sexual economy (i.e., Kristeva (1982), Clover (1987), Creed (2002), and Arnold (2013)). Women's bodies have been regarded as terrifying objects due to an intersectional relationship between abject bodily waste via menstruation, and the embodiment of an impending threat of castration via an absence of a phallus (Creed 2002). According to Kristeva (1982), it is precisely these physical differences between female and male bodies that disturb male identity, and as a consequence align the female body with the abject. Subsequently, in order to protect patriarchal order from the fear projected by the female body, women have either been represented as monstrous subjects needing to be terminated or as harmless, desirable objects. Although the relationship between the female body and abjection is not new, it has found explicit expression within the horror genre. Consequently, women's bodies, within horror films, have been exploited as sites for slashing, raping, bludgeoning, and mutilating, while simultaneously occupying a site of macabre romance and desire. Therefore, the female figure within horror cinema is a messy and ambiguous symbolic figure which has spawned a plethora of feminine horror tropes.

Among others, one prevalent trope that has emerged from Western horror literature is that of the beautiful corpse which traditionally represents dead women as beautiful or exquisite. This phenomenon has been extensively theorized in Elizabeth Bronfen's formative book *Over her Dead Body: Death, Femininity and Aesthetic* (1992) which investigates imagery of the beautiful corpse in various forms of literature. She concluded that the convention of the beautiful corpse undermines female agency through the use of objectification as a means to dismantle the abjection associated with the female body in a patriarchal sexual economy (Bronfen 1992). Bronfen argued that this is further complicated and extended through the naturalized abjection of the corpse. As a result, this phenomenon is attributable to the fetishization of dead female bodies by representing female corpses as beautiful, sensual, and erotic. Bronfen adeptly observes this relationship, reflecting that

> Femininity and death cause disorder or stability, mark moments of ambivalence, disruption or duplicity and their eradication produces a recuperation of order, a return to stability. The threat that death and femininity pose is recuperated by representation, staging absence as a form or re-presence, or return, even if or rather precisely because this means appeasing the threat of real mortality, of sexual sufficiency, of lack of plenitude and wholeness [Bronfen 1997, xii].

Most examples of the beautiful corpse maintain a firm boundary between the incorruptible and decomposed. Either a character is presented as an object of the sublime dead, uncorrupted by the effects of death or as the subjective, abject monster whose rotting body is a terrifying sight to behold. Objectivity is explicitly achieved through protecting the female form from signs of rot and decay; preserving the feminine body as pristine and pure. Her body must remain still, a time capsule of beauty that is incorruptible by any signs of decay, to achieve a spectacle of objectification. The terror generated from an abject woman is diminished through an idealistically romanticized form, transforming the monstrous feminine into a "passive object" that "privilege[s] tropes of masculine imagination and desire" (Bronfen 1997, 141). Furthermore, the pristine female corpse transforms into an untouchable signifier through its preserved construction, which occupies a moment of "jouissance as nostalgia, within reach but lost forever" (Bronfen 1997, 99). Therefore, the fear produced by the abject nature of the dead female body is undercut by representing the female corpse as an object of the male ego, resulting in an oppositional representational binary which limits and collapses nuance within representations of the feminine experience.

Conversely, the pristine, objectified female corpse can reclaim agency through undergoing, or revealing signs of decomposition and decay. A woman's desirability is undermined by the decay of a dead body, instigating "control and power, given that of the woman's self-disintegration also becomes an act of self-construction" (Bronfen 1997, 141). Ultimately, her body must remind the viewer that she is dead, thus seeking power through her abject nature. Her rot signifies acceptance of death, providing power to the demeaned female form within the symbolic realm of the beautiful corpse. Her spoilt body transcends into subjectivity, rather than objectivity via a loss of male desirability (Bronfen 1997, 141). Consequently, the feminine corpse within literature must reveal signs of decomposition to assert an objective position. The feminine corpse must liberate itself from objectification through a celebration of the cruelties of death, as "a woman can gain a subject position only by denying her body" (Bronfen 1997, 143).

One such example, which revives a sense of agency through the decaying female form, is the character of Emily, who is a subversive animated version of the beautiful corpse within the musical stop motion film *Corpse Bride* directed by auteur Tim Burton (2005). Burton's eccentric gothic style retells the classic Yiddish/Russian folk tale *The Finger* (Mancini 2016), which centers upon the notion of the beautiful corpse. Burton's version follows the journey of the young groom Victor (voiced by Johnny Depp) who when reciting his vows accidentally slips his wedding ring onto the finger of a corpse, Emily (voiced by Helena Bonham Carter), which brings her to life. Initially repulsed by her, Victor tries to escape from Emily, but as their story continues, he begins to respect and care for her. The film is resolved when Victor marries his first betrothed, Victoria (voiced by Emily Watson), and Emily finds peace in understanding how and by whom she was murdered.

Emily's subversive representation marks her as both a beautiful corpse and as not, thus rendering her as a modern example of the beautiful corpse. Although Emily's physical construction is marked by decay and rot, she is still strikingly feminine. The softness of her design exudes femininity. Her body bends elegantly, substituting the harsh, angular lines associated with post-mortem rigidity with softer, plumper, and rounder shapes. Her costume evokes an idealistic notion of virginal purity. A dried flower crown rests upon her long matted blue hair, keeping her lace veil in place. An unmistakable hourglass figure is adorned by a once delicate white lace wedding gown, which has become tattered and torn with time spent aging beneath the soil. Below an ample bosom, a series of ribs subtly peek through a small tear in her gown. A gloved right hand shows signs of decay by revealing her raw arm bones beneath. Although her high cheekbones are angular, there is a softness to her face. Long, thin eyebrows curve around long-lashed, framed eyes, making her appear kind and welcoming. Furthermore, a small green maggot resides in her eye socket. Her soft, wide smile is accentuated by plump lips which are colored an unnatural pink for a decomposing corpse. Emily's pale blue complexion epitomizes the appearance of a still-cold corpse, as oxygen deprivation has caused her skin to change to a soft blue color, but simultaneously evokes western ideals of pale skin beauty.

Notably, Emily's white wedding dress and pale skin borrow from the iconography associated with the purity of white passive females. Within a western cultural sphere, the intersectional relationship between whiteness and feminine gendering produces problematic imagery, which aligns white females with purity, passivity, and objectivity (Dyer 1996; Strokes 2001; Boris and Janssens 1999). Mason Strokes argues that women are valued according to puritanical ideals of maidenhood which are "rooted in a patriarchal system of control" (2001, 34). The cultural repertoire of white feminine passivity is produced in order to empower the male subject as a protective figure (Boris and Janssens 1999, 115). This is signaled through the whiteness of female skin and symbols associated with chastity. One explicit symbol is the white wedding dress. Emily's white wedding dress epitomizes virginal purity, as a subtle and silent pledge of the wearer's abstinence. This signifier becomes more complex when combined with her pallid-bluish skin which marks her as a passive white female in need of care and protection.

However, despite her virginal feminine appearance, Emily's body is simultaneously represented as a site of monstrous abjection. Unmistakably, her body has sustained decay and rot which characterize her as dead. Her corpse-like representation is considered "the ultimate in abjection" (Creed 2002, 70) within the symbolic realm. In order for a living body to survive and thrive, it must remove waste both internally and externally by removing waste from the body itself (through breathing, defecation, urination, vomiting, etc.), and be able to distance itself from the source of excreted waste (Creed 2002, 70). Subsequently, the immobility of a corpse renders it helpless to the pollutants of the waste it produces. Furthermore, the corpse is considered the final waste product of the soul, as the soul leaves behind the corporal body, which renders the body left behind as an 'excretion' within western Christian theology (Bakhtin 1984, 51). Therefore, Emily's decomposing body is symbolically a caged vessel of putrid waste, unable to escape contaminants produced by the body, which is meant to be secreted by the soul when leaving the body. Her body becomes a symbolic reference of the abject.

Consequently, the clashes between the representational binaries of dead and alive, natural and unnatural, and feminine and dead construct her as an ambiguous and liminal figure. Each satirical symbol culturally marks Emily as feminine, and as a result desirable to the male gaze, but this is undermined by the clear design choice to mark her body as both dead and alive. Therefore, Emily's construction is distinctly transcendent as she adheres to and undercuts the problematic ideologies attached to the iconography of the beautiful corpse. Emily's physical representation can be interpreted as an example of the beautiful corpse, whose construction contributes toward a problematic representation of objectified women within horror literature. However, this representation simultaneously undermines the objectivity of the beautiful corpse via her physical representation which embraces the abject through the iconography of a decaying corpse. Therefore, Emily's body is marked with complexity as she navigates the multifaceted intersection between the body, the object, the subject, agency, and passivity through her representation as an exquisite corpse.

Operating within a camp horror framework, the next aspect I discuss is how the employment of grotesque humor generates a degree of agency and subjectivity within Emily's character. Analysis focuses explicitly on Emily's engagement with grotesque corporeal humor and intertextual humor which subvert traditional horror codes and conventions. Exploiting grotesque and intertextual humor ultimately undermines Emily's abject nature without undermining her subjectivity, which liberates her from the objectification associated with the beautiful corpse. The inclusion of grotesque and intertextual humor in representing Emily furthers her ambiguous and liminal nature by distorting the binaries between object and subject, and what is terrifying and what is not. Aligning femininity with grotesque humor produces an exceptional and rare instance of ambivalence within the monstrous female form, within the horror genre. Therefore, Burton's reimagining of Emily as the beautiful corpse generates a subjective and agentic representation of femininity. However, first I locate and explain the camp horror and the grotesque body as a framework of analysis.

It is necessary to understand the subgenre of camp horror, as both intertextual and corporeal humor function, within *Corpse Bride* (Burton 2015), through camp horror conventions. To define camp horror, one must first consider the phenomena of camp aesthetic. Camp as an aesthetic practice was first investigated by Susan Sontag's seminal work *Notes on Camp* (1964). Through a series of fifty-eight "jottings," Sontag argued that camp should be considered as "a certain mode of aestheticism" that is achieved through a "degree of artifice, of stylization" (1964, 2). Sontag argued that the practice of camp undermines high culture through an explicit desire to "dethrone the serious" (1964, 10). Therefore, camp rejects the banality and superficiality of high art culture by celebrating alternative imagery, situated within the exaggerated, subversive, absurd, and flamboyant, in order to promote an empowered, emotive aesthetic practice that is situated within the gutter of low culture.

Sontag's camp philosophies have voyaged beyond fine art and have found particular purchase within the scholarship of the horror subgenre camp horror. One such scholar is David MacGregor Johnstone whose book *Kitsch and Camp and Things That Go Bump in the Night; or, Sontag and Adorno at the (Horror) Movies* (2010) advanced Sontag's sentiments via a study of camp as a subversive aesthetic practice that has empowered the gap between low and high art within horror cinema. Johnstone acknowledges the subversive nature of camp horror, and how the subgenre has become synonymous with cult cinema. Johnstone reflected on the subversive nature of camp horror via the interplay of intertextual humor. Camp horror utilizes the 'seriousness' of horror films codes and conventions but subverts these qualities through a combination of homage and mockery, therefore producing a genre concerned with "style over content" (MacGregor Johnstone 2010, 237). This is achieved through camp horror's employment of stylistic codes as humorous intertextual references of the horror genre. Johnston illustrates this through cult classic horror films such as Mel Brooks's *Young Frankenstein* (1974), which draws on the gothic tale of Frankenstein's Monster, and *Attack of the Killer Tomatoes* directed by John De Bello (1978), which is inspired by 1950s sci-fi films.

Although most camp horror humor is generated through intertextual pleasures, some camp horror films utilize the spectacle and shock of the grotesque body to neutralize and subvert horror codes and conventions. Understanding the grotesque body is the prescribed focus of Mikhail Bakhtin's pivotal work *Rabelais and His World* (1984), which has become influential within horror scholarship. Bakhtin argued that the grotesque body centers on three pivotal moments within life, these being sexual intercourse, birth, and finally, death (Bakhtin 1984, 353). These moments offer a degree of liminality and transcendence by bridging the gap between life and death; opposing forces that inhabit a shared space within the body. These transcendent periods are experienced inwardly; however, Bakhtin argued that these experiences are expressed through the physical, as seen through the body experiencing involuntary spasms, tensions followed by stillness, sweating, screaming, and convulsions.

Therefore, the grotesque body is determined by a principle he terms the "material bodily value," which refers to an assumed natural connection between the body and the earth (Bakhtin 1965, 18). Bakhtin explicitly aligns the visual representation of the body with that of "degradation," as the body is bound to become united with the ground in death (Bakhtin 1965, 19). Degradation refers to the ambivalent act of the body coming "down to earth" (Vice 1997, 155), which is signaled through the body's signs of decay. Therefore, Bakhtin argued that the body and earth are connected and that the body's connection back to earth in death should be a period of festivity and celebration (Bakhtin 1984).

Moreover, in order for the grotesque body to be considered as a part of the grotesque aesthetic, the construction of the body must border the liminal line between funny and terrifying. For artworks to be considered grotesque, they must induce a response of laughter, disgust, or horror, or a combination of these reactions (Harpham 1976, 463). The grotesque is a culturally and temporally specific aesthetic which produces momentary shock or laughter through a visual style reliant on decay and distortion. However, moments of decay or fragmentation are holistically viewed, blurring the binaries between wholeness and brokenness, aimed to subvert conventional representations. This is achieved through the aesthetic representational practices which are concerned with distortion and deformation which is often embraced via the construction of monstrous creatures within the horror genre.

Consequently, most grotesque images are dependent on physical deformity, as counter imagery relies on "our conventions, our prejudices, our commonplaces, our banalities, our mediocrities" (Harpham 1976, 462). Therefore, grotesque imagery distorts the body, depending on what images are culturally considered subversive. Specifically, the grotesque body is dependent on a spectator's gullibility or humor in order to enact its "structure of estrangement" (Harpham 1976, 462). One must occupy a degree of familiarity that is "suddenly subverted or undermined" (Harpham 1976, 462) to produce a sharp shock or surprise that is essential to the feelings of estrangement. This moment of destabilization is not met with terror but rather with humor. Grotesquery's countercultural nature aims to "instill fear of life rather than fear of death" (Harpham 1976, 462). The grotesque is, therefore, the "ambiguous mixture of hilarity and terror, the anxiety, the bewilderment" (Harpham 1976, 466).

As a result, the landscape offered by the intersection between camp horror and grotesque produces subversive humor which is reliant on both intertextual and corporal humor. Both the camp horror genre and the grotesque body simultaneously utilize and subvert traditional codes and conventions of the horror film genre. Camp horror's tactical balance between a degree of homage and parody of horror films produces a genre focused on the humorous exploitation of horror iconography. Furthermore, camp horror embraces traditional horror iconography and transforms these icons into subversive figures through the utilization of terribly cheap, cheesy, and exaggerated stylistic cinematic conventions. This is specifically achieved through the humorous engagement with traditional grotesque bodies seen within the horror genre. As a result, camp horror films deploy intertextuality as a form of subversive humor concerned with mockery, the uncouth, and the grotesque. Ultimately, camp horror and the grotesque body offers an alternative lens through which to engage with horror film tropes, especially for films such as *Corpse Bride* (Burton 2005) whose formats do not necessarily fall within traditional live-action horror genres.

Shifting focus from situating and explaining the relationship between camp horror and the grotesque body, I now explore how Burton employs a sense of playful mockery and simultaneously homage to older horror conventions. Specifically, I analyze how Burton's subversion of the beautiful corpse through the grotesque body produces humor which undercuts Emily's monstrous construction.

By examining Emily's construction through a grotesque lens, her positioning as a beautiful corpse is further undercut and repositioned, as her vivaciously decaying corpse elates her from stilted passivity through erotic objectification, while simultaneously destabilizing abject fear through the threat of the monstrous. Although Emily's body is released from the beautiful corpse through signs of decay, her body is not viewed as monstrous due to her grotesque, humorous construction as a celebration of death. The grotesque construction of her rotting corpse is a celebration of death, rather than a moment of fear. Although her body's putrefaction signifies death, it is not completely destroyed and exudes the spirit and vigor of the living. The grotesque body epitomizes the duality between life and death, which celebrates these dichotomies through the signified animated corpse. Therefore, Emily's construction navigates the oppositional boundaries between life and death, as her fragmented but still complete body dissolves the line shared between the binaries of wholeness and brokenness, thus obscuring the conventions of life and death. Emily's body is the embodiment of the noble or honorable (a feminine body) which is undermined through its revolting, degraded, and disgusting appearance. Her animated corpse exemplifies the liminality of death and life which share a sacred space within the body. The unification of her decaying body with the soil is a source of festivity, as death is undermined and conquered through her grotesque body.

Specifically, Emily's abjection and potential passivity are undercut by ridiculous and laughable moments which are marked by the grotesque body. The manner in which Emily dismantles and acknowledges her decaying body provokes a macabre sense of grotesque humor. For example, Emily unhinges her fibula to throw for Victor's dog, Scraps, who enthusiastically bounds off in search of the bone. This camp moment presents itself as humorous as she unexpectedly disassembles herself to play a trivial game of fetch. Subsequently, Emily instils a degree of agency within her construction by deconstructing her own decaying body. Emily is able to dismantle herself due to her rotting body, which has given her the control to manipulate her body as she feels fit. Simultaneously, this elicits a moment of sudden shock and destabilization, which causes laughter. Within the grotesque, laughter is generated through ambivalence between pleasure and displeasure. Temporary displeasure is caused by Emily's loss of limb; however, the playful way in which she engages with her loss creates enjoyment in the audience. Therefore, laughter here is universal and expansive and is what the grotesque aims to achieve to dismantle previous power structures by eliciting laughter through the previously feared.

Furthermore, Emily's degree of agency is furthered by the grotesque, "intertextual worm" that resides in her body. The aptly named Maggot is a small, vivid green worm who inhabits Emily's eye socket. Although Maggot is an entity of his own, he forms part of Emily's body and reiterates the grotesquery seen in Emily's figure. His appearance borders on fascinating and repulsive. A caricature face of the iconic horror film actor Peter Lorre (from such cult classics as *Mad Love* [1935], *The Face behind the Mask* [1941], and *Tales of Terror* [Corman 1962]) is grafted onto a squat green worm torso, which is sculptured to mimic the knots of vertebrae in the human spine. Maggot's sickly, puffy eyes bulge from his skull and are framed by two expressive black eyebrows, while his two gap-teeth protrude from a wide, sly mouth. His soft, nasal voice parodies Lorre's creepy and somber vocal timbre. Maggot relies on his vocal texture, expressive eyes, and the occasional point of his tail to create gestures.

Maggot's construction is further complicated via the deployment of inter-textual humor, which is embraced by the camp horror genre, which in turn complicates Emily's construction as the beautiful corpse. Lorre's distinct vocal quality and facial features have become iconized as villainous, as he became the antagonist in most horror films in which he performed. This association is playfully reinterpreted, as Lorre's caricatured Maggot is con-structed as an amicable character, who poses little threat to those around him due to his small stature. Intertextual humor is explicitly utilized to undermine the unnerving performances of Lorre through the body of a small, pathetic worm, thus embodying the intertextual subversion of horror conventions that are deployed in camp horror films. At other times, he becomes a humorous and helpful sidekick, such as when he alerts Emily to her leg which has fallen off while dancing ("Psst, hey, I think you dropped something"). Moments of abjection are undercut by his humorous remarks through the ridiculousness of the statements, as well as the acknowledgement of Emily's decay.

Furthermore, intertextual humor is similarly employed to parody the sani-tized Disney experience. Maggot functions similarly to Disney's rendition of Jiminy Cricket as a conscience in *Pinocchio* (1940). However, here Maggot fails to offer morally righteous and respectable advice, but rather incites debauched and unscrupulous counsel such as threatening to kill the Barkis Bittern ("Let me at him!") or commenting on Victor's feelings on his wed-ding night ("After all, he couldn't get far—with those cold feet"). Maggot signifies the impetuous voice inside all of us that we have become condi-tioned to ignore, especially in sanitized Disney films.

Maggot symbolically undercuts Emily's objectification as the beautiful corpse through the construction of his grotesque body. Although these im-ages of Maggot and Emily may seem disturbing, they are met with laughter. Maggot is revealed when Emily's eye pops out, yet spectators are not ter-rified, but rather only momentarily shocked by the humorous spectacle.

Often, grotesquery is constructed via distortion, usually through animalis-tic characteristics that blur the human form, in the form of a human figure, or through facial features that protrude or gape (Bakhtin 1984, 306). Hybridiza-tion between a human and animal form is perhaps the oldest form of grotes-query, and Maggot is an example of this blending. He is constructed as a human-worm hybrid distorting the boundaries between animal and human, and his facial features uncomfortably protrude and gape from his small, oval face. The mouth, wide and agape, produces the grotesque through distortion. Bakhtin argues that the eyes have "no part in these comic images" as they are not essential to the grotesque, as they express individuality (Bakhtin 1984, 316) unless the eyes protrude or bulge, which they do in both Maggot's and Emily's construction.

Finally, camp horror conventions are further deployed in the way in which Maggot subverts fears of castration anxiety associated with the eye, within horror literature, by poking fun at the notion of the phallic eye. The phallic eye is located in a Freudian psychoanalytical framework, where the loss of an eye is a symbolic substitute of castration anxiety, which suggests a loss of power or agency (Freud 1919, 7). Consequently, eyes become a fruitful symbolic terrain which allows female protagonists to explore agency. As a simultaneous example, and reimagining of the beautiful corpse, Maggot is a subjective male voice embedded within the complex subjective and objectified female body of Emily. His physical construction as a 'seminal worm' is implicated as phallic, and this perhaps imbues Emily with a symbolic phallus, thus instilling her subjectivity further through a patriarchal lens. However, his presence is not overwhelming or autonomously commanding. He becomes secondary to Emily's thoughts and opinions. He is easily ignored, as he is pulled from his hiding spot in her eye and is often told to mind his own business. Audiences never see his perspective, but he is included in the perspective gaze of Emily's eye when she is surveying her surroundings. His presence undercuts her femininity and objectivity by neutralizing her gendered body, and by masculinizing her form. Therefore, Emily's objectivity is further complicated via Maggot's presence within her body. Although it is problematic to only align female agency with the symbolically imbued phallus, Emily is a particularly complex case study who further complicates this relationship through her decaying body. Her body is a space for his survival, but he remains simply as a guest and not as a vehicle of subjectivity, but rather another trope which complicates the possible eroticization of Emily as the beautiful corpse.

In summary, Emily from Burton's *Corpse Bride* (2005) is a notable figure within popular culture whose representation offers a complex site of investigation. She is able to artfully navigate the problematic relationship between death and the feminine aesthetic, by both adhering to the objectification of the female body and liberating femininity from the power of the male gaze. As evidenced through this analysis, Emily's construction is one riddled with ambiguity. Her construction as a beautiful corpse fulfills problematic horror tropes and clichés rooted in unconscious patriarchy. However, these are simultaneously undermined through Burton's reimagining of the beautiful corpse trope through symbolic language and the visual, cinematic treatment of her body as grotesque. Emily's beautiful corpse body is injected with a degree of agency, and thus has reimagined the stereotypical horror genre trope of the objectified, beautiful corpse. This is explicitly achieved through the way in which she embraces decay and death with joviality, which is produced through grotesque corporeal humor and intertextual humor within a camp horror framework. In some ways, this restores agency and autonomy to the monstrous female, but in an innovative, gentle way that is unparalleled to that of how female power is typically rendered in horror (as both dangerous and aggressive). Emily is not simply a site of the monstrous, nor is she fully released from the objectification of the beautiful corpse. She is a subtle rendering of both, subconsciously navigating and commenting on previous feminine horror tropes. As a result, Burton refreshingly offers a powerful, alternate female horror figure, whose agency lies within ambiguity, subversion, and humor of the macabre.

BIBLIOGRAPHY

Arnold, Sarah. 2013. *Maternal Horror Film: Melodrama and Motherhood*. New York: Palgrave Macmillan.

Bakhtin, Mikhail. 1984. *Rabelais and His World*. Bloomington: Indiana University Press.

Boris, Eileen and Janssens, Angélique. 1999. "Racialized Bodies and Citizenship in Twentieth Century Germany." In *Complicating Categories: Gender, Class, Race and Ethnicity*, edited by Eileen Boris and Angelique Janssens, 150–62. Cambridge: Cambridge University Press.

Bronfen, Elisabeth. 1992. *Over Her Dead Body: Death, Femininity and the Aesthetic*. Manchester: Manchester University Press.

Brooks, Mel, director. 1974. *Young Frankenstein*. 20th Century Fox.

Burton, Tim, director. 2005. *Corpse Bride*. Warner Bros., Tim Burton Animation Co., and Laika Entertainment.

Clover, Carol. 1987. "Her Body, Himself. Gender in the Slasher Film." *Representations, Special Issue: Misogyny, Misandry, and Misanthropy* 20(1): 187–228.

Corman, Roger, director. 1962. *Tales of Terror*. American International Pictures.

Creed, Barbara. 2002. "Horror and the Monstrous Feminine, an Imaginary Abjection." In *The Film Reader*, edited by Mark Jancovich, 67–76. Routledge: London.

De Bello, John, director. 1978. *Attack of the Killer Tomatoes*. NAI Entertainment.

Dyer, Richard. 1996. "'There's Nothing I Can Do! Nothing!' Femininity, Seriality and Whiteness in *The Jewel in the Crown*." *Screen* 37(3): 225–39.

Florey, Robert, director. 1941. *The Face Behind the Mask*. Columbia Pictures.

Freud, Sigmund. 1919. *The Standard Edition of the Complete Psychological Works of Sigmund Freud*. London: Hogarth Press and the Institute of Psycho-Analysis.

Freund, Karl, director. 1935. *Mad Love*. Metro-Goldwyn-Mayer.

Harpham, Geoffrey. 1976. "The Grotesque: First Principles." *The Journal of Aesthetics and Art Criticism* 34(4): 461–68.

Kristeva, Julia. 1982. *Powers of Horror: An Essay on Abjection*. New York: Columbia University Press.

MacGregor Johnstone, Davi. 2010. "Kitsch and Camp and Things That Go Bump in the Night; or, Sontag and Adorno at the (Horror) Movies." *The Philosophy of Horror*, edited by Thomas Fahy, 229–44. Lexington: University Press of Kentucky.

Mancini, Mark. 2016. "12 Lively Facts about Corpse Bride." *Mental Floss*. Accessed January 10, 2019. http://mentalfloss.com/article/89345/12-lively-facts-about-corpse-bride.

Luske, Hamilton and Ben Sharpsteen, directors. 1940. Walt Disney Productions.

Stokes, Mason. 2001. *The Color of Sex: Whiteness, Heterosexuality, and the Fictions of White Supremacy*. Durham: Duke University Press.

Sontag, Susan. 1964. "Notes on Camp." *Monoskop*. Accessed January 8, 2019. https://mono skop.org/images/5/59/Sontag_Susan_1964_Notes_on_Camp.pdf.

Vice, Sue. 1997. *Introducing Bakhtin*. Manchester: Manchester University Press Series.

Chapter Eleven

Sexual Encounters Between the Living and the (Un)dead in Popular Culture

Matt Coward-Gibbs and Bethan Michael-Fox

Depictions of sexual encounters between the living and the (un)dead have become increasingly prominent in popular culture. Following in the footsteps of *Buffy the Vampire Slayer* (1997–2003), vampires have sex with the living in *Twilight* (2011, 2012), *The Vampire Diaries* (2009–2017) and *True Blood* (2008–2014). Zombiism is in part a virulent sexually transmitted disease in *iZombie* (2014–2019). The living are perpetrators of sexual violence against the (un)dead in *Deadgirl* (2008) and an (un)dead girlfriend returns for three-somes in *Nina Forever* (2015). A number of the examples given here are adaptations, and where a range of literary and visual genres have proved highly successful in fueling the spread of sex between the living and the (un)dead from the page to the screen, monsters—not exclusively (un)dead ones—have frequently been utilized as a way for society to "safely represent and address anxieties" (Levina and Bui 2013, 1). Many of these issues and anxieties relate explicitly to gender and sexuality. Bram Stoker's *Dracula* (1897) is famed for playing into Victorian anxieties about "female sexuality and gender roles" (Swartz-Levine 2016, 345). Kee (2014, 177) has empha-sized how zombie films often "toy with fantasies of miscegenation without explicitly dealing with the subject." In the twenty-first century, the social anxieties and concerns about sexuality and gender signaled in texts where the living have sexual encounters with the (un)dead are as varied as the texts in which they feature.

The #timetoshine advertising campaign for Orbit Chewing Gum in 2019 provides an apt example of the breadth of the living/(un)dead coupling now pervading popular culture. It proposes that rather than running from a zombie on prom night, a teenager might want to kiss one. Only fifteen seconds in length, the advert is a nod to the well documented dominance of zombie narratives in the current cultural moment (Luckhurst 2016). It also testifies to the increasing presence of representations of sexual encounters of the living/ (un)dead kind within our cultural lexicon. The advertorial vignette features a living teenage male saying to a rotting teenage female zombie "I don't know if we should kiss. I mean, you're a zombie." The zombie female pops a chewing gum in her mouth and responds, "but I'm kinda hot." Sexually suggestive music with the lyrics "do you wanna go to my bed" plays as the two kiss. Through a critical lens, the brief depiction might prompt a range of questions about transgressive sexual encounters, femininity, masculinity, normative gender roles, liminality and bodily monstrosity. As we seek to demonstrate in this chapter, the depiction of sexual encounters between the living and the (un)dead in popular culture can offer auspicious opportunities for analysis.

We focus on sexual encounters between the living and the (un)dead in three television series, namely: *In the Flesh* (created by Dominic Mitchell for BBC Three and aired 2013–2014), *The Strain* (created by Guillermo del Toro and Chuck Hogan for FX and aired 2014–2017) and *American Horror Story* (created by Brad Falchuk and Ryan Murphy for FX and airing 2011–present). Television can be understood as a particularly apt space for social-science fiction, where issues central to lived experience can be negotiated and explored (Reed and Penfold-Mounce 2015; Penfold-Mounce, Beer, and Burrows 2011). Similarly, television may be understood to "constitute a gigantic empirical archive of human sense-making" ripe for analysis (Hartley 2003, xviii). The three texts examined here can be understood to offer spaces in which complex issues are negotiated in "safe spaces" but also as ones that are actively involved in processes of "sense making" both for and with audiences. In their complex multiplicities of meaning, the texts considered can be understood as both "subversive of and complicit in dominant culture and ideologies" (Jowett 2005, 2). Despite their immediately apparent implications of transgression and necrophilia, many of them perpetuate a range of dominant cultural and social gender norms and heteronormative ideals. The figurative images of "monstrous males" and "fatal females" on which this collection focuses are both upheld and subverted in the sexual encounters examined.

Throughout the chapter the plural "audiences" is adopted to acknowledge the plurality of audiences in the twenty-first century and the ways in which different audiences make sense of television in different ways (Livingstone 1998). Being female or male, for example, "will mean different things to different people" (Jowett 2005, 6). Similarly, individual experiences and subject positions will shape the reception of the texts examined here. The term (un)dead has been selected for two reasons. First, to denote the breadth of the characters represented in these series who rarely conform to and often complicate established categories of the (un)dead such as zombies or vampires. Second, to emphasize that these characters, though evidently not the "real" dead, are often positioned as "dead people" who are sometimes monstrous rather than as "monsters" because they are dead. Similarly, monstrosity is figured not only of the (un)dead in these series but also of the living, typically as a consequence of monstrous actions toward either the living or the (un)dead.

IN THE FLESH

In the Flesh is premised on the idea that being a zombie (known as Partially Deceased Syndrome in the series) can be managed with a treatment. As the treatment is not curative, the (un)dead require rehabilitation before being reintegrated into society. In principle, they are able to go about their lives in relatively similar ways to the living. However, they are visibly "other." They have pale skin and white eyes with small, pinprick pupils. At treatment centers, they are instructed on how to wear contact lenses and a cover-up mousse in order to appear "alive." Philip, who is alive, and Amy, who is (un)dead, offer the most sustained representation of a sexual relationship in the series. In season one, they are seen in Amy's bed with the implication they had a "one-night stand." The sex is heterosexual and between two cisgender characters. It is notable, however, that Amy has, as she explains, gone "*au naturale*" by not wearing cover-up mousse. Visually, it is clear she is (un)dead. Philip had, the night before, tried to segregate Amy in a part of the local pub cordoned off for the partially deceased, but it was clear Philip was sexually attracted to Amy. Amy has little interest in Philip and has spent the night with him as a consequence of being bored and lonely. As Philip leaves, he insists "this, what happened last night, can't get out." Philip explains: "I'd lose my job. . . . Oh Jesus, there'd be hell to pay."

The sex here is taboo in line with Douglas's ([1966] 2002) framework of the interrelationship between pleasure and taboo. That is, that sex is, primarily, a pleasurable experience, yet across societies globally it is mired with rules, regulations and purification rites (Douglas, [1966] 2002). Sex within Douglas's ([1966] 2002) framework might also be seen to become taboo when the aim of sexual activity does not align with that of society writ large. Here, no reproduction could take place given that the (un)dead Amy could not become pregnant. More broadly, a relationship of any kind between the living and (un)dead is positioned as highly undesirable and risky in this series where members of the community's Human Volunteer Force are seen to execute the (un)dead for their "otherness."

When audiences witness the aftermath of Amy and Phillip's one-night stand, Amy is quick to point out that she was not satisfied with the sexual encounter either, asking Philip: "You think I want it known I shagged someone like you?" She is signalling Philip's reputation as "uncool," officious, and aligned with those against the reintegration of the (un)dead into communities. Philip, evidently offended, responds: "Good. Keep your mouth shut. People round here found out I slept with a rotter I'd be strung up." Here too, Amy's position as "rotter" and Philip's attraction to her draws on the framing of the taboo-based paradox associated with sex. Philip's explicit reference to potentially violent community retaliation against him also echoes the series' broader concerns with "othering" and the ways in which sexual relationships deemed to be transgressive have historically been—and continue to be—met with severe repercussions. Similarly, Philip's concerns about community retaliation demonstrate how Amy can be read as a "fatal female." Any sexual contact with her poses a threat.

The sex between Amy and Philip is clearly consensual, if not necessarily highly desirable for Amy. Not only is she not particularly attracted to Philip, but we later discover that Amy and the other (un)dead characters have not been able to "feel," raising questions about whether it has been possible for Amy to experience physical sexual pleasure. Later in the episode Amy experiences what might be interpreted as an incidence of gendered violence. Gary, a local member of the Human Volunteer Force who fought the dead in their rabid zombie state, arrives at Amy's house to paint "PDS" on it in red paint. He sees that she is not wearing cover-up mousse and before leaving, grabs her from the bed, drags her to her dresser and smudges the make-up over her face. He shouts "In this village, yer cover up yer rotter face! Got it!" The risk of sexual assault by an unknown man entering her house and bedroom without permission are likely to be in audiences' minds. Gary asks Amy: "You're not like other girls are you?" This, according to Moore (2016, 306) "might refer to her rejection of constructions of femininity that require women to perform and conform to standardized notions of beauty by applying make-up." In the first season of *In the Flesh,* Amy is positioned as sexually desirable (to Philip, and potentially to Gary) but also as monstrous—failing to conform to the community's expectations of the (un)dead and of women.

Shame is often apparent in the sexual encounters between the living and the (un)dead in this series. Season two features an undead brothel. Philip has been visiting the brothel and asking an (un)dead woman to dress up like Amy, opting for the full "girlfriend experience." The sex-worker takes off her make-up, which she has used to make her look living for the other customers, so that she can look like the *"au naturale"* Amy—this again marks out Philip's sexual desires as deviating from the norm. It emerges that a local woman has been filming those entering and leaving the brothel. The implication is that those who are caught will be doubly shamed, first for using a brothel, but also for using a brothel in which the sex-workers are (un)dead. As Seal and O'Neill (2012, 6) have explained, in the cultural history of prostitution the sex-worker often emerges as a "body-object symbolized by liminality, abjection, commodification and desire." In this series, the (un)dead state of the sex-workers concerned furthers the ways in which these marginal characters, who are all female, can be read in terms of liminality and abjection. Yet here an interesting character development occurs for Philip, who sacrifices his role as a respected member of the local community. As the Human Volunteer Force drag the sex-workers and customers out of the brothel and line them up along the wall outside to be photographed, Philip arrives and attempts to give a rousing a speech. Though received with ridicule, Philip's speech in season two, episode four of *In the Flesh* reveals his personal growth:

> I know how it feels to shout about bad things and bad people. It's nice. It's as if it's making you a purer person inside. But it's not real [. . .] you can only pretend for so long and then you're back stuck with yourself [. . .]. And all the things you're ashamed of. That you know you'll do again. What I'm trying to explain is that idea that you were ever a pure person just makes everything worse. It makes you so disappointing [. . .]. People aren't pure [. . .]. We're not good any more than they're evil or they're inhuman [. . .]. If we could accept our real selves and live with who we really are and love ourselves then maybe we could accept . . . and live with . . .

Philip goes to stand with the other customers lined up outside the brothel, demonstrating to the community that he too has been paying to engage in sexual activity with the (un)dead. Much of his speech is cliched, awkward and poorly articulated, in line with his characterization as a young man who has never quite fitted in. Yet he is also positioned here as reflective and open to change in a speech that echoes a series of ideas about purity, "othering" and us/them rhetoric related to miscegenation and sexuality, championing both self-acceptance and the acceptance of others.

Later in season two, episode four, Amy finds Philip alone. Impressed by his honesty at the brothel, she approaches him and jokes:

> terrible news about the full disclosure on your sex-life by the way. Not going down brilliantly with the townsfolk. Your reputation's in tatters. What with the necrophilia and fancying rotters [. . .] prepare yourself for some sort of lynching or social ostracism.

Amy's explicit reference to necrophilia is positioned as comedic because Amy and the sex-workers are evidently "alive" even if they are dead. The choice of the words "townsfolk," "lynching," and "social ostracism," are all indicative of the conservative, "old fashioned" views held by the community. The two go on to have a loving relationship and this development is indicative of why sex between the living and the (un)dead on television can be especially interesting, given "the seriality of TV lends itself to moral complexity" and "to a perceived sense of intimacy between audiences and TV characters as we watch their lives unfold on a daily or weekly basis" (Jowett and Abbott 2013, 202). Audiences see Philip shift from a conformist, self-righteous young man into a confident and accepting one who rebels against his community's views. As the second season comes to a close, Amy begins to rehumanize. Amy seems to reveal her own anxieties over whether Philip loves her, or whether he does have a specific sexual interest in the (un)dead, asking: "Are you still gonna like me? [. . .] Now I'm, uh, warming up?" Philip responds with: "Amy, I'd like you cold. I'd like you hot. I'd even like you tepid [. . .]. You're still you. Dead or alive." Amy's re-humanizing as a consequence of finding "true love" echoes a series of fairy-tale narratives where a young woman is "saved" by a man. As such it might be understood as equally as normative in terms of established power dynamics in sexual relationship as the depictions of (un)dead female sex-workers in the series. Yet the focus on the individual, on Philip's love for Amy because she is Amy and not because of a constructed category into which she fits, also echoes recent cultural discourses around the dissolution of categories of gender and biological sex and the ways in which these oppositions, not without critique and dissent from varying quarters, are being "challenged in social and cultural life" (Nicholas 2014, 1).

THE STRAIN

The Strain, an FX television series based on a trilogy of books by Guillermo del Toro and Chuck Hogan, presents a world as it enters "the end times." Within *The Strain*, sex is predominantly a non-issue for the (un)dead because the vampiric life of the series, known as the *strigoi*, experience the atrophication of their genitals during the transitory process, and gain what is known throughout the series as a "stinger," a long, fleshy proboscis which sits under the tongue, used to consume blood and infect others striking from the yonic opening formed in the *strigois'* throats. In this section, we draw on two story arcs across the series. The first is the transformation to *strigoi* of Gabriel Bolivar, a musician and presumed "sexual player" (season 1). The second is the kidnapping of programmer Dutch Velders by the *strigoi* Thomas Eichorst (season 2). In framing the place of the "stinger" by considering the narrative of Bolivar, we consider the way in which it is used as a form of assault by Eichorst.

The infected but not yet fully (un)dead, transitional Bolivar is pictured in his bathroom, where he proceeds to crush and snort medication for erectile dysfunction before returning to three women, in various states of undress, on his bed. The four parties caress one another before Bolivar takes one of them and places her on her back, standing between her parted legs. He becomes removed from the events taking place concentrating on the pulsing vein in the woman's neck before reaching down and biting her. As he is yet to transform into a *strigoi* his teeth break the skin, but this does not kill her. Audiences return to Bolivar's private bathroom in the next episode. Having just returned from a performance he stares at himself in the mirror, his eyes bloodshot red. As he removes his wig, we see his hair has almost entirely gone. As he begins to remove the grey/white makeup he is shocked to find that his skin is almost the same color. Seemingly unfazed by these changes, Bolivar walks over to the toilet and begins to urinate. We hear a loud splash as his testicles and penis fall from his body into the bowl of the toilet. Still seemingly unfazed, he flushes the toilet before turning around to the camera revealing a fleshy flat surface where his genitals had once been. Later in the episode a urologist visits his apartment in order to check up on his condition at the request of his personal doctor. Bolivar sits in the dark, his body twitching. We hear a loud thud as the urologist screams. Bolivar's fleshy proboscis has attached to her and is throbbing as Bolivar screams "mine" repeatedly and drags her across the floor.

Erectile dysfunction has been recognized across many sources as having a detrimental effect on an individual's sense of self (Potts, et al. 2006; Marshall and Katz 2002). As Foucault (1978, 103) attests, sexuality and acts of sex

> appears rather as an especially dense transfer point for relations of power . . . sexuality is not the most intractable element in power relations, but rather one of those endowed with the greatest instrumentality . . . capable of serving as a point of support, as a linchpin, for the most varied strategies.

Power, and the loss of phallic power, as such presents Bolivar with a crisis of identity in which what he has previously used as a marker of his power and competency is dwindling. Bolivar, even though positioned across the early series by his phallic power and sexual allure and competency, appears completely unphased at the loss of his penis—shrugging and flushing the toilet. In essence, it could be argued that Bolivar is in fact welcoming his transformation replacing the dysfunctional penis with the proboscis, the phallic like "stinger." Both, per se, offer the opportunity for a form of reproduction, with the "stinger" acting as a way to transfer the viscous white fluid containing small worms that act to transfer the vampirism from the host to the victim. Bolivar's lack of virility is replaced by the strength of the "stinger," demonstrated as being strong enough to be able to drag a human being. Sexual lust is replaced with blood lust.

Although, across some vampire television there are aspects of consensual blood consumption (cf. *Shadowhunters,* 2016–2019), Bolivar's actions against the urologist take place without consent. Blood, however, is used throughout vampire television and cinema for its tabooed, yet reproductive quality (Tenga and Zimmerman 2013). Foucault (1985, 125–27) notes that historically there was a contention that semen itself was just foaming blood, caused to foam by the vigors of sex. However, this developing relationship between blood and semen becomes particularly poignant when considering sex between the human and the (un)dead and the way in which blood is engaged with during "monstrous" intercourse. What remains consistent in Bolivar's sexual encounters regardless of whether he is alive or (un)dead is his treatment of women as sexual objects, as "his," there to entertain him and for his own gratification with no agency or their own. In this representation of sexual contact between the living and the (un)dead, the male is monstrous both (un)dead and alive, and for the women involved this can prove fatal.

In the latter part of season two, Dutch Velders, a female hacker, is being held hostage by one of the leading antagonists, *strigoi* Thomas Eichorst. Throughout the series Eichorst's sadistic character has been well-founded, primarily via his status as the Commandant of the Treblinka Concentration Camp. Eichorst, like Bolivar, is positioned as monstrous both alive and (un)dead. Eichorst, having chained up Dutch in a padded cell, enters the room drunk (achieved by force feeding alcohol to a host before drinking their blood) and proceeds to become enraged at Dutch, stating "you enjoy being looked at" and that her clothes and hair are "all very calculated." The implication here is that Dutch "uses" her sexuality as a weapon and enjoys having "power" over men through her sexually attractive appearance. Just like with Bolivar, Eichorst's genitals have atrophied and, with that, comes a lack of identity. As the plot is unwoven, it is revealed that Dutch reminds Eichorst of a Jewish woman he once dated, to which she mockingly asks if he became a Nazi because he couldn't get laid. As Scaptura and Boyle (2019) state, "when a man's gender identity is threatened, he is more likely to endorse traditional gender roles, overcompensating to appear more masculine."

As the episode progresses Eichorst's treatment of Dutch becomes more traumatic. Eichorst enters the room demanding that Dutch remove her pants, before screaming "now" in her face. The defensive Dutch, making explicit the threat of rape implied here, retorts "I know you lost your dick seventy years ago, so what're you gonna do?" She resentfully complies and Eichorst exclaims that it is a "night for trying new things" before grabbing Dutch's face and crudely applying red lipstick to her mouth as she struggles. The parallel here with *In the Flesh* is notable, as in both series a scene in which a male forces a female to wear make-up in a gendered act of violence emphasizes the ways in which women's visual appearance can be interpreted as both a threat to, and something to be controlled within, patriarchal hierarchies. Eichorst congratulates himself on his application of the lipstick before laying down on the ground and forcing Dutch to spread her legs and bend over. As she does, Eichorst licks his lips before his "stinger" emerges from his mouth and begins to strike across Dutch's inner thighs. Just before he begins to actively sexually assault Dutch with his "stinger," she reaches round and hits him in the eyes with a can of pepper spray. Bauman (1998) may regard this interaction with the "stinger" as being an example of a "sex-substitute," that is where sex is stripped of its reproductive purposes, to be defined around male pleasure. What is evident in these sexual encounters between the living, always female, and the (un)dead, always male, in *The Strain* is the ways in which male power is constructed as dependent on power over a woman. Eichorst, in particular, is positioned as both emasculated and threatened by Dutch and more broadly by women, whose emancipation over his extended life course troubles him. His attitudes toward Dutch can be understood in terms of the anxieties of Men's Rights Activists around shifting gender norms and standards of consent (Gotell and Dutton 2016). Though women including Dutch are positioned as powerful in *The Strain,* the threats and physical and sexual violence women are subject to from the "monstrous" living men in the extratextual world in which *The Strain* is situated remain consistent when the threat is from an (un)dead male within this text.

AMERICAN HORROR STORY

American Horror Story (*AHS*) is an anthology horror series developed by Ryan Murphy and Brad Falchuk, the first season of which premiered in 2011. In this section we consider *AHS: Coven*, the third season of the series. The series, set in contemporary New Orleans, explores the relationship between a group of witches in their search for their next leader, known as the Supreme. The series centers, at least initially, on the initiate to the coven Zoe Benson who discovers her abilities during her first penetrative sexual encounter, which is entirely consensual, sweet and even loving. The pair kiss gently and as he penetrates her, asking if she is okay. His nose begins to bleed. He violently falls back onto the bed, his body convulsing and begins to haemorrhage before dying. Benson is sent to the coven in an attempt to learn how to control her powers, where she forms a connection with a boy named Kyle Spencer who she meets while attending a fraternity house party with fellow witch Madison Montgomery. At the house party, Madison is raped. As the fraternity leave the party in a bus, Madison uses her powers to flip it, killing all of them bar one. Zoe visits the hospital in hope of seeing if Kyle was the one who lived. She finds Madison's rapist, comatose but alive in a small hospital ward. She closes the door of the room and proceeds to straddle and have sex with his lifeless body, intentionally killing him in the same way that her boyfriend had previously died.

Zoe, in these scenes, underpins the literality of the fatal female. Histories of female sexuality tend to associate women with both power as well as submission. Within *AHS: Coven* what we find is that sex is initially inverted and used as a tool for Zoe in order enact revenge against Madison's rapist. Across the *AHS* narrative women tend to be placed into positions of sexual dominance and empowerment. Relationships are formed between sex, power and revenge. As Henry (2013, 169) explains, "the rape-revenge genre has had a surge of popularity and prolificacy in the post-2000 period." Zoe and Madison's rape-revenge is enabled by their supernatural powers as witches, complicating Zoe's relationship to the power that has been both burden and opportunity for her. Zoe's first and loving sexual encounter is traumatic given her powers violently kill her partner during sex. In enacting rape-revenge on Madison's behalf, Zoe literally weaponizes her sexuality by raping and killing the unconscious attacker. Zoe is simultaneously victim (she has not asked for her destructive magical powers and cannot control them) and perpetrator (of sexual violence and murder). She is "fatal" and "monstrous." According to Broedel (2003, 183) witches have historically been constructed in certain texts as "the personification of deviant or "bad" female sexuality." Here, Zoe's use of deadly sex to enact rape-revenge seems to play explicitly into current cultural discourses around women who supposedly use sex and sexuality as a weapon, just as her magical powers being "triggered" by penetrative sex seem suggestive of long-established ideas about the dangers and risks of sexual activity for young women.

As a way of thanking Zoe for her support, Madison agrees to help Zoe bring Kyle back to life. They visit the morgue in an attempt to uncover his body and find that the bodies of the fraternity are all in separate pieces. Madison convinces Zoe that they should take various "boy parts" in order to craft Kyle into the "perfect boyfriend." Kyle returns and lives alongside the coven where Madison and him bond over the fact that they are both, in essence, returned from the dead, Madison having recently been brought back to life after having been murdered. Their bond grows stronger with Zoe walking in to find them having rough sex against a wardrobe. Later, in a confrontation between Madison and Zoe, they agree that the two of them would effectively share Kyle, sealing the agreement by engaging in a threesome. This is made possible by both Kyle and Madison effectively being undead, meaning that Zoe's power has no effect on them. As with Jones's (2013) writing on the film *Deadgirl*, the zombie, or (un)dead, becomes an object for sex. In *Deadgirl*, the rape of a female zombie by young men is portrayed as necrophilic and monstrous. Kyle, however, consents to the extent that his (un)dead self can. He has been "made" from "boy parts" by the two witches, rendering Kyle's body an object crafted and to be used for pleasure in a way that is suggestive of a "gender reversal," signalling the ways in which women's bodies have so often been constructed, altered, and decorated to adhere to socially and culturally specific sexual ideals.

Complicating matters further, the parts from which he has been made include those of the dead men deemed culpable in Madison's rape and as such can be understood in terms of ideas about reclamation, consent and revenge. As Weedon (1997, 120) argues, "the failure to understand the multiplicity of power relations focused in sexuality will render an analysis blind to the range of points of resistance inherent in the network of power relations, a blindness which impedes political resistance." Though in some ways *AHS: Coven* might be understood as normative and to perpetuate problematic depictions in its representation of a threesome including two stereotypically sexually attractive (slim, young, white) women as well as its portrayal of vengeful women "weaponizing" their sexuality, it might also be read as a subversive text that critiques and complicates ideas about women's agency, sexual desire, consent, and the ways in which female sexuality can simultaneously be experienced and depicted as a burden and as empowering. Zoe's (un)dead sexual partners become, in this context, a "safe space" in which Zoe might discover and experiment with her own sexuality without fear of fatal consequences. Given that *AHS: Coven* is set within an all-girls school, Miss Robichaux's Academy for Exceptional Young Ladies, the parallel being drawn with homosexual female encounters seems clear. The popular motif of young women in same sex contexts such as girls' schools or sororities engaging in sexual activity with each other, without fear of the repercussions of unwanted pregnancy or of male perpetrator rape, seems to be being signalled in Zoe's sexual activity with the (un)dead.

CONCLUSION

If television can operate as an imaginative space in which the unpicking of complex societal issues can occur within a frame of relative safety (Livingstone 1998; Penfold-Mounce 2018), the sexual encounters between the living and the (un)dead in the three series examined here suggest that it might be a space for negotiating both shifting and enduring ideas about gender and sexuality in popular culture more broadly. A commonality of distinctive power dynamics and social stigma prevail throughout each of the examples, where ideas about "fatal females" and "monstrous males" apply to both the living and the (un)dead, all positioned as capable of violence for different reasons. Despite the necrophilic underpinnings and the transgressive persuasion of the sexual encounters between the living and the (un)dead examined here, they are often portrayed in a highly normative manner; both in terms of gender and sexuality. The sexual encounters examined across this chapter take place almost exclusively between cis-gendered individuals and almost exclusively in the context of heterosexual sexual interaction. As Jowett (2005) has argued, television can open up possibilities for alternative sexualities whilst simultaneously continuing to present heterosexuality as the "norm." Although in some of the cases the sex discussed above is consensual in nature, it is still portrayed as being tabooed. This is not solely because one partner is (un)dead and therefore suggestive of transgression, necrophilia and miscegenation. Taboos around sex-work and ideas about the "weaponization" of women's sexuality and male violence and misogyny all feature heavily in these series in the sexual encounters between the living and the (un)dead. Arguably, these texts both reflect and serve as commentary on some of the key debates about gender and sexuality within the wider social context in which they operate.

BIBLIOGRAPHY

Bauman, Zygmunt. 1998. "On Postmodern Uses of Sex." *Theory, Culture & Society* 15 (3–4): 19–33.

Broedel, Hans Peter. 2003. *The Malleus Maleficarum and the Construction of Witchcraft.* Manchester: Manchester University Press.

Douglas, Mary. 1966/2002. *Purity and Danger: An analysis of Concepts of Pollution and Taboo.* London and New York: Routledge.

Foucault, Michel. 1978. *The History of Sexuality. Vol 1: An Introduction.* New York: Pantheon Books.

Foucault, Michel. 1985. *The History of Sexuality. Vol 2: Uses of Pleasure.* New York: Pantheon Books.

Gotell, Lise and Emily Dutton. 2016. "Sexual Violence in the 'Manosphere': Antifeminist Men's Rights Discourses on Rape." *International Journal for Crime, Justice and Social Democracy* 5 (2): 65-80.

Hartley, John. 2003. "Foreword: 'Reading' Television Studies." In *Reading Television*, edited by John Fiske and John Hartley, ix–xxii. London and New York: Routledge.

Henry, Claire. 2013. "Challenging the Boundaries of Cinema's Rape-revenge Genre in Katalin Varga and Twilight Portrait." *Studies in European Cinema* 10 (2-3): 133–45.

Jones, Stephen. 2013. "Gender Monstrosity: Deadgirl and the Sexual Politics of Zombie-Rape." *Feminist Media Studies* 13 (3): 525–39.

Jowett, Lorna. 2005. *Sex and the Slayer: A Gender Studies Primer for the Buffy Fan.* Middletown: Wesleyan University Press.

Kee, Chera. 2014. "Good Girls Don't Date Dead Boys: Toying with Miscegenation in Zombie Films." *Journal of Popular Film and Television* 42 (4): 176–85.

Levina, Marina and Diem-My T. Bui. 2013. "Introduction: Toward a Comprehensive Monster Theory in the 21st Century." In *Monster Culture in the 21st Century A Reader*, edited by Marina Levina and Diem-My T. Bui, 1–14. London: Bloomsbury.

Livingstone, Sonia. 1998. *Making Sense of Television: The Psychology of Audience Interpretation*, 2nd ed. London: Routledge.

Luckhurst, Roger. 2016. *Zombies: A Cultural History.* London: Reaktion Books.

Marshall, Barbara L. and Stephen Katz. 2002. "Forever Functional: Sexual Fitness and the Ageing Male Body." *Body & Society* 8 (4): 43–70.

Moore, Allison. 2016. "I Don't Take Orders from a Lad Wearing Make-up." *Critical Studies in Television: The International Journal of Television Studies* 11 (3): 299–314.

Nicholas, Lucy. 2014. *Queer Post-Gender Ethics. Genders and Sexualities in the Social Sciences.* London: Palgrave Macmillan.

Penfold-Mounce, Ruth, David Beer, Roger Burrows. 2011. "The Wire as Social Science—Fiction?" *Sociology* 45 (1): 152–67.

Penfold-Mounce, 2018. *Death, The Dead and Popular Culture*. Bingley: Emerald.

Potts, Annie, Victoria M. Grace, Tiina Vares, Nicola Gavey. 2006. "'Sex for Life'? Men's Counter-Stories on "Erectile Dysfunction," Male Sexuality, and Ageing." *Sociology of Health & Illness* 28 (3): 306–29.

Reed, Darren and Ruth Penfold-Mounce. 2015. "Zombies and the Sociological Imagination: *The Walking Dead* as Social-Science Fiction." In *The Zombie Renaissance in Popular Culture*, edited by Laura Hubner, Marcus Leaning, and Paul Manning, 124–38. London: Palgrave Macmillan.

Scaptura, Maria N. and Kaitlin M Boyle. 2019. "Masculinity Threat, 'Incel' Traits, and Violent Fantasies Among Heterosexual Men in the United States." *Feminist Criminology* 15 (3): 278–98.

Seal, Lizzie and Maggie O'Neill. 2012. *Transgressive Imaginations: Crime, Deviance and Culture*. London: Palgrave Macmillan.

Stoker, Bram. 2004 [1897] *Dracula*. London: Penguin.

Swartz-Levine, Jennifer A. 2016. "Staking Salvation: The Reclamation of the Monstrous Female in Dracula." *The Midwest Quarterly* 57 (4): 345–61.

Tenga, Angela and Elizabeth Zimmerman. 2013. Vampire Gentleman and Zombie Beasts: A Rendering of True Monstrosity. *Gothic Studies* 15 (1): 76–87.

Weedon, Chris. 1997. *Feminist Practice and Poststructuralist Theory*, 2nd edition. Oxford: Blackwell.

Part V

Reanimation without Sentience

There's no reasoning with a zombie.
The reanimated corpse of fiction, or the enslaved human of mythology,
they are single minded and relentless.
Better protect your braaaiiiinnnnzzzz . . .

Chapter Twelve

Behind the Door

Sukuma Mitunga *(Zombie) Narratives as Social Critique in Northwestern Tanzania*

Amy Nichols-Belo

Imagine an unexpected or premature death. The mourners, residents of Northwestern Tanzania, weep over the body of a young man, sobbing and touching the corpse. And yet there is no corpse; instead they grieve over the body of a dog or a log bewitched to resemble the deceased. More horrifyingly, the man is not dead at all, but is trapped behind the door (*nyuma ya mlango*[1]), unable to cry out that he is still alive. He is bewitched, his tongue made numb through magic or removal. In the days that follow the burial, he will become a kind of zombie laborer toiling in the shadows between life and death at the behest of a witch (*mchawi*). In the past, his labor-in-death would have involved hoeing or planting, but in contemporary Northwestern Tanzania, he is just as likely to be made into a *litunga* (pl. *mitunga*, "bound ones") because, as one interlocutor explained, of his skill "as a computer repairman, mechanic, engineer, or driver."[2] *Mitunga* stories portray individual witches profiting from illicit labor or describe a shadow reality that inverts many of the everyday experiences of life in Mwanza, Tanzania's second largest city, and its environs. While *msukule* (pl. *misukule*) is the Kiswahili term used across the nation, *litunga/mitunga* is the Kisukuma term most commonly used in Mwanza, which while now a multiethnic and increasingly cosmopolitan space, is still thought of as the capital of Sukumaland.[3]

In Tanzania, stories about not-dead, bewitched laborers (or what English speakers might gloss as zombies) circulate among a number of ethnic groups including the Ihanzu (Sanders 2003, 2008), Kaguru (Beidelman 1963), Fipa (Willis 1968), and Sukuma (Bessire 2000; Stroeken 2001, 2010; Rasmussen

2009; Tanner 1956), as well as in other multiethnic cities such as Dar es Salaam (Hasu 2009) and Iringa (Lindhardt 2009). While, these stories overlap, with other African (Comaroff and Comaroff 1999, 2002; Isichei 2002; Shaw 1997) and Haitian (Ackerman and Gauthier 1991; Davis 1988; Rath 2018; Simpson 1945) constructions of the undead, they differ in compelling ways. After a brief review of zombie narratives in Tanzania and elsewhere, I turn to the ways that Sukuma *mitunga* stories demonstrate pan-African ideas about the amorality of witchcraft and illicit consumption, while offering local critiques of everyday life in Tanzania and failures of the postcolonial state. I also call attention to the ways that gender, race, and hunger figure into these accounts. In making my argument, I analyze interviews, carried out in Mwanza between 2004 and 2010, with both people who knew of *mitunga* and those who believed that they had narrowly escaped zombification. [4]

ZOMBIE NARRATIVES IN OTHER CONTEXTS

Historians Luise White (2000) and Elizabeth Isichei (2002) encourage Africanists to treat rumors about witchcraft, vampires, and zombies as "symbols [that] reflect the real tragedies of lived experience" (Isichei 2002, 3) and as forms of "subjugated knowledge." Indeed, White's (2000) analysis of East African rumors vampires demonstrates a link between experiences of colonial extraction, labor migration, and stories about European collection and consumption of blood. I contend that zombie narratives are particularly good to think with and illustrate both global and local anxieties, whether they be the harbingers of infectious disease and the collapse of society in American popular culture or a reflection of inequalities in many sub-Saharan African contexts including Tanzania.

Isichei's (2002) broad-ranging analysis of the "poetics of rumor" and "poetics in memory" across sub-Saharan Africa and—via the transatlantic slave trade—in the New World demonstrates the importance of supernatural storytelling as a source for history. Because witchcraft and sorcery often feature spirits, sacrifice, and illicit accumulation, historians and anthropologists of the Atlantic World have compellingly argued that the trauma of the Middle Passage lives on in accounts of undead slaves (*zombi*) in Haiti (Ackerman and Gauthier 1991; Davis 1988; Simpson 1945) or in hypermodern witch cities in Sierra Leone (Shaw 1997). Rath (2018) questions the familiar argument that the figure of the Haitian *zombi* is the result of an imported West African concept made salient among the enslaved on Caribbean plantations. Instead, she argues that some of the earliest descriptions of *zombi* draw on European ideas of witchcraft as well as African origins. While Rath (2018) might agree that Haitian *zombi* narratives reflect the memory of enslavement, she argues that scholars' insistence on locating *zombi* antecedents in Africa minimizes European antecedents and reinforces stereotypes of "Africa as a 'place of sorcery and the occult' and Haiti as a 'place of cannibals and evil magic'" (2018, 394).

In Mwanza, Tanzania more generally, and in South and East Africa, zombie narratives reflect more recent colonial and postcolonial anxieties about labor, gender, race, and citizenship. While some East and Southern Africans were enslaved, including Sukuma who were trafficked in the Indian Ocean slave trade, the making of zombies is just one of the many ways that witchcraft serves as a "negation of life-giving material, sexual, and social exchange" (Comaroff and Comaroff 1999, 289). More simply, witches engage in violence that is rooted in both jealousy and greed. This logic may seem paradoxical: witches are understood to cause harm because they are jealous of kin and neighbors' relationships, personal successes, and financial achievements, yet witches are thought of as greedy individuals who use medicine (*dawa*) and power (*nguvu*) to facilitate amoral accumulation. Jealousy and greed run counter to the sociality and reciprocity considered ideal in many sub-Saharan African societies.[5]

Despite Ishichei's (2002, 94) assertion that zombie owners are male, most authors writing about Africa describe zombie-making witches as aberrant women. In post-Apartheid South Africa, for example, witches produce zombies instead of kin and hoard wealth rather than contributing:

> In place of fertile procreation, and the forms of wealth that benefit a wider community, the witch makes ghost workers out of the able-bodied. She thrives by cannibalizing others, robbing the rising generation of a legitimate income and the wherewithal to marry or to establish their own families indeed, of becoming fully adult. (Comaroff and Comaroff 1999, 289).

Similarly, Ihanzu witches "both reproduce and invert . . . images [of domesticity] by illicitly creating a zombie 'family' that ensures the ongoing [economic] production and reproduction of her household" (Sanders 2008, 187). Similarly, in Iringa, wealth-generating "witchcraft comes at a high price, such as the sacrifice of a human relative, who is either eaten by witches and their *majini* [Islamic spirits] or kept as a kind of zombie spirit (*msukule*) that can be put to work in fields or shops" (Lindhardt 2009, 42).

In Cameroon, African zombie-makers are viewed as entrepreneurs, participants in organized crime, or as *nouveaux riches* (Ciekawy and Geschiere 1998). Writing primarily about Nigeria, but rooting his analysis in examples from across the continent, McNally (2011, 186) suggests that zombie narratives traveled from Africa to Haiti to Hollywood before being reimagined as "fables of modernity" in contemporary African contexts. McNally is particularly committed to the idea that zombie-making witchcraft is relatively recent (within the last thirty years) and reflective of (global) capitalist exploitation.

While I am sympathetic to this perspective and the large body of anthropo-logical scholarship on modernity and the occult (e.g., Geschiere 1997; Meyer and Pels 2003; Moore and Sanders 2001; West and Sanders 2003) that in-forms it, in this piece I want to examine the ways that zombie stories in Northwestern Tanzania both reflect and respond to *local* anxieties. Of course, local anxieties are themselves products of "modern" contexts, but here I want to both acknowledge the longevity of zombie stories in the region and avoid reifying the trope of global modernity. Instead, I argue that Sukuma zombie stories offer an unintentional social critique of contemporary everyday life and the failings of *ujamaa*, Tanzania's unique form of African socialism that promoted development through self-reliance and collective labor. Despite the depiction of terrifying events, these narratives also describe otherworldly alternatives where women have more agency, Africans have more power than South Asian Tanzanians, and justice is meted efficiently and transpar-ently. This fairness, at times, inadvertently and nostalgically references the failed promises of *ujamaa*.

MAKING *MITUNGA* IN SUKUMALAND

While stories about *mitunga* are common today, Tanner (1956) references cases dating back to the early 1920s. In his account of the practices of Sukuma "sorcerers,"[6] Tanner describes the making of *mitunga* alongside the use of "magic medicines" that cause physical symptoms, "unseen blows," and "poltergeist pranks" (1956, 438–39). In contrast with contemporary ac-counts he views this magic as a form of resurrection whereby "the newly dead (*litunga*) are resurrected to work for the sorcerer [and] . . . retained in a vacuum until allowed to die by the release of the sorcerer's power over their spirits" (439). While he mentions loss of speech elsewhere, he does not attach it to zombification, writing instead that, "At night and at midday the sorcerer is said to call his victim by name, and if he answers, he is struck dumb" (438). Early accounts rarely specify the forms of labor carried out by *mitunga* but suggest the power of witches who are able to control them. For example, Bessire (2000) provides a third-hand account of an elderly Sukuma woman who refused to move to a government village during "villagization," an *ujamaa* planning project that included collectivized agriculture and deliv-ery of electrification, schools, and other amenities. While villagization was originally imagined as a choice, over-zealous government officials particu-larly in Northwest Tanzania, began forcibly removing and resettling resi-dents. According to the story, when officials were unsuccessful in burning down her house, they entered and found *mitunga* (described as "skeletal spirits hanging down"), concluded that she was a witch, and left her alone. While most of these earlier accounts do not specify forms of labor, I was told a story in 2007 that suggested that nonagricultural work was also "done" by *mitunga* in the 1970s or 1980s. The interlocutor, a woman who I estimated to be in her forties, told me of a girl she had known as a child whose grandmother had a tiny house that was full of a dozen *mitunga*, all working as tailors. The witch running this spectral sweatshop was getting rich off illicit labor, but was unable to display her wealth for fear of producing jealousy in her family and neighbors.

Contemporary accounts include several differences. First, *mitunga* seem to be more "undead" than "resurrected." Instead, as the opening anecdote and the ones below demonstrate, *mitunga* are humans transformed and bound to labor for their creators. Rasmussen describes a story shared by an interlocutor (a Bible school student) about a friend laid out for burial:

> The face was definitely the child he had played with, but the body looked much older and wrinkled and as if it had been dead for longer. The child's father came with an axe that had been treated by a healer. He split the body apart like wood with everyone watching. It turned into the core of a sisal tree. When the father did this, his son came out from behind the door inside the house [Rasmussen 2008, 130].

Second, while *mitunga* lose the power of speech and often their sense or wits (*akili*), they are not all trapped in the "vacuum" that Tanner (1957) describes, but sometimes return to the everyday world after losing their utility as laborers. These returned *mitunga* appear in a diminished state with unkempt hair, long fingernails, and soiled clothes. One of the Pentecostal ministers that Steve Rassmussen (2008) and I interviewed described the difficulty in attempting to minister to these individuals who seem to lack understanding (*fahamu*) and are bereft of speech. As I describe below, the returned are distinct from those who escaped zombification.

Finally, while *mitunga* might be made and kept by individuals, many recent narratives situate *mitunga* in either the hypermodern "witch-city" of Gumbush (or Gamboshi) imagined as having "tarmac roads . . . two storied houses, cars and many lights. . . . Just like Ulaya (Europe)" (quoted in Stroeken 2001, 285). In Stroeken's analysis, Gamboshi is "an invisible village where legendary dance leaders, witches and sorcerers reside and feast" (2001, 285), but also a real village located in Bariadi District, a marginal and rural area several hours from Mwanza. Rumors about its shadow identity as a hidden witch-city date to the 1950s (Stroeken 2001). Other sources suggest that these stories began to circulate in the 1980s (Rasmussen 2008). For example, a rural district cultural officer told me in 2007 that at least "20 years ago, there was a village like Gumbush in . . . [our district]. It was never proved, but people would say that early in the morning, they saw lots of buildings and motor cars." Magulu, a then-forty-six-year-old produce seller, told me about his own experience with Gamboshi. As a young man, he and a group of companions had "gotten lost" while visiting the area for a dance competition. On their journey home, he explained:

> I heard bird noises, cattle, and cars. . . . At 7:00 am, we had to stop traveling, because we saw lots of dead people hidden there. The dead people were either walking or hiding. . . .[Gumbush] was a village, not like a city because I couldn't see it. It was like a village, but you can see the witches. You can only see it if you are given medicine because they must want you to see it and then they keep you. You can hear [car] horns and see buses, but then they disappear.
>
>   . . . I stopped dancing in competitions [because of it]. If you don't have a sponsor to protect you, they [witches] will take you to use your talents there. My younger brother and I stopped dancing there because we didn't have an advocate in Gumbush. Lots of dead people are seen there. Party members from far away contribute *mitunga*. They have meetings and conferences where they contribute cows or children. They write "IOUs" that say things like, "next week, you can take my son."

Magulu's account ascribes the sounds of modernity—cars and buses in a part of Tanzania where vehicles are rare, especially at night—to Gumbush. It is also a place where "the talented" are taken by witches as contributions to "the party." While multiparty democracy has flourished in Tanzania in recent years, there has yet to be a president elected from any party but the Chama Cha Mapinduzi (CCM), the ruling party since independence. Magulu describes both the sacrifice of kin and the indebtedness of witches who are required to make contributions to the party, perhaps in exchange for power.

While Gamboshi has a particular rural and peripheral location, the notion of "Gumbush," an invisible realm that can rarely be glimpsed by non-witches, is an essential feature of *mitunga* narratives. I was told that each district seemed to have a central place where witches meet, study, and employ their zombie laborers. Dr. Pascal, a traditional healer, described Gumbush as "like a college for big witches to put their zombies. At the college, [*mitunga*] . . . learn different techniques. After finishing their studies, they stay there." Moreover, he explained that in Gumbush, "the industries are making zombies and learning the science of witchcraft." Like Shaw's (1997) informants' descriptions of a witch-city in Sierra Leone, Gumbush marks a remarkable disjuncture from the reality of village (and even urban) life. At the time of these interviews, Mwanza, Tanzania's second largest city had only one traffic light and few paved roads. Despite its depiction as a terrifying place where witches engage in sacrifice, descriptions of Gumbush are usually presented with a mix of humor and aspirational ideas about the Global North and Tanzania's potential for "development." As Esther's story (described below) illustrates, in Gumbush, citizens may even achieve *maendeleo* (development), an elusive concept that Tanzanians often describe as something that can be acquired like a commodity (Sanders 2003; Snyder 2005).

Ironically, however, the very "existence" of Gumbush is thought to suppress development. Speaking of his home village, Magulu, the Mwanza-based sweet potato seller, said, "Life is really bad there. They still can't make *maendeleo* there because [Gumbush]" is located nearby. The existence of a parallel world with its successful economy and political structure may in effect trap Tanzanians behind the door to fair participation in the larger economy.

ZOMBIES OUT OF PLACE

Whether dead, disappeared, or returned without speech, *mitunga* are unable to describe their experiences as illicit laborers.[7] Below, I share stories about several individuals who narrowly escaped zombification. While often told in the conspiratorial tone of a good story, these narratives and similar accounts were presented as truthful.

I first learned of Esther, a then thirty-three-year-old teacher, from her uncle, a lively and energetic storyteller. In our 2007 interview, Esther's uncle described her escape from a zombie village and subsequent rescue by a teacher who found her wandering in Sengerema Town. I subsequently interviewed Esther many times over the following months about these and other experiences relating to bewitchment and a long and incurable illness marked by treatments by biomedical practitioners, traditional healers, and Pentecostal preachers. During this period of suffering, Esther was kidnapped by a male cousin who took her to Sengerema District (several hours away by ferry and bus) to be treated by a traditional healer (*mganga*). Esther believed that the healer was actually a witch and that her cousin, a fisherman, had traded her for magic that would increase his yield.

After several failed attempts, Esther escaped from the healer's compound and found herself traveling at night and on foot through unfamiliar countryside. After some time, Esther arrived in a village that was occupied by *mitunga* and powerful witches. Esther explained:

> And there in the bush, I saw some people who were different. They couldn't communicate. Some could speak, but their tongues were stuck inside their mouths so they couldn't speak well. . . . It was a town . . . where people had been finished, taken, been bewitched. Their bodies were looking like those of humans, but defective in their minds. . . . They don't remember home and how to do things.

The village where they lived resembled many villages in that part of north-western Tanzania. The *mitunga* lived in houses and kept trying to bring her to a healer for "treatment," which Esther believed would transform her into a *litunga*. After an attack by a vicious animal, she continued to wander the countryside where she came across other people who could not speak. She arrived at a different village that had houses, shops, cars, motorcycles, and farms, but was similarly populated by witches and their *mitunga*. In this village, she learned that if she wanted a car—a rare luxury for most Tanzanians—"you have to work like the rest of them. There are farms and you can work it, or you can get people to do work for you." The residents of the village told her, "If you come here, you can never leave. If you have a car or a house [here], you can't return again [to the place that you came from]." The residents of this village took her to the *balozi* (ten-cell leader) for registration:

> [The *balozi*] started asking me questions. They asked my name to register it, but I lied about my name. I lied about the name of my father and the name of my mother. I lied about all three names. . . . And the *balozi* asked me "Where do you come from?" I didn't tell the whole truth, because if I told the truth, I knew they would arrest me. So I told them some lies.

The *balozi* informed her that she couldn't leave and told her, "We have already registered you. You should marry, you should get a fiancé here, and give birth here." Esther was despondent. "After hearing that, I began crying and thinking about my children, my husband. I cried, 'Mama, I'll come back. Mama, I'll see you again. Eh! Mama, I am suffering so much.'" When she awoke, she wondered if there was any way out. She thought, "[my new *litunga*-husband and] I can find ourselves a farm or they could give us one at the village because we are starting life at the village. Or you can go to do labor for someone, in order to get money and development."

Esther discovered that her clothes had been buried in the ground. She believed that this was a form of symbolic burial that effectively trapped her in that place. Suffering from a headache, she went to a small shop owned by a powerful witch where she was sold medicine that resembled Hedex, a commercial headache remedy widely available in Tanzanian pharmacies. While she was there, she overheard people talking about how they wanted to replace one of the rice paddy farmers with her. The ineffective worker was either of European (*Mzungu*) or of Indian descent (*Mhindi*) and didn't "know how to prepare the farm or to plant rice . . . [and was] messing things up."

Trapped in this bizarre place for several days, Esther was forced to eat under-seasoned food served and eaten in a strange manner. The *mitunga* "living" in that place ate their *ugali* (stiff porridge) with their palms facing downwards like shovels. *Ugali* is usually pressed into a ball, held in the fingers, and used as a "spoon" for stew or sauce, but as many people told me, *mitunga* eat their *ugali* using the tops of their hands like "shovels." She felt like she had lost her wits and became convinced that she had to consume a mixture of ashes and urine. She finished the story:

> After drinking the ashes and urine, my tongue stopped coming out. I was fine, Ah! So ashes are like a medicine helping me. I decided to leave. I went to the road and saw lots of big tractors and big motorcycles. Amazing! . . . If you wanted to cross the bridge, you could see terrifying insects that will swarm you or lots of tanks (*vifaru*, literally rhinoceroses). So I decided to cross to the other side to a village by Karebezo.

While presented as a true and terrifying experience, Esther's zombie village both mirrors and inverts everyday life. A headache is treated with a commercial remedy, and a bureaucrat registers newcomers. Esther's account describes an alternate universe where people are unable to speak, eat properly, or wear normal clothes, but engage in relatively normal activities. If anything, the village that Esther describes represents an idealized rural setting where people work in order to get "money and development" and where she and her *litunga*-husband would be given a plot of land and a car simply for agreeing to participate in the village economy. Importantly, this dream is rarely realized in contemporary capitalist Tanzanian life where unemployment is high and social and economic development needs remain unmet. Indeed, in their depiction of diverse forms of labor including farming, tailoring, and specialized technical fields, Gumbush is perhaps the only place in Tanzania with full employment. It recalls the promises of ujamaa villagization with effective provision of work, land, and in some narratives, technology and education. Esther's experience also references the often-frustrating layers of Tanzania's bureaucracy that citizens have negotiated since the nation's socialist inception. In order to get her plot, she must sign registration books and deal with party bureaucrats. At the same time, as someone who is out of place, she is able to escape the village relatively unscathed.

A similar story was told to me in 2007 by Edgar, a man in his sixties who lived in Buswelu, a peri-urban village about 15 km from Mwanza. According to Edgar, a teenage boy had returned from Gumbush about six years prior and two years after his burial. He had grown a bit and his skin had become lighter,[8] but was otherwise unchanged. The boy reported that he had been allowed to leave Gumbush, because he had been wrongly taken there. The person who had brought him there was not a relative and according to the Gumbush administrator (*mtawala*), the youth hadn't done anything to deserve banishment to Gumbush. Rasmussen (2008) describes a similar story told to him by a woman who was kidnapped by a classmate's parents when she was a child and nearly taken to Gamboshi. The parents placed medicine on her forehead that made her invisible and gave her domestic work to do. Then:

Her family came looking for her. The village was alerted. They hid her under the bed. Her family came into the hut looking for her. They could not see her. She could not speak to them or move to touch them. Later, her uncle who was a pastor prayed. Then a neighbor saw her pounding grain. This was reported to her family who came looking for her. They again did not find her and left because a rainstorm was coming. Those who were keeping her told her that their daughter was supposed to have taken her to Gamboshi, but since the daughter had delayed, she would have to leave. They put her out in the road in the middle of the night. She found her way home and lay down in the kitchen. When her uncle found her, she could not speak. So he beat her. . . . Then she was better [2008, 132].

In both of these stories, youth are allowed to leave because they, like Esther, are out of place, and don't belong in Gumbush. This suggests both a peculiar code of ethics for sacrifice and in the boy's case, a critique of Tanzania's notoriously inefficient bureaucracy, since it took two years for local government to discover the error in placing the youth in Gumbush. Contemporary stories about *mitunga* thus reference both an idealized social-ist postcolonial nation that provides land, employment, and opportunities for development and contemporary inefficiencies and bureaucracy. *Mitunga* and Gumbush stories also offer subtle critiques of other social issues including gender and racial inequalities and food insecurity.

It is worth noting that in *mitunga* narratives, witches are usually women and laborers are usually men. Witches behave in illicit, consumptive ways and serve as producers, landowners, and controllers of capital. In the every-day world, however, men continue to maintain control over most land and capital despite decades of land tenure reform meant to mitigate gender in-equality. In the shadow world of Gumbush, women have power, and, indeed, even a potential zombie recruit like Esther is able to exercise agency in marriage and labor that belie the everyday experiences of many women. Hasu (2009) describes zombie (*misukule*) testimonials given by young wom-en at Dar es Salaam's Glory of Christ Tanzania Church.[9] While testimonials of sin, traditional healing, and spirit possession are a regular feature of Pente-costal services in Tanzania (and Africa more broadly), claiming "deliverance from being a zombie" is quite unusual and, indeed, their stories look quite different from the *mitunga* narratives that I'm familiar with. While Hasu focuses largely on the content of their testimonials and deliverance, we could also look at these accounts as a form of female empowerment whereby young women gain religious and social capital through public testimony.

Stories about zombies also make visible Afro-Tanzanian frustrations about race and inequality. In Mwanza, shopkeepers are predominantly of Indian descent (*Wahindi*). These shopkeepers often sit in the back of shops and bark orders at their hardworking African clerks, criticizing them for their "inefficiency" or "unintelligence." Most industries in Mwanza are also run by ethnically Indian Tanzanians or expatriate Whites working with Afro-Tanzanian partners. In Esther's zombie village, by contrast, she hears of an ineffective laborer who is either White or Indian, who needs to be replaced by an Afro-Tanzanian who knows how to plant rice properly. In all of the stories that I collected about zombies in Sukumaland, people assured me that zombies could be men, women, or children, Black, White, or Indian, but that witches were African. As in the gendered inversion of land tenure, Gumbush also inverts racial hierarchies as powerful witches, who are always of African descent, run shops and delegate labor. At the same time, zombies returned home after being rejected by witches or because they don't belong are often described as having "white skin"—where whiteness signifies not wealth and power, but the pitiable existence of one who is returned in diminished form. Zombie stories reference racial stereotypes in other key ways. Edward, a driver who had worked in an expatriate mining camp, told me that he had been offered 20 million Tanzanian shillings (about $20,000 at the time) by a white man to acquire the fat of a zombie (*mafuta ya mitunga*).[10] The white man, Edward said, regularly sold the zombie fat for a profit in Uganda. Edward's offer symbolizes the reality of unequal relationships between Whites and Africans. During the period of that interview, the gold and copper mining industries were dominated by European, North American, South African, and Australian corporations. The influx of White laborers and investment in the first decade of the twenty-first century had increased demand for Tanzanians as sexual, domestic, or otherwise laboring bodies.

Hunger is also an important theme in Tanzanian zombie narratives with Rasmussen's informants describing returned *mitunga* collapsing from starvation. The church testimonials that Hasu (2009) often included claims of consumption of human flesh during the period of zombification. Even Esther's description of poorly seasoned *ugali* and the repeated claim that *mitunga* are unable to eat *ugali* properly suggest a preoccupation with food, both as a form of sociality and as an increasingly hard thing to come by. Famine is a feature of rural Tanzanian life (Phillips 2018) and in urban areas, food costs have risen dramatically in the twenty-first century. Phillips (2018) writes of "subsistence citizenship . . . a particular relationship between smallholder farmers and the twenty-first century state that is both constituted and constrained by the project of meeting basic needs" (4). Like the other tangibles that constitute development, food, in Tanzania, is intimately connected with the state. The preoccupation of what zombies consume offers yet another form of state critique.

CONCLUSION

Like White (2000) and Isichei (2002), I have chosen to treat rumor and fantastical stories of witchcraft, Gumbush, kidnapping, and persons returned from the dead as narratives worthy of analysis. I have described the ways that *mitunga* stories differ from depictions of zombies elsewhere in Tanzania and Africa, while making clear that witchcraft in the region is rooted in both greed and jealousy. I have described how *mitunga* stories have long been about illicit gains, but also offer a local critique of inequalities and inefficiencies. In particular, I have analyzed Gumbush, in its many forms, as more than just emblematic of modernity and development, but as a mythical realization of the dreams of *ujamaa* and promises of villagization. While terrifying, Gumbush, as experienced by Esther and others, offers education, employment, and the ability to access land, resources, and even development. Moreover, despite its reputation, Esther and others' escapes prove that Gumbush has a certain fairness, not always found in everyday life. In particular, I have argued that Gumbush mirrors many aspects of Tanzanian everyday life, while inverting particular experiences of gender and race. Indeed, Gumbush is a place where women have power and ownership of capital and Afro-Tanzanians compel the labor of Indian and Tanzanian *mitunga*.

NOTES

1. With the exception of the Kisukuma word litunga (pl. *mitunga*) and the Haitian word zombi, all other italicized words are Kiswahili.

2. All interviews were carried out by me with the assistance of Steven Bugumba between September 2006 and September 2007 or in June–July of 2010. All interlocutors are referred to by pseudonyms.

3. Sukumaland is a nonpolitical designation, but instead refers to the geographic area historically occupied by the Sukuma. At 13 percent of the population (University of Pennsylvania African Studies Center n.d.), the Sukuma are the nation's most populous ethnic group but have not been considered to be politically powerful.

4. I first visited Mwanza in 2001 as a master's student and subsequently carried out fieldwork on witchcraft beliefs and anti-witchcraft practices during the summer of 2004, September of 2006–September of 2007, summer of 2010, and summer 2015. More recently, I have traveled to Mwanza with Mercer University students.

5. *Sukuma Law and Custom*, a colonial guide to Sukuma customary law, describes only two crimes punishable by death, witchcraft and theft. Both are profoundly asocial crimes and rooted in greed. Interestingly, however, murder could be adjudicated through payment of a fine (Cory 1953).

6. Witches would be the current translation.

7. The returned *misukule* described by Hasu (2009) seem not to lack speech; perhaps *misukule* do not lose speech when zombified.

8. Edgar said his skin color was similar to my tanned, white skin.

9. Hasu describes Glory's pastor (Pastor Gwajima, a Sukuma resettled in Dar) as a self-proclaimed expert in raising the dead who claimed in 2008 to have "brought back at least 150 people from *msukule*).

10. This comment presaged Northwestern Tanzania's "epidemic" of occult murders of persons with albinism, whose body parts were thought to have magical properties (Bryceson 2010; Brocco 2016; Nichols-Belo 2018).

BIBLIOGRAPHY

Ackermann, Hans-W. and Jeanine Gauthier. 1991. "The Ways and Nature of the Zombi." *The Journal of American Folklore* 104(414): 466–49.

Beidelman, T.O. 1963. "Witchcraft in Ukaguru" In *Witchcraft and Sorcery in East Africa*, edited by John Middleton and E. H. Winter. 58–98. London: Routledge.

Bessire, Aimee Holloway Conlin. 2000. "Negotiating Cultural icons: Sukuma Art, History and Colonial Encounter in Tanzania." PhD diss., Harvard University.

Brocco, Giorgio. 2016. "Albinism, Stigma, Subjectivity and Global-local Discourses in Tanzania. *Anthropology and Medicine* 23(3): 229–43.

Bryceson, Deborah Fahy, Jesper Bosse Jønsson, and Richard Sherrington. 2010. "Miner's Magic: Artisanal Mining, the Albino Fetish and Murder in Tanzania. *Journal of Modern African Studies* 48(3): 353–82.

Ciekawy, Diane, and Peter Geschiere. 1998. "Containing Witchcraft: Conflicting Scenarios in Postcolonial Africa." *African Studies Review* 41(3): 1–14.

Comaroff, Jean and John L. Comaroff. 1999. "Occult Economies and the Violence of Abstraction: Notes from the South African Postcolony." *American Ethnologist* 26(2): 279–303.

Comaroff, Jean and John L. Comaroff. 2002. "Alien-Nation: Zombies, Immigrants, and Millennial Capitalism." *South Atlantic Quarterly* 101(4): 779–805.

Cory, Hans. 1953. *Sukuma Law and Custom*. Oxford: Oxford University Press for the International African Institute.

Davis, Wade. 1988. *Passage of Darkness: The Ethnobiology of the Haitian Zombie*. Chapel Hill: University of North Carolina Press.

Geschiere, Peter. 1997. *The Modernity of Witchcraft: Politics and the Occult in Africa*. Charlottesville: University Press of Virginia.

Hasu, Päivi. 2009. "The Witch, the Zombie and the Power of Jesus: A Trinity of Spiritual Warfare in Tanzanian Pentecostalism." *Suomen Antropologi—Journal of the Finnish Anthropological Society* 34(1): 70–83.

Isichei, Elizabeth. 2002. *Voices of the Poor in Africa*. Rochester, NY: University of Rochester Press.

Lindhardt, Martin. 2009. "The Ambivalence of Power: Charismatic Christianity and Occult Forces in Urban Tanzania." *Nordic Journal of Religion and Society* 22(1): 37–54.

McNally, David. 2011. *Monsters of the Market: Zombies, Vampires and Global Capitalism.* Leiden: Brill.

Meyer, Birgit, and Peter Pels, eds. 2003. *Magic and Modernity: Interfaces of Revelation and Concealment*. Stanford: Stanford University Press.

Moore, Henrietta L., and Todd Sanders, eds. 2001. *Magical Interpretations, Material Realities: Modernity, Witchcraft, and the Occult in Postcolonial Africa*. New York: Routledge.

Nichols-Belo, Amy. 2018. "'Witchdoctors in White Coats': Politics and Healing Knowledge in Tanzania." *Medical Anthropology* 37(8): 722–36.

Phillips, Kristin D. 2018. *An Ethnography of Hunger: Politics, Subsistence, and the Unpredictable Grace of the Sun*. Bloomington: Indiana University Press.

Rasmussen, Steven Dale Horsager. 2008. "Illness and Death Experiences in Northwestern Tanzania: An Investigation of Discourses, Practices, Beliefs, and Social Outcomes, Especially Related to Witchcraft, used in a Critical Contextualization and Education Process with Pentecostal Ministers." PhD diss., Trinity International University.

Rath, Gudrun. 2018 "Zombi Narratives: Transatlantic Circulations." In *Reshaping (G)local Dynamics of the Caribbean: Relaciones y Deconexiones—Relations et Déconnexions—Relations and Disconnections*, edited by Anja Bandau, Anne Brüske, and Natascha Ueckmann, 385–96. Heidelberg, Germany: Heidelberg University Publishing.

Sanders, Todd. 2003. "Invisible Hands and Visible goods: Revealed and Concealed Economies in Millennial Tanzania." In *Transparency and Conspiracy: Ethnographies of Suspicion in the New World Order*, edited by Harry G. West and Todd Sanders, 148–74. Durham, N.C.: Duke University Press.

Sanders, Todd. 2008. *Beyond Bodies: Rainmaking and Sense Making in Tanzania*. Toronto: University of Toronto Press.

Shaw, Rosalind. 1997. "The Production of Witchcraft/witchcraft as Production: Memory, Modernity and the Slave Trade in Sierra Leone." *American Ethnologist* 24(4): 856–76

Simpson, George E. 1945. "The Belief System of Haitian Voudoun." *American Anthropologist* 47(1): 37–59.

Snyder, Katherine A. 2005. *The Iraqw of Tanzania: Negotiating Rural Development*. New York: Westview Press.

Stroeken, Koen. 2001. "Defying the Gaze: Exodelics for the Bewitched in Sukumaland and Beyond." *Dialectical Anthropology* 26(3–4): 285–309.

Stroeken, Koen. 2010. *Moral Power: The Magic of Witchcraft*. New York: Berghan Books.

Tanner, R. E. S. 1956. "The Sorcerer in Northern Sukumaland, Tanganyika" *Southwestern Journal of Anthropology* 12 (4): 437–43.

West, Harry G., and Todd Sanders, eds. 2003 *Transparency and Conspiracy: Ethnographies of Suspicion in the New World Order*. Durham: Duke University.

White, Luise. 2000. *Speaking with Vampires: Rumor and History in Colonial Africa*. Berkeley: University of California Press.

Willis, R. G. 1968. "Kamcape: An Anti-sorcery Movement in South-west Tanzania." *Africa* 38(1): 1–15.

Chapter Thirteen

Does Death Destroy the Binary?

A Look at Gender Roles during Human/Zombie Interaction in the World War Z *Universe*

Rebecca Gibson and James M. VanderVeen

INTRODUCTION

Max Brooks's novel *World War Z: An Oral History of the Zombie War* (2006) and the subsequent graphic novel *The Zombie Survival Guide: Recorded Attacks* (Brooks 2009) are arguably some of the most detailed and extensive formulations of the zombie mythos. *Recorded Attacks* (2009) details historical zombie outbreaks and shows how individuals dealt with them as they occurred. *World War Z* (2006) is a collection of oral interviews with forty-four survivors of the zombie apocalypse, from the initial outbreak in China to the final days of victory where international teams work in the spring thaws to beat back the last zombie stragglers. The world has weathered the storm, but has the gender binary survived in the roles people assume? Or has the struggle to defeat the undead, preserve humanity, and recreate a living human civilization resulted in an "all hands on deck" lack of defined roles or role reversal?

In this chapter, we will explore the cultural ideas about gender roles and the way they change as the living inhabitants of the world learn of, react to, and fight against the undead. We will look at all aspects of male/female interactions, both human and zombie, and discern if the zombies are seen as gendered by the human protagonists and how that affects their efforts to eradicate the threat. Some questions we will ask include: Are parents inclined to protect their children, even after zombification, and is this filtered through the lens of gender? Do the undead follow any norms of society or are they now free from all societal rules? Are zombies immune from being seen as sexual beings, due to their undead state, or do human survivors retain feelings and desires for former companions? Furthermore, does the act of killing zombies have a sexual or gendered component, and does that affect either the reluctance or the desire to see them dead?

The stories are global, but the majority of action is centered in the West (North America and Europe). As such, we will examine the "traditional" gender roles of those cultures as compared to the beliefs and actions of those who survive the zombie apocalypse. Perhaps zombies are not human enough to have gender as it is normally perceived. In the books, there is little to no presence of living genderqueer or nonbinary people. It speaks to the power of culture (or at least the view of an author writing from within that culture) that, at least on the surface, the representation of women as domestically oriented caretakers and men as providers/protectors remains relatively unchanged even while all other aspects of daily life are drastically altered. Some of the most striking images in the books are those of people behaving in unexpected ways with regards to established cultural rules. Our goal is to describe the depiction of gender in the aftermath of a crisis.

ZOMBIES AND SURVIVORS: A NEW BINARY?

The organization of *World War Z* (Brooks 2006) focuses on individual survivor narratives, which form a coherent plot—from the onset of the zombie outbreak, to the relative peace of the aftermath, when the survivor's efforts are turned to cleaning up and rebuilding. It is a compilation of voices from mostly men and a few women who the fictive author interviewed at various points in the war. There are six named female survivors, although we will only be looking at four. Each survivor will be paired with a theme common among the narratives, for the purpose of analysis. However, before commencing that analysis, we will take a look at various ideas about gender and society that will serve as a scaffold for our understanding of how the metanarratives of zombies and war changed those ideas.

It is widely acknowledged in the American theoretical and scholarly musings about gender, and has been for a considerable time, that gender is on a spectrum—a cline—with no distinct binary divisions and with multiple categories into which one can identify or not, as one chooses (Rubin 1984; West & Zimmerman 1987). These multiplicities include not merely the traditional (to the West) male and female, but also bigender, agender, and various gender expressions such as butch, femme, masculine, and many others. Many people, and many authors, still conflate gender with sex, seeing two (and often only two) distinct categories—male and female, rooted in outward physical gender expression. In *World War Z* (Brooks 2006), this binary is strictly upheld, with no mention of genders other than male and female, and only one positive instance of homosexuality (though many gendered insults, which we will return to later in this chapter). Yet the book does offer up a third category for our contemplation, a category that disrupts this preconceived binary: the undead.

In much of the Western world, the state of death can also be seen as a binary: one is, or one is not. This is not a universal distinction, with various cultures around the world recognizing liminal periods which last for periods of time ranging from moments (see any "near death" experience), to years, in the case of the people of South Sulawesi, in Indonesia (Doughty 2017). After these periods, though, the state of death is absolute—the transition is completed, and the living person has become the dead person. This is a one-way journey, with no return ticket; the dead remain dead.

Death does not wipe out previous distinctions, either—a dead body is human, a dead body is female or male (or other gender categories), a dead body has the race that was socially recognized in life, a dead body retains its connections to the living through ancestry relations and the family's memory. However, death is not undeath. When a zombie occurs, as a result of the "Solanum virus" (Brooks 2003), it becomes a third category that only partially retains the previous distinctions—the undead. These undead are distinct from so-called "spiritual" zombi(e)s, those of Haitian voudou (Charlier 2014), where the zombified subject is still alive. Solanum zombies are physically dead, decaying at a slowed rate, and retain very little humanity, lacking the ability to comprehend or follow orders, procreate, or eat anything but various kinds of flesh. Their singular purpose is to feed. Known as zombies, Zs, Zack, ghouls, Gs, the walking plague, or "it," zombies are both humanized and dehumanized, gendered and nongendered, "us and not us" (Webb and Byrnand 2017), and yet they occupy their own unique category as well, a category that the mind struggles to acknowledge. Zombies break the binaries.

One commonality in the discussion of binaries and why we cling to them, though they are often false, is that humans find defined oppositions comforting, and the space between those oppositions to be disquieting (Levi-Strauss 1964). We wish to know what something is, and one way to that knowledge is to define it in opposition to something else. Zombies, like other fictionalized monsters, thrive in the space between categories. They are not alive but possess some of the traits of the living. They are no longer "us," but we can still identify them as once members of our species and our families. Thus, in the new order of the world in *World War Z* (Brooks 2006), the opposition manifests quite literally, with the survivors against the zombies.

SURVIVORS AND TROPES: THE WOMEN OF WORLD WAR Z

The gender binary is firmly reified in *World War Z* (Brooks 2006) and *Recorded Attacks* (Brooks 2009), and the voices heard therein are over-whelmingly male. As a result, two clear analytical categories were formed upon a close reading of the text: the experiences of the female survivors and the ways in which gender is used in either stereotypical or non-stereotypical ways. In recognition of that, each of the four female survivors (and one unfortunate victim) chosen for analysis will be paired with the analytic category that is most similar to their own personal story.

Survivor: Barati Palshigar
Location: Ulithi Atoll, Federated States of Micronesia
Trope: Zombies as Agender

One question we asked in the introduction to this chapter was whether zombies in *World War Z* (Brooks 2006) retain gender. The evidence for and against depends on which character in the text is speaking at the time, and their own ideas, prejudices, and goals. A commonly discussed motif is that of the posthuman; the human beyond human, the cyborg, the changed human (Haraway 1990; Vint 2017). We all, to a degree, may be posthuman. We all rely on enhancements, technology, modern conveniences, to exist in our world. None of us are exclusively human, particularly in the postcolonial developed world (Shaw 2018). Yet, we are arguably also not the undead. Social and/or medical gender transitioning is becoming more normalized and accepted in the United States and the world, as is the concept of being without gender, or waiting until gender is self-identified before assigning a gender and/or sex markers to legal identification (Wells 2018; Ziedler 2017). Yet even in death (Doughty 2014), even in spiritual zombification (Charlier 2015), the person does not lose gender, something often seen as integral to identity (Probyn 1993).

As previously mentioned, however, physical zombies are their own category. For the most part, in *World War Z* (Brooks 2006), they form a collective identity. They are spoken of as a group, with individuals referred to only on a momentary basis—the one being shot, the one doing the attacking, the one who reanimated. When identified in such a way, most zombies are not given verbal gender markers, and are instead, dehumanized. On various pages, a zombie is referred to as "it" (Brooks 2006, 20 and 102) and "the thing" (20). They are referenced as "ghouls" (Brooks 2006, 90), as "G" or "Z" (96). Yet one character argues that this practice has beneficial outcomes for the survivors.

Survivor Barati Palshigar, a translator who served aboard the UNS Ural where Radio Free Earth was broadcast, argues for dehumanizing the zombies. As a translator she participated in putting out correct information about the capabilities of the zombies, stating "People wanted so badly to anthropo-morphize the walking blight. . . .There were so many misconceptions: zom-bies were somehow intelligent; they could feel and adapt . . . carried memo-ries of their former existence . . . communicated with and trained. . . . It was heartbreaking having to debunk one misguided myth after another" (Brooks 2006, 196–97). In this, she is accurate: as zombies have ravenous hunger, a drive to continue to feed no matter the obstacle, and very little else in terms of humanity, the instinct to anthropomorphize them becomes a short-sighted one, if the character wishes to survive the War. Yet what happens when that instinct is insurmountable? What occurs when survivors identify too much with the undead, or when the undead are intimately familiar?

Survivor: Sharon
Location: Topeka, Kansas, USA
Trope: Zombies as Gendered

Patient zero, the oldest identified case of Solanum infestation in *World War Z* and the hypothesized originator of the outbreak, is male, while the first examined patient is female—one of his relatives. The relative became in-fected when tending to the young boy, who then bit her. Her nonrecognition of the severity of the situation led her to take care of him, even though "he'd rubbed off the skin around his bonds [yet] there was no blood. . . . The boy's skin was cold and gray. . . . I could find neither his heartbeat nor his pulse" (Brooks 2006, 7). The caring behavior is one example of a theme: when zombies are gendered, they are so because the survivor, or the person describing them if not a survivor, identifies with or has a personal stake in their humanity.

Another example is that of the feral child, Sharon. Sharon is a very young survivor of an attack on her church, and the events of that day were burned in her memory. Having the "mind of a four-year-old girl" (Brooks 2006, 73), Sharon describes her attack to the fictive author in haunting detail. She mimics the voices of her mother, her mother's friends, the pastor of the church, even the moans of the zombies—a sound so inhuman that it is seen as merely a relic of their residual respiration systems. What makes a feral child, or other feral human survivor, is deep trauma and a failure to metaphysically cope with the lack of continued state of war. They have PTSD, but a version where they relive their circumstances over and over. In this case, Sharon is not identifying with the zombies as people. Instead, she has seen the people do things as monstrous as the zombies, and in addition to reliving her circum-stances, she is unable to make a clear mental distinction between the killing done by the zombies, and the killing attempted by those who would be her protectors.

While at first this does not directly conflate the gender identity of zom-bies, it does address why that gender identity is so tenuous, and indeed, how

the live humans' identities qua humans are also tenuous. Sharon's own attacker was no zombie, but her living, breathing, caring mother—" [*She goes
back to stroking her own face, her mother's voice has become harder.*]
[Brackets sic, italics changed from bold in original text to maintain emphasis,
eds.] 'Shhh . . . it's okay, baby, it's okay . . .' [*Her hands move down from
her face to her throat, tightening into a strangling grip.*] 'I won't let them get
you. I WON'T LET THEM GET YOU!'" (Brooks 2006, 75). With that one
action, her mother becomes the monster, and the zombies at the door become
almost more humane; at least their actions are driven by their own survival,
and they do not turn on each other. However, other humans are driven to
survive in ways that are more constructive.

Survivor: Mayor Mary-Jo Miller
Location: Troy, Montana, USA
Trope: Women in Male Roles

Foregrounded in *World War Z* (Brooks 2006), the theme of post-capitalism
and the drive to consume things that cannot be replenished (Larsen 2017)
ends up in dissolution of typical gender roles. At least on one axis of those
roles: the ability for women in the United States to hold political power. The
need for an all-hands-on-deck warfare resolves into stereotypical male and
female roles being jumbled together, with women rising high in the hierar-
chy, taking leadership positions that outstrip those which they might have
aspired to before the War.

One such woman is Mary-Jo Miller, the Mayor of Troy, Montana. At the
time of this writing, females make up only about 20 percent of the mayors of
cities with populations over 30,000 (Center for American Women in Politics
2018). Miller becomes her city's mayor rather by default. Her husband did not
survive the zombie attack on their home, and she found herself needing to build
a new life for her children. Not just the Mayor of Troy, but its developer, Miller
pioneered a new city plan for resistance and rebuilding in the new world.

In this more male role, taken due to necessity, she is joined by many un-
named women throughout the course of the book. Whether through economic
necessity, lack of available men, or just the pressure of the moment, women
stepped up and did what was necessary. A good many women are mentioned
merely as adjuncts of their husbands, but those who are not are cast as doctors,
technical trainers, film narrators, fighter pilots, and more. A former Catholic
nun, "Sister Montoya," is a comrade in arms, just as lethal on the zombie killing
field as the male survivor highlighted in the chapter titled "Denver, Colorado."
Additionally, the commander of the Deep Submergence Combat Corps is female, affectionately referred to as the "Sturgeon General." This nickname does
not show disrespect, but rather emphasizes the power of the position, and the
distance from the man speaking, who is several ranks lower, though still quite

high ranking, at Master Chief Petty Officer. Finally, the impetus for the entire book's premise is driven by a woman.

The fictive author states that he had raw data floating around in the form of interviews and stories after his official report, and when he vehemently protested to his "boss" that the stories should be kept alive, she replied "Who's stopping you from keeping these stories alive in the pages of your own (expletive deleted) [sic] book?" (Brooks 2006, 2). The use of quotation marks around boss in the text contains significance; it is not that the fictive author cast aspersions on female leadership. Quite the opposite, in fact. Based on evidence in the first few and last few pages (Brooks 2006, 1–3 and 337), his boss is most likely the post-war president of the United States. She is mentioned in passing—no name, simply the title, and as the book is near-ing its end (page wise and chronologically), the reader may assume that she, the new president, will be the one to guide the United States into the post-zombie, post-capitalist future, to help the survivors learn to live with minimal consumption in all its various forms. Regrettably, this progressive trend does not show up in changes in the language of the survivors—there are still considerable amounts of gender-based insults used.

Survivor: Colonel Christina Eliopolis
Location: Parnell Air National Guard Base, Tennessee, USA
Trope: Gender Based Insults

Survivor Christina Eliopolis, the aforementioned fighter pilot, is unique among her fellow survivors. A woman in a male job, though not from finan-cial need, she reproaches herself for displaying "womanly" qualities. This stems from her training at the military academy in Colorado Springs. The purpose of the training is to turn any person, regardless of gender, into a soldier, to strip away weakness, to temper individuality, and to create a person who can follow orders and do their job well, up to and including killing others (Linneman et al. 2014). She states: "You wanna talk about being alone in a hostile environ-ment try my years at Colorado Springs. *But there were other women . . .* [italics changed from bold in original text to maintain emphasis, eds.] Other cadets, other competitors who happen to have the same genitalia. Trust me, when the pressure kicked in, sisterhood punched out" (Brooks 2006, 174). The training was "the only thing [she] could count on" when her plane crashed in zombie territory (Brooks 2006, 174).

Why did the plane crash? She does not know, but she blames herself—she was taking a bathroom break, and, speaking to the fictive author, she states "I wasn't doing my job. I was squatting over a bucket like a goddamn girl!" (Brooks 2006, 175). This use of gender coded language repeats throughout the chapter, with her purported savior, the radio operator "Mets Fan," eventually motivating Eliopolis to save herself by screaming at her "'Move your ass, you fuckin' bitch!'" then "'What are you, some weak little victim?'" and finally "'What are you, your fucking mother!?!'" (Brooks 2006, 183). The conflation of female and weakness carries on in the larger narrative, as well, used both self-reflexively by characters, and as disparagements about other characters.

These disparagements take pretty standard forms, like "impotent" (Brooks 2006, 46), "eunuchs" (48), "cunt" (58), "pussies" (61), and "dumb bitch" (152), used as insults, but also there are more creative or subtle constructions that the reader must tease out or deconstruct in order to fully see what they say about gender during the War. There are two particularly memorable ones, the first of which occurs relatively early in the book, on page 24. The fictive author is interviewing a doctor, who had helped perform a heart transplant that infected the recipient. After learning of the infection, the doctor returned to the hospital to eliminate the new zombie, and brought his gun with him: "*You carried a gun?* [italics changed from bold in original text to maintain emphasis, eds.] I lived in Rio. What do you think I carried, my 'pinto'?" (Brooks 2006, 24). "Pinto" has several meanings in Portuguese, from baby chicken to a common surname. Here the reference is clear. The doctor is emphasizing his own machismo by using a slang term for penis. Reiterating the machismo theme, the doctor "gave her [a nurse] a good one across the cheek" (Brooks 2006, 24) to stop the nurse from a fit of hysterics, and then had to be slapped in return after shooting the zombie. The gun itself has distinct masculine traits, particularly its size. "It was a 'Desert Eagle,' Israeli, large and showy, which is why I'd chosen it" (Brooks 2006, 25).

The second instance is more subtle, a linguistic construction that emphasizes the perceived weakness (read: womanliness) of so-called "quislings" or humans who identified with zombies so much that they 'joined' them and acted like the living dead. The character speaking in this chapter also said the aforementioned "dumb bitch" (Brooks 2006, 152), and in this case refers to the quislings as "a Patty Hearst/Stockholm Syndrome-type" (156). The significance here lies in the fact that due to the ever-shifting nature of language, and the destruction of most historical documents/communication systems in the War, the survivors are in an era where there are more people who will recognize Stockholm Syndrome than who will understand its intrinsic relationship to Patty Hearst. Thus, the formulation of the sentence must be meant to feminize the quislings, emphasizing their weak spirits.

Victim: Sharon Parsons
Location: Joshua Tree National Park, California, USA
Trope: A Woman's Place Is in the Home

Brooks expands the *World War Z* universe with the graphic novel *Recorded Attacks* (2009), where twelve stories of possible zombie outbreaks in the past are described. Occurrences from eastern Africa in 60,000 BC to western

North America in AD 1992 are recounted in panels with narration. Amidst their temporal and geographic differences, the stories have one striking similarity with regards to the portrayal of gender: females are shown primarily in domestic settings and in the background. In fact, there is only one instance of a named woman in the entire book. Unfortunately, this woman, identified as Sharon Parson by the driver's license found near her mutilated body, is the victim of a zombie attack. Her remains were recovered near a tent, her temporary home while experiencing the natural splendor of a national park. Her head is caved in by a rock, and her body displays human bite marks. The narration includes an autopsy finding that Sharon consumed at least a part of her now-missing boyfriend before she was dispatched.

Almost every other woman shown in *Recorded Attacks* (Brooks 2009) is dehumanized, whether she is a zombie or still alive. Regardless of the time period, the females are always part of a larger group, working in the home (often with children nearby) or serving others in the village. In two instances, the women are shown as enslaved people. As zombies, the women are only depicted as part of the larger horde. They are not the focus of action. The males are the ones biting or being beheaded. Female humans and female zombies are both presented essentially as scenery, filling up space in the background of the panel, without detailed features, and playing no roles in the story other than as "extras." The characters in Brooks's *Recorded Attacks* (2009) match up with the artistic representations of Cro-Magnon males and females reported by Diane Gifford-Gonzalez. She, too, found that authors and illustrators tended to privilege certain groups over others, depicting adult females much less often than adult males and almost never showing female-only scenes (Gifford-Gonzalez 1993). The story involving Sharon is the only one to have a living woman playing a role outside of taking care of the house, the children, or the men in the scene.

Further, among zombies, there is only one story with a "leading character" who was a female. Cossack men are rampaging through Siberia in AD 1583. They find themselves without food during the harsh winter and must resort to uninterring bodies from a local cemetery. A corpse is removed from the tundra. She was a young female with hands and feet bound and with her mouth securely gagged. The men thaw her by the fire of their hearth. Once warmed and animated, she bites one of them. She is summarily chopped into pieces, roasted, and eaten. The next panel finds the men turned to zombies themselves (Brooks 2009). Even in death, and as the undead, the female gender role of food producer remains cliché.

CONCLUSIONS

Although there are only a half dozen instances of zombies being individually identified as male or female in *World War Z* (Brooks 2006), and even fewer in *Recorded Attacks* (Brooks 2009), each speaks to the very nature of identifying with the remains of the zombie's humanity. This earned derision from certain survivors: "That's how the media portrayed them. . . . Gs in business suits and dresses, like, a cross section of everyday America, only dead. That's not what they looked like at all" (Brooks 2006, 97). Todd Waino, who helped orchestrate the successful Battle of Yonkers, gives an account of a zombie family seemingly working together (though that happens due to mere proximity of reanimation): "There were five of them, a man, a woman, three kids, they had him pinned on his back, the man was on his chest, the kids had him by the arms trying to bite through his suit. The woman tore his mask off, you could see the terror in his face. I'll never forget his shriek as she bit off his chin and lower lip" (Brooks 2006, 101–2). In this we see that the former family group reemphasizes how much society has changed—the family, a mythical place of support and love, is turned upside down by zombification. In the rest of his chapter, Waino refers to the zombies in uniformly dehumanizing terms: Zs, Gs, ghouls, and Zack.

While Zack might be considered a form of gendering, the dehumanizing aspect (seen in other wars as Jerry for Germans or Charlie for the Viet Cong) overpowers the fact that Zack is a male name. The use of the nickname is not a gendering aspect; it represents the uniformity of the zombie hordes. Showing the validity of this interpretation, many times when a survivor ascribes gender to a zombie, the next description of it, sometimes in the same sentence, contains a dehumanizing marker—as though the survivor wants to self-correct, to emphasize that in killing the zombie, they did not kill a human. In describing a female zombie, a male survivor states "I centered my sight between her shrunken, milky blue eyes . . . it's not really the eyes that make them look all cloudy. . . . Zack doesn't make any tears" (Brooks 2006, 278). With conventional gender roles being followed, and the zombie identified as a woman, the term Zack can only be there to act as a way of distancing the survivor from the act of killing.

All wars involve horrible acts. Monsters, by definition, are horrible as well. A common response to horrific events, whether real or fictional, is the process of dehumanization. A goal of soldiers in battle is to strip the personhood from their intended targets. Phrases like "collateral damage" are euphemisms that are intended to reduce the moral culpability of military action. Likewise, by stripping away the gendered identity of zombies, survivors of an apocalypse can attempt to assuage their guilt and lessen the impact of any behavior that breaks conventional norms. Thinking of the monsters as "not us" and removing any characteristics associated with "us" is meant to complete the process of killing the living dead once and for all.

BIBLIOGRAPHY

Brooks, Max. 2003. *The Zombie Survival Guide: Complete Protection from the Living Dead.* New York: Broadway Books.

Brooks, Max. 2006. *World War Z: An Oral History of the Zombie War.* New York: Broadway Books.

Brooks, Max. 2009. *The Zombie Survival Guide: Recorded Attacks.* New York: Three Rivers Press.

Charlier, Philippe. 2015. *Zombies: An Anthropological Investigation of the Living Dead.* Gainesville: University of Florida Press.

Center for American Women in Politics. 2018. "Women Mayors in U.S. Cities 2018." Accessed October 10, 2018. http://www.cawp.rutgers.edu/levels_of_office/women-mayors-us-cities-2018

Clifford-Gonzalez, Diane. 1993. "You Can Hide, But You Can't Run: Representations of Women's Work in Illustrations of Palaeolithic Life." *Visual Anthropology Review* 9(1): 22–41.

Doughty, Caitlin. 2014. *Smoke Gets in Your Eyes: And Other Lessons from the Crematory.* New York: W.W. Norton & Company.

Doughty, Caitlin. 2017. *From Here to Eternity: Traveling the World to Find the Good Death.* New York: W.W. Norton & Company.

Haraway, Donna. 1991. *Simians, Cyborgs and Women: The Reinvention of Nature.* New York: Routledge.

Larsen, Lars Bang. 2017. Zombies of Immaterial Labor: The Modern Monster and the Consumption of Self. In *Zombie Theory*, edited by Sarah Juliet Lauro, 157–70. Minneapolis: University of Minnesota Press.

Levi-Strauss, Claude. 1964. *The Raw and the Cooked: Mythologies Vol. 1.* Chicago: University of Chicago Press.

Linneman, Travis, Tyler Wall, and Edward Green. 2014. "The Walking Dead and Killing State: Zombification and the Normalization of Police Violence." *Theoretical Criminology* 18(4): 506–27.

Probyn, Elspeth. 1993. *Sexing the Self: Gendered Positions in Cultural Studies.* London: Routledge.

Rubin, Gayle. 1984. "Thinking Sex: Notes for a Radical Theory of the Politics of Sexuality." In *Culture, Society, and Sexuality: A Reader,* edited by Richard Guy Parker and Peter Aggleton, 143–78. London: Routledge.

Shaw, Debra Benita. 2018. *Posthuman Urbanism: Mapping Bodies in Contemporary City Space.* London: Roman & Littlefield.

Vint, Sherryl. 2017. "Abject Posthumanism: Neoliberalism, Biopolitics, and Zombies." In *Zombie Theory*, edited by Sarah Juliet Lauro, 171–81. Minneapolis: University of Minnesota Press.

Webb, Jan and Sam Byrnand. 2017. "Some Kind of Virus: The Zombie as Body and as Trope." In *Zombie Theory,* edited by Sarah Juliet Lauro, 111–23. Minneapolis: University of Minnesota Press.

Wells, Ashlee Dean. 2018. "I'm Raising My Child Gender-Neutral and What I've Learned Is It's Not Enough." Accessed October 10, 2018. http://www.upworthy.com/i-m-raising-my-child-gender-neutral-and-what-i-ve-learned-is-it-s-not-enough

West, Candace and Don H. Zimmerman. 1987. Doing Gender. In *Gender and Society* 1(2): 125–51.

Zeidler, Maryse. 2017. "Parent Fights to Omit Gender on BC Child's Birth Certificate." Accessed October 10, 2018. http://www.cbc.ca/news/canada/british-columbia/parent-fights-to-omit-gender-on-b-c-child-s-birth-certificate-1.4186221

Afterlife and Afterword

James M. VanderVeen

As evinced by the chapters in this volume, cultures around the world have long told stories about supernatural beings. Although scary stories may differ in their specifics, there are commonalities that date back to the first recorded figurative drawings. Upper Paleolithic cave paintings and rock engravings from Europe, South Africa, and Australia all show possible therianthropes (Dayton 2001). The combination of human and animal forms into a supernatural being can be seen in the sphinx in Egypt and in Vishnu in India. *The Epic of Gilgamesh* and the *Beowulf* saga recount battles against monstrous hybrids, as do many of today's best-selling science fiction novels (although the modern combination is more likely that of a machine and a human). It could be argued that stories about monsters are as close to a universal as we have.

Those supernatural beings are part of our physical world, interacting with us on the plane of existence, but they also span a time before and after our own personal experiences. Many monsters are ghost-like, having a spirit form present after death. Others, like vampires and zombies, retain their corporeal bodies even if they no longer adhere to the norms of being alive. Monsters can also be artificially imbued with traits resembling life (like the creature made by Dr. Frankenstein or as seen in an advanced robot, a spaceship, or a haunted house). The monsters that we create are, according to Foucault (2002), at a distinct point between that which we know—the ordered and classified world—and that which we do not yet understand—the undifferentiated and that in process. In other words, they represent that which cannot be completely articulated. By being human-like but not human, by not being completely dead nor fully alive, by interacting with the natural world but being from the supernatural, these creatures are liminal forms between states.

Just as scary stories have been told since antiquity, the study of such stories has a long history. They are popular *culture* and speak to what we feel is important. For that reason, scholars regularly mine folklore to learn about norms and expectations. People used to sit around a campfire and talk of monsters not just to arouse fear, but to educate. We still share stories with the same purpose, although the light of the fire has often been replaced by the glow of a television or movie screen. These legends help to socialize. Folklore provides moral lessons that anchor a culture in its past and prepare its members, usually children but not exclusively, for what is expected of them in the present. The tales we tell are passed down to us from previous generations, and they passed from us to ensure our culture carries forward.

One tale not shared in the previous pages is that of Zora Neale Hurston's search for a "real," not purely supernatural, monster: the Haitian zombie. Hurston was trained as an anthropologist by Franz Boas, one of the founders of the field in the United States. Her fellow students included such luminaries as Margaret Mead, Ruth Benedict, and Ella Deloria. They all worked to document cultures across the globe and show that humanity is more undivided than we had thought. Hurston's interests included the folklore of African Americans and black Caribbean islanders. She wrote *Tell My Horse: Voodoo and Life in Haiti and Jamaica* (Hurston 2009), a travel book about the non-Spanish Greater Antilles. It included ethnographic material concerning the practices of the inhabitants of those nations, but it was also a type of memoir for Hurston. The book (and, for a time, its author) were marginalized or ignored by the academy. Neither fit neatly into a recognizable genre or disciplinary field. They were liminal, so to speak, or at least transformational. As was the topic. Hurston writes, "Here in the shadow of the Empire State Building, death and the graveyard are final. It is such a positive end that we use it as a measure of nothingness and eternity. We have the quick and the dead. But in Haiti there is the quick, the dead, and then there are Zombies" (2009, 179).

Hurston provides a firsthand account of the mysteries of Voodoo, including her encounter at a mental hospital with "the broken remnant, relic, or refuse of Felicia Felix-Mentor" (2009, 179), a woman alleged to be a zombie. Haitian zombies are people with speech and will power destroyed through sorcery (possibly aided by psychology and pharmacology). They become an enslaved person, although they are no longer seen as a "person" at all by their family or friends. They have lost their identities, including—at least for Hurston—their gender. She refers to Felix-Mentor variously as "it" as well as "her." She writes, "They are bodies without souls" (2009, 179) and "From an educated, intelligent being to an unthinking, unknowing beast" (2009, 181). In this case, for Hurston and her informants, zombies are no longer human and therefore no longer assigned a gender. In another famous instance, however, gender most definitely plays a role. Hurston tells, at length, the story of

Marie M., a beautiful daughter of a prominent family who dies "in the bloom of youth" (2009, 194). Five years after her death, a rumor reaches a priest through a confessional. A person believed to be Marie M. was living in the hills above the town. She is soon recovered, wild and demented, and has given birth to three children. If this was Marie M., and she was made a zombie by a sorcerer, then she was also made into a sexual creature.

The Caribbean Zombies of popular culture in the 1920s–1950s were often turned that way for reasons relating to sex (Paravisini-Gebert 1997). These zombies are not infected by some virus and are not transformed by a bite. They are carefully selected by a *bokor* (sorcerer) who, through the use of both magic and poison, places them into a state resembling death. After burial and disinterment, the victim remains under the control of the bokor for his personal gain and also as a social sanction. Zombies in the movies of that time are turned as a punishment for oversexed white females, to become the victim of the sinister lust of the bokor, or as a stand-in for subverting race and class barriers between ill-fated lovers (Paravisini-Gebert 1997). Of course, the form of the monster evolves. The supernatural has proven quite versatile over time, but, as Zora Neale Hurston observed, "gods always behave like the people who make them" (2009, 219).

Regardless, the purpose of the monster is to define what it means to be a good person. Academic research, like that done by Hurston as well as those in this volume, intersects with popular culture in an effort to better understand proper behavior. Supernatural creatures are a device against which members of a group measure their status in terms of ethical choices and agency (Erle and Hendry 2020). Our monsters function as signs and symbols for societal problems and, as such, are ideal fodder for research. But when we experience the monster's emotional impact on us, when we get physically afraid, they become real (Cohen 1996).

What makes the stories scary is the conflict that exists between right and wrong behavior. Inappropriate thoughts and actions in humans are addressed through the proxy of the characters in the tales. Their punishments are shown with the hope that we, the living, will improve. The most spine-tingling of tales, those that involve death or its potential, "allow us to indulge our fears and desires without penalty" (Bell 2017, 3). These stories are comforting when the protagonist succeeds over the monster. They are also thrilling, exhilarating, even—at times—titillating because we, the audience, have faced that fearsome threat and escaped unharmed. We indulge that which terrifies us through popular culture. The threats change over our own lives and across different eras, but the thrill remains the same. Leo Braudy (2016) has distilled our fears into some general groups, all of which were discussed with specific examples in this volume. There is the fear of the monster from nature, like the Spider Queen from *Love, Death & Robots*, that represents a world that humans only think they have harnessed. There is the fear of the monster we built and believe we control, like the creature from Frankenstein or cyborgs, that threaten us by becoming all too human. Another monster we fear is produced by our repressed minds, our own dark psychology, represented by an otherwise normal house turned evil from within. The monster from our past, such as a vampire, signifies the fear we have of losing our modernity: the present day's technological improvements, medical progress, and societal change. The most recent monster on the scene, the zombie, is an impersonal danger. It symbolizes that which can overwhelm our safe society: an epidemic of disease, of commercialism, of faceless anonymity behind devices, of groups of people different than yourself.

The authors of the chapters found in this book demonstrate that we have supernatural creatures tied to death, the monsters of folklore, because having them makes us feel safe. Along the same lines, they approach the volume's central question of gender in the undead (or, more specifically, in the "not living," because of the ships, houses, and cyborgs) as an extension and expression of our selves. The focus is not really the creatures, but instead it is the humans who interact with them. Buffy, evil scientists, sorcerers, and punk metal bands are all part of the society that constructs the identities of these monsters. Gender remains in the supernatural creatures, whether they are living or dead or something in between, because the people they haunt remain. People make the monsters, and our societies have decided to construct a certain identity for the monsters. They reflect our fears but also our political situations, our religious ideals, our personal desires, and ourselves. We make the monsters who, in turn, make us look inward at our beliefs and outwards at our norms. Gender roles, like much else in society, will change over time and in different cultures, but they will always be the lines inside which the monsters will be colored.

BIBLIOGRAPHY

Bell, Susan. 2017. "Monsters on Our Minds: What Our Fascination with Frightful Creatures Says About Us." *USC News.* Published October 30. https://news.usc.edu/130364/monsters-on-our-minds-what-our-fascination-with-frightful-creatures-says-about-us/.

Braudy, Leo. 2016. "Why We'll Always Be Obsessed With—and Afraid of—Monsters." *The Conversation.* Published October 28. https://theconversation.com/why-well-always-be-obsessed-with-and-afraid-of-monsters-65080.

Cohen, Jeffrey Jerome, editor. 1996. *Monster Theory: Reading Culture.* Minneapolis: University of Minnesota Press.

Dayton, Leigh. 2001. "Animal-headed Humans Appear in Earliest Art." *New Scientist.* Published November 21. https://www.newscientist.com/article/dn1590-animal-headed-humans-appear-in-earliest-art/.

Erle, Sibylle and Helen Hendry. 2020. "Monsters: Interdisciplinary Explorations in Monstrosity." *Palgrave Communications* 6, 53. https://doi.org/10.1057/s41599-020-0428-1.

Foucault, Michael. 2002. *The Order of Things: An Archaeology of the Human Sciences.* London: Routledge Classics.

Hurston, Zora Neale. 2009. *Tell My Horse: Voodoo and Life in Haiti and Jamaica.* New York: Harper Perennial Modern Classics.

Paravisini-Gebert, Lizabeth. 1997. "Woman Possessed: Eroticism and Exoticism in the Representation of Woman as Zombie." In *Sacred Possessions: Vodou, Santería, Obeah, and the Caribbean*, edited by Margarite Fernândez Olmos and Lizabeth Paravisini-Gebert, 37–58. New Brunswick: Rutgers University Press.

Index

abject, 12, 23–24, 34–38, 49n6, 149, 150–151, 153, 154, 156–158, 161

agency, 28, 31, 76, 97, 128, 135, 141–143, 145, 150–160, 167, 171, 180, 186, 205

alien/aliens, 10, 24, 25, 31, 33, 35–36, 38, 42, 44, 54, 93

American Horror Story (AHS), 162, 169–171

androgyny/androgynous, 113, 126

automata/automaton, 3, 29

beast, 4, 15, 24–26, 140, 204

beauty/beautiful, xii, 4, 12, 18, 24, 26, 27, 30, 33, 37, 110, 114, 143, 149–154, 156, 158–160, 164, 205

Blodeuwedd, 12–13

blood, xi, 14, 16, 26, 30, 61, 85–86, 88–92, 95, 98n3, 101, 103–106, 108–111, 114, 118–120, 124–125, 127–130, 140, 161, 166–168, 178, 195; menstrual, 88, 150

Bram Stoker's Dracula, 97, 117, 125

Bride of Frankenstein, 140

Bride of Frankie, 144–145

Buffy the Vampire Slayer, 67–83; Angel, 71, 74–75, 77, 78, 81; the Slayer, 67–82; Watchers, 67, 74, 76–79, 82

Butler, Judith, 69

cannibalism, 8, 9, 179

castration, 23–27, 35, 150, 158

Christianity, 7, 86–89, 91, 93, 97, 153, 186

colonial, 6, 14, 29, 34, 41–44, 46, 48, 49n1, 49n9, 50n18, 56, 138, 178, 179, 186, 188n5, 194

contagion, 6, 95

Corpse Bride, 149–160; Emily, 152–154, 156–159; Maggot, 157–159

corpses, 6–7, 9, 15, 17, 33, 42, 89, 90, 103, 105, 106, 149–150, 152–154, 156–160, 177, 199

creations/creatures, 4–7, 9–13, 15, 18, 24, 25, 31, 33, 35–36, 38, 44, 48, 69, 73, 85, 93, 96, 97, 103, 105, 108, 126, 135–143, 146, 155, 203

culture/cultural, 4, 7, 17, 28, 35, 36, 41, 43, 48, 54, 68, 69, 73, 85–86, 89, 92–94, 101, 102, 104, 108, 111n5, 116, 125, 129, 130, 136–138, 152–156, 159, 162, 165, 166, 170, 171, 181, 191–193, 203, 204, 206

cursed, 4, 12, 13, 16, 58, 61, 82

cyborg/cybernetic, xii, 23–24, 26, 28, 30–32, 36–38, 41, 45, 194, 206

dead, xi, 5–9, 14–18, 24, 26–28, 35, 67, 70, 85, 105, 106, 109, 117, 136, 144, 150–151, 153, 163–166, 170–171, 177, 180–183, 188, 188n9, 192, 193, 198, 200, 203, 204, 206

Deadpool, 11

death, xi, xii, 4, 6–7, 9–12, 14–18, 26–28, 32, 33, 41, 43, 46, 47, 54, 60–62, 70,

73, 77, 85–87, 89, 90, 95, 105, 106,
108, 110, 113, 114, 119, 120, 127, 135,
141, 143, 149, 151–152, 155–157, 159,
177, 188n5, 193, 194, 200, 203–206
de Bodard, Aliette, 41–44, 46
decay, 14, 90, 151–153, 155–159, 193
deception, 24, 26, 28, 32, 33, 36, 38, 57
demon/demonize, 17, 28, 55, 60, 67,
69–70, 76, 78, 80–82, 86–88, 91, 98n2,
98n3
devil, 36, 87, 89–91, 93, 98n1, 104
Dracula: Abraham Van Helsing, 92, 117,
118; character, 85, 92–93, 97, 117–119,
123, 127, 130; Johnathan Harker, 117;
Lucy Westenra, 92, 117, 118, 125;
Mina Harker, 117, 118, 125; novel, 85,
91–93, 95, 97, 113, 117, 119, 129, 130,
161

erotic, 28, 59, 92, 96, 108–110, 140, 149,
151, 156, 158
evil, 12, 15–16, 29, 30, 36, 58, 70, 75,
86–91, 98, 98n1, 110, 130, 165, 179,
206

femininity/feminine, 23–25, 28, 31, 69,
72–75, 78, 79, 81, 82, 106, 114–120,
124–129, 137, 139, 145, 149–154,
157–160, 162, 164
feminist/feminism, 23, 27–28, 31, 37–38,
50n18, 68, 71, 82–83, 107, 135, 136,
138–146
femme fatale, 15, 24, 26, 28, 33, 38, 114
Foucault, Michel, 70, 167, 203
*Frankenhooke*r, 143–144
Frankenstein, 135, 138, 139, 144–146,
203; creation/Adam, 5, 12, 13, 138,
140, 203; Elizabeth, 141–144; film
(1910), 139–140; film (1931), 140; film
(1957), 141; Justine, 141–142; monster/
creature trope, 5, 9, 140, 206; novel, 12,
135, 136, 138, 139; Victor
Frankenstein, 12, 136, 138–143

gender, xii, 23, 41–46, 49n10, 49n15, 53,
62, 67–69, 71–72, 74, 80–83, 86–87,
89, 91, 97, 103, 106–108, 114–118,
129–130, 137–138, 145, 146n4, 149,
152, 158, 161–164, 166, 168, 171–172,
178–179, 186–188, 191–198, 200–201,
204, 206; roles, 23, 36, 48, 55, 57, 73,
81, 115, 135, 137, 139–141, 145, 161,
162, 168, 191–192, 196, 199, 200, 206
A Girl Walks Home Alone at Night, 114,
119, 130; the Girl, 114, 119–124, 130;
the Junkie, 119, 121–123, 130; the love
interest, 119, 121–123, 130; the Pimp,
119–123; the Prostitute, 119–122; the
Street Urchin, 121, 122
ghost, 17, 54–60, 86, 93, 102, 179, 203
ghoul, 9, 102, 103, 108, 193, 194, 200
Gilman, Charlotte Perkins, 54, 56
Ginger Snaps, 7
golem, 13
Gothic, 53, 56, 71, 73, 75, 101, 102, 111n3,
152, 154
grotesque, 33, 37, 105, 109, 150, 153–159

hallucination, 6–8, 11, 61
Hannibal Lecter, 8
Haraway, Donna, 31, 45
haunted house, xii, 53–55, 58–60, 62, 203
haunting, 43, 56, 58
The Haunting of Hill House, 54–56, 60–62
heteronormativity, 48, 72, 81, 162
heterosexual/heterosexuality, 26, 30, 35,
37, 50n19, 108, 162, 163, 172
HIV/AIDS, 95, 110
homosexuality/gay/lesbian/bisexual,
25–28, 96, 99n5, 101, 108–111, 129,
140, 171, 179
humanity, xii, 4–7, 12, 16, 27, 29, 41, 42,
94, 98, 105, 119, 124, 129, 130, 191,
193, 195, 200, 204
human remains, 5, 8, 198
humor, 104–106, 153–160, 182

impurity, 86, 109
incubus/incubi, 86
Interview with the Vampire, 110–111, 130;
book, 130; movie, 110, 130
In the Flesh, 162–166, 168

Jackson, Shirley, 54–56, 61, 62

lamia, 86, 88
Leckie, Ann, 47
Lilitu/Lilith, 23, 88

liminality, xii, 4–12, 14–18, 43, 48, 68–70, 73, 75, 79, 98, 114, 118, 150, 153, 155, 157, 162, 165, 193, 203, 204

love, 4, 11, 12, 24, 28, 29, 32, 33, 36, 56, 60, 75, 77, 79, 85, 95, 96, 105, 114, 115, 117–119, 121–123, 125–127, 136, 140, 141, 144, 145, 165, 166, 200, 205

Love, Death & Robots, 24, 29, 32, 205

madness/hysteria, 18, 54, 56, 61, 80, 90, 118, 198

masculinity/masculine, 24, 59, 62, 69, 74, 75, 77, 81, 103, 106, 108–110, 115–120, 125–130, 136–146, 146n3, 151, 158, 162, 168, 192, 198

The Matrix, 5, 8, 9

memory, 8, 10, 41, 43, 46, 47, 56, 178, 193, 195, 198

monster/monstrous, 3–7, 9, 11, 14–18, 23–29, 31–38, 42, 47, 59, 60, 61, 67, 69, 70, 73, 85, 86, 88, 90–92, 94–98, 103, 108, 111n8, 140, 149–151, 153–156, 159–160, 161–171, 193, 195, 200–201, 203–206

motherhood, 13, 54, 57–58, 60–62, 75, 77, 79–81, 89, 114, 118, 121, 122, 124, 141, 143, 145, 195

mutation, 4, 6–7, 11, 12, 17

mutilation, 25, 27, 29–32, 89, 150, 198

mythology, xii, 4, 7, 8, 12, 13, 23–24, 27, 29, 35, 36, 85–86, 88–90, 92, 93, 96–98, 102, 129, 139, 188, 191, 195, 200

nature/natural, xii, 3, 4, 28, 35, 86, 94, 126, 127, 136–140, 142, 143, 145, 151, 153, 155, 200, 203, 205

nonbinary, 44, 45, 192

Nosferatu, 113

Only Lovers Left Alive, 114, 119, 124–129; Adam, 114, 119, 124–129; Eve, 114, 119, 124–130

paranormal, 55, 59

patriarchy/patriarchal, 23–24, 27–28, 31, 36, 37, 48, 54, 55, 62, 63, 79, 149, 150, 152, 158–159, 168

penetration/penetrative, 25, 26, 28, 110, 114–115, 117–120, 124–127, 129–130, 169–170

phallic/phallus, 25, 27, 31, 36, 60, 118, 150, 158, 167

plague, 90, 95, 193

prostitution/whore/sex work, 30, 36, 87, 104, 119, 120, 143, 164–165, 172

Queen of the Damned, 113, 115, 125–126

queer, 24, 25, 27, 28, 41, 43–45, 48, 49n8, 49n14, 50n18, 56, 96, 97, 99n5–99n6, 101, 103, 105, 108, 110–111, 192

quisling, 198

rape/raping, 24–28, 36, 38, 60, 97, 122, 142, 150, 168–171

reality, 8, 14, 33, 43, 45, 80–82, 95, 106, 107, 119, 135, 137, 138, 143–146, 177, 182, 187

reanimated/reanimation, 5–7, 15, 103, 144, 194, 200

Resident Evil, 11–12

revenant, 7, 102

Rice, Anne, 94, 130

robot/robots/robotics, 9–10, 30–32, 44, 45, 203

romance/romantic: genre, 91, 102; relationships, xi, 4, 32, 45, 46, 50n19, 73, 74, 77, 95, 97, 141, 143, 145, 150, 151

sacrifice, 4, 10, 58, 62, 88, 98n3, 165, 178, 179, 182, 186

Sektor Gaza, 101–111, 111n9

sex/sexual/sexualization, 15, 23–24, 29–33, 35–37, 45, 55, 59, 61, 73, 86, 88–89, 91–97, 101, 103, 104, 106–111, 114, 115, 117, 118, 120, 121, 125, 130, 137, 139, 140, 142–144, 149–151, 155, 161–172, 179, 187, 192, 205; sexual violence, 24–29, 31, 58–60, 75, 78

shapeshifting, 4, 16, 24, 29

Shelley, Mary Wollstonecraft, 127, 135–143, 145, 146

Silent Hill, 14–15

Star Trek, 5, 9, 10, 31, 49n5; Borg, 5–6, 31; Data, 9–10, 13; *The Next Generation*, 10

Stoker, Bram, 85, 91–93, 161
The Strain, 162, 166–169
succubus/succubi, 29, 86
suicide, 4, 6, 56, 58, 60–62, 87, 89, 114, 125, 127
supernatural, xi–xii, 4, 9, 12, 53, 55, 56, 58, 60–62, 68, 71, 91, 93–95, 104, 105, 108, 111n8, 170, 178, 203–206
survivor/survive, 24, 25, 27–28, 30–32, 36, 37, 41–44, 46, 74, 78, 79, 124, 127, 153, 158, 191–198, 200, 201

Tanzania, 177–180, 182–188, 189n10
technology, xii, 5, 23, 26, 29, 31, 33, 44, 94, 111n7, 185, 194, 206
Tepes, Vlad/Vlad the Impaler, 92–93, 117
transformation, 3–10, 12–18, 27, 29, 31, 43, 69, 82, 86, 89, 92, 93, 96, 97, 109, 118–119, 125, 130, 151, 156, 166, 167, 181, 184, 204, 205
trauma, 15, 27, 32, 36, 41, 45–48, 168, 170, 178, 195
Twilight, 161

unclean, 73, 86
undead, xii, 87, 91–92, 95, 102, 105, 118, 130, 161–172, 178, 181, 191–195, 200, 206
Underworld, 113, 115, 119, 129
upyr'/upyri, 101–103, 105, 106, 108–111, 111n2, 111n12

vagina, 35, 144; *vagina dentata*, 35
vampir/vampiry, 101–103, 106, 108–110, 111n2

vampire, xi, xii, 16, 60, 85–98, 101–103, 105, 106, 108–111, 111n2, 111n8, 111n12, 163, 167, 178, 203, 206; *See also A Girl Walks Home Alone at Night*; *Angel*; *Bram Stoker's Dracula*; *Buffy the Vampire Slayer*; *Dracula*; *Interview with the Vampire*; *Nosferatu*; *Only Lovers Left Alive*; *Queen of the Damned*; Rice, Anne; Stoker, Bram; Tepes, Vlad/Vlad the Impaler; *Twilight*; *Underworld*; *upyr'/upyri*; *vampir/vampiry*
vengeance/revenge, 4, 8, 12, 24–32, 36, 60, 114, 136, 170, 171
violence/violent, 24–33, 36, 47, 58–59, 73, 75, 77–81, 83, 87, 95–97, 104, 108, 110, 115, 117–120, 124, 125, 127, 129–130, 137, 138, 140, 141, 144, 145, 161, 164, 168–172, 179

witch/bewitch, 29, 30, 36, 88, 90–91, 98n3, 104, 105, 111n8, 169–170, 177–179, 180–184, 186–188, 188n4–188n6; *Mchawi*, 177
World War Z, 191–201

"The Yellow Wallpaper," 54, 56
Young Frankenstein, 142–144

zombie, xi–xii, 7, 11, 72, 102–103, 105, 108, 161–164, 170, 177–180, 182–183, 185–188, 191–201, 203–206; *litunga/mitunga*, 177–178, 180–188, 188n1

About the Editors and Contributors

ABOUT THE EDITORS

Rebecca Gibson is an adjunct professor in the department of sociology and anthropology at Indiana University South Bend and the department of anthropology at American University. Her published works include *Desire in the Age of Robots and AI: An Investigation in Science Fiction and Fact* (2019) and *The Corseted Skeleton: A Bioarchaeology of Binding* (2020). She holds a PhD in anthropology from American University, and when not writing or teaching can be found reading mystery novels amidst a pile of stuffed animals.

James M. VanderVeen is an archaeologist and professor of anthropology at Indiana University South Bend, where he teaches classes about everything from Aztecs to zombies. He is also the assistant director of the university's center for teaching and learning. He has won several awards for his own teaching and has published on pedagogical innovations in the classroom. Outside of the classroom, his research focus is the interaction between cultures at contact. He has conducted excavations of pre- and post-Hispanic settlements across the Caribbean and pre- and post-industrial domestic residences in northern Indiana.

ABOUT THE CONTRIBUTORS

Alex Claman (they/he) is a master's student at Texas Tech University studying ancient Mediterranean archaeology, geography, and reception of Mediterranean antiquity in speculative fiction. Their essay, "The Avenging Mother: Essun, Clytemnestra, and Intergenerational Trauma in N. K. Jemisin's

Broken Earth Trilogy," has been published in *Strange Horizons*, with several other articles on archaeological and literary topics in preparation. They are an active member of the Sinis Archaeological Project and the Small Cycladic Islands Project.

Matt Coward-Gibbs is an associate lecturer in the Department of Sociology at the University of York and a part-time lecturer in sociology at York St John University. His research, in broad terms, focuses on culture and community, death and dying, pleasure and leisure, and deviance and transgression. Coward-Gibbs is the editor of *Death, Culture and Leisure: Playing Dead* (Emerald, 2020), book reviews editor of *Mortality*, and a steering group member of the *Death & Culture Network* (www.york.ac.uk/dacnet). @MattCowardGibbs

Freya Fenton is a scientist, ancient historian, and researcher. She holds an honours degree in Egyptology and ancient history from Swansea University, and an MSc in museum studies from the University of Leicester. Her undergraduate dissertation investigated the modern reconstruction of an Egyptian temple garden, primarily based on the gardens of the mortuary temple of Hatshepsut at Djeser-Djeseru; and her MSc the replacement of contested human remains in museums through 3D printing techniques, using the remains of Charles Byrne at the Hunterian as a case study. Her personal research interests include folklore and mythology, the changing of perspectives on death and human remains over time, the cultural impact of nuclear technologies, the gothic, and Archaeogaming as a discipline. Having worked as a conservation assistant, laboratory scientist, archaeology technician and many other varied roles over the years, she is currently a haplogroup and panel researcher for a personal genomics company. In her spare time, she enjoys video games, knitting, kickboxing, and spending time with her partner and cats.

Agustín Fuentes, trained in zoology and anthropology, is a professor of anthropology at Princeton University. His research delves into the how and why of being human. Ranging from chasing monkeys in jungles and cities, to exploring the lives of our evolutionary ancestors, to examining what people actually do across the globe, Fuentes is interested in both the big questions and the small details of what makes humans and our closest relatives tick. His current projects include exploring cooperation, creativity, and belief in human evolution, multispecies anthropologies, evolutionary theory and processes, and engaging race and racism. Fuentes is an active public scientist, a well-known blogger, lecturer, tweeter, and a writer and explorer for National Geographic. Fuentes's books include *Race, Monogamy, and Other Lies They Told You: Busting Myths about Human Nature* (University of California),

The Creative Spark: How Imagination Made Humans Exceptional (Dutton), and *Why We Believe: Evolution and the Human Way of Being* (Yale).

Victor Hernández-Santaolalla (vhsantaolalla@us.es) holds a PhD in communication studies. He is currently associate professor of the Department of Audiovisual Communication and Advertising of the University of Seville (Spain). His research interests focus on the effects of mass communication, ideology and popular culture, political communication, propaganda, and surveillance and social media. He has published papers in collective books and international journals like *Information, Communication and Society*, *European Journal of Communication*, *International Journal of Media & Cultural Politics* or *The Journal of Popular Culture*, among others. Recently, he has published a book about mass media effects (2018). He has also edited two books about *Breaking Bad* (2013) and *Sons of Anarchy* (2017) tv shows, and another about the representation of serial killer in contemporary television series (2015).

Bethan Michael-Fox is an associate lecturer in the Faculty of Arts and Social Sciences at the Open University, where she is also an honorary associate in the School of English and Creative Writing. She is also a visiting research fellow at the University of Bath's Centre for Death and Society. She is the editorial officer for the journal *Mortality* and a representative for the Association for the Study of Death and Society. Michael-Fox is a senior fellow of the HEA and a fellow of the RSA. Please feel welcome to connect on Twitter @bethmichaelfox or via LinkedIn. For a full list of publications please see her Orcid page https://orcid.org/0000-0002-9617-2565.

Amy Nichols-Belo is associate professor of anthropology and global health studies and chair of the International and Global Studies Department at Mercer University in Macon, Georgia. She has conducted research in Mwanza, Tanzania, on witchcraft belief and anti-witchcraft practices since 2003. Nichols-Belo also researches best practices in service-learning and undergraduate global health pedagogy.

Lev Nikulin is a postgraduate research associate in Slavic literature at Princeton University. He recently defended a dissertation on horror in the work of Nikolai Gogol, in which he analyzes Gogol's poetic contributions to horror fiction and argues for Gogol's inclusion in horror studies. In addition to working on the nineteenth-century Gothic, he researches the proliferation and mixing of genres in the late Soviet period in film and music, including considerations of gender and sexuality. He teaches on Gogol and on Russophone and global horror in film and literature.

Chelsi Slotten holds a PhD in anthropology from American University. Her PhD work focuses on how gender impacted lived experiences and identity formation during the Danish Viking Age. She is dedicated to increasing public scholarship through her work as cohost of the *Women in Archaeology* podcast. She is a lifelong sci-fi nerd and has periodically appeared on the *Podcapers* podcast to discuss the intersection of comics, heroes, and anthropology.

Devi Snively is a former ballerina turned filmmaker, published fiction author, and part-time film academic, and a proud alumnus of American Films Institute's (AFI) Directing Workshop for Women and invited participant to the 2017 inaugural AFI/Fox Studios Bridge program. Her screenplays have placed in such competitions as the Nicholl Fellowship, Slamdance, and PAGE Awards, and her films have screened at over five-hundred festivals worldwide, garnering awards, distribution, and critical acclaim. She is also a cofounder/writer of *Beyond the Bechdel*, a feminist cinema blog.

Sarah Stang is a PhD candidate in the Communication & Culture program at York University in Toronto, Ontario. She is the editor-in-chief of the student-run journal *Press Start* and the essays editor for the academic middle-state publication *First Person Scholar*. She approaches the study of digital games and other media from an interdisciplinary, intersectional feminist perspective. Her published work has focused on interactivity, game adaptations, gender representation, fatherhood and familial bonds, representations of madness, and the monstrous-feminine in digital games. Her current research explores the symbolic representation of marginalized bodies as hybrid monsters in digital games, tabletop roleplaying games, and science fiction and fantasy media.

Holly Walters is a cultural anthropologist whose ethnographic work focuses on pilgrimage and politics in the Nepal Himalayas as well as on material culture, divine personhood, and ritual practice in South Asia. Drawing on theoretical frameworks in religion, psychological/medical, and linguistic anthropology, her current research addresses the roles of sacred landscapes and digital religious revival in the relationships between Hindus, Buddhists, and Bonpos who venerate sacred ammonite fossils, called Shaligrams. She also has specific interests in the anthropology of media, semiotics, and popular culture which appear in her regular contributions to *The Familiar Strange*. Her first book, *Shaligram Pilgrimage in the Nepal Himalayas*, is available from Amsterdam University Press.

Gillian Wittstock completed her bachelor of dramatic arts, honours equivalent in 2016 at *The University of the Witwatersrand*. She was awarded the Postgraduate Merit Award Scholarship in 2017 and went on to finish her master's by Dissertation in Dramatic Art at Wits in 2019. Her thesis titled *The Uncanny, Grotesque, and Carnivalesque in Animation: Reimagining Stop Motion Horror* investigated how the use of stop motion animation, as a medium is especially adept at facilitating the intersection between the uncanny, carnivalesque, and grotesque. She currently works as a part-time co-lecturer and teaching assistant and research assistant within the *Interdisciplinary and Cultural Studies Department* at Wits University.

www.ingramcontent.com/pod-product-compliance
Lightning Source LLC
Chambersburg PA
CBHW022310280326
41932CB00010B/1051